ECONOMIC GROWTH

Theory, Empirics and Policy

For Silvia

ECONOMIC GROWTH
Theory, Empirics and Policy

Benigno Valdés
Professor of Economics
ICADE
Universidad Pontificia Comillas, Spain

Edward Elgar
Cheltenham, UK • Northampton, MA, USA

Published by
Edward Elgar Publishing Limited
Glensanda House
Montpellier Parade
Cheltenham
Glos GL50 1UA
UK

Edward Elgar Publishing, Inc.
6 Market Street
Northampton
Massachusetts 01060
USA

A catalogue record for this book
is available from the British Library

Library of Congress Cataloguing in Publication Data
Valdés, Benigno, 1953–
     Economic growth : theory, empirics and policy / Benigno Valdés.
     Includes index.
     1. Economic development. 2. Economic policy. I. Title.
HD75.V35 1999   98–31059
338.9—dc21   CIP

ISBN 1 84064 0030

Printed and bound in Great Britain by MPG Books Ltd, Bodmin, Cornwall

Contents

List of Figures

List of Tables

Preface

My friends will not believe that I have written this book: they know that as a graduate student I hated this stuff. "This" stuff? No, "that" stuff: the one containing tons Hamiltonians, "turnpike theorems," exaggeratedly heated "capital controversies" and so on; by contrast (and personal exasperation), it seemed to me that its *economics*, by which I mean theory about "the facts" of the real world, testing of the theories and policy advice (or, at least, policy speculations) was not *in-pari-materia* with its mathematical complexity.

This was in the mid eighties, but the problem had begun much earlier. In 1956 Solow and Swan, independently of each other, devised a beautiful piece of economic growth theory which provided a much needed analytical framework for many valuable (but informally made) theoretical insights and empirical results, particularly on the sources of economic growth. (See Nelson, 1997, for an excellent account of this and related research. On this article, more below.) Almost immediately, however, the (perhaps excessive?) emphasis on mathematical rigor of the time swept the theory of economic growth much as it did other areas of economics: in my opinion, that was not all for the good because, at least to some degree, the necessary balance between mathematical rigor and theoretical relevance was lost in favor of the former.

I hope not to be misunderstood: my complaint in my years as a graduate student was not against the mathematization of economics, much less against the effort put into the development of mathematical tools, however removed these might have being from the analytical necessities of the time. I knew then, and still believe now, that sooner or later we have to "stand on the shoulders" of tool-developers. It was the abovementioned *lost balance* which troubled me; in particular, I found it impossible to come to terms with the fashion of expressing an economic idea in a complex mathematical way when it can be conveyed with easy math. So I used to call this subject "economic ballistics" instead of Economic Dynamics, which was the official title, mostly because its mathematics, which I perceived as too often (although not always) unnecessary, had been "developed in the context of the American and Soviet missile and space programmes" (Jones, 1976).[1]

On the other hand, I finished my PhD in the Spring of 1986, precisely the year in which Paul Romer published his 1983 thesis, which *did* add to the "stock of knowledge" in this field new and very promising ideas. Needless to say, I missed it by a few months. Then I became employed in academic activities having to do more with business-oriented students from Eastern Europe (a satisfying albeit exhausting experience, for I was forced to "recycle" myself in that direction) than with pure economics "freaks." Therefore, I too missed the publication of the immensely valuable data banks compiled by Maddison (1989) and Summers and Heston (1991), as well as their empirical "exploitation" in the early nineties (by a host of authors quoted in the text). Of course, I also missed Romer's (1990) remarkable paper.

In short, by 1993 a lot of new and very relevant information, which had given a complete turn to this field, was unknown to me. It was in the summer of that year, during a short visit to the London School of Economics, that Christopher Pissarides brought to my attention the existence of these new developments in a (shortly before) dead area of economics. This event changed my whole appreciation for the field of long-run macroeconomics. In a way, it also changed my life. For, having received an invitation from the University of Salamanca to teach a one semester course in this area to senior undergraduate students (the same course, basically, that I designed for my seminars at ICADE), I accepted the challenge and went back to my intellectual background: economics.

The task, though, turned out to be more difficult and time consuming than I could imagine. In both ICADE and the University of Salamanca, we have very good students in economics. But not all of them know (nor should they, at this level, be expected to know) the sophisticated "mathematical methods developed in the context of the American and Soviet missile and space programmes." Thus, I had to introduce them to the basic new ideas in economic growth without using optimal control theory. Moreover, in my teachings I did not like the use of the new-fashioned "intertemporally-

---

[1] It might be possible that this loss of balance between mathematical rigor and theoretical relevance contributed to the slowdown of devotion to the subject during the 1970s and most of the 1980s, for two reasons: First, it may have put off students of economics; and second, much of the research done in this area during those years, not following the canons of the time, was mostly ignored in teaching, let alone promoted as a proper subject for graduate dissertations. (Another, not less influential reason, was of course the fact that the irruption of the rational expectations revolution in economics shifted the interest of the profession away from almost any subject other than the theory of the business cycle. This, I must say, I still regard as a price worth paying, for we learned a lot from the rational expectations insight.)

optimizing representative agent" unless it was *strictly* necessary. In fact, I do not see the need for this guy to be *always* there, other than, as Solow (1994) says, making the whole thing unnecessarily complex. (This would not be so, however, if we were talking of the theory and policy of the business cycles, where the use of intertemporal optimization does make a difference for the results.)

Hence, this book contains neither calculus of variations nor (for the most part) the "intertemporally-optimizing representative agent." It was written to be used in a one semester course for senior undergraduate students in economics (or as an introduction to the subject for first year graduates) who *do* know simple Lagrangian calculus and elementary econometrics, micro- and macroeconomics. Now, I do not know to what extent I have succeeded in my purpose, though I can say that my own students at Salamanca, ICADE and (occasionally) elsewhere seem to follow up quite nicely.

It is now only ten years since "the current wildfire revival in growth theory [began]" (Solow, 1994). In the history of science, ten years is nothing, and yet this is what would have happened had I tried to write this book at that time: Chapters 1, 2 and 6 would not have taken the same format; Chapters 3, 4, 7 and 8 would not exist; and finally, Chapter 5 would exist, but most likely its *economics* would have been overshadowed by the mathematics. There is no doubt, therefore, that much progress has been made in this field by conventional scientific standards. Moreover, the contents of this book by no means exhaust the results of the new wave of research in growth theory. Far from it. But for the advanced graduates, professional devotees, and so on, an excellent consulting manual by Barro and Sala-i-Martín (1995) already exists. With the present book I have only tried to make what we think are "new basic ideas" accessible to the newcomers, that is, to put economic growth theory and policy back into the standard economist's curriculum.

I would be grateful to students and instructors who let me know their suggestions for improvement (which surely will be needed). For example, during the last stages of the book I have asked myself many times the question of whether the book is "complete." Surely, what has been included is not superfluous; but much of value has been left out. So, for instance, should I have included specific chapters on such issues as "Bounded Learning by Doing," "Economic Growth Through Creative Destruction" and "Leaders *vs.* Followers in R&D," instead of the short summaries of Section 8.5? In the end, I took the decision to leave the book as it is now, mostly because (I thought) otherwise the main line would be lost (and the book have gotten too long for a one semester teaching). Regrettably, one cost of this decision is that some important contributors to the recent revival of economic growth theory had to be bypassed. I apologize for that, and am willing to rethink the matter if suggested.

When this book was ready for print, Richard W. England, of the University of New Hampshire, sent me a precious new article by Richard Nelson (Nelson, 1997) which bears on many of the issues treated in the book. Upon reading this article, I was tempted to introduce a number of qualifiers to some of the things I say in the book. But I have decided not to do it because from a pedagogical point of view it will be better that the readers of this book not yet acquainted with Professor Nelson's article, be "shaken up" by its reading afterwards. I eagerly encourage them to read this article. I will certainly ask my own students to do it as their last assignment for the course (and do hope that Professor Nelson's message permeates the profession).

Finally, I would like to devote a few lines to what (possibly) is good advice to the students. Although this book is short in length, it contains more material than seems apparent at first glance, and it must be covered in four months, so please do not postpone its reading for too long.

Acknowledgements

In writing this book I have benefited from many friends and colleagues, unfortunately (or should I say "fortunately?") too numerous to name at length. Among them, I would like to mention Christopher Pissarides, of the London School of Economics, whose teachings reconciled me with the subject; David Anisi and Ignacio Mauleón, of the University of Salamanca, whose fellowship "boosted" me in those difficult moments one goes through while writing a book (I suppose any book); Cesar Rodriguez, of the University of Oviedo, for the careful reading he did of the equations in the first draft of the book and other related comments; Angel de la Fuente, of the Spanish Center for Advanced Scientific Research (CSIC) in Barcelona, for his readiness to help whenever I needed his advice; and Richard W. England, of the University of New Hampshire, for giving me, as he always has, encouragement and ideas (many of which, particularly those that relate to actual or potential "environmental and resource constraints" in the process of economic development, I am *not equipped* to tackle).

Professors Jordi Caballé, of the Universitat Autònoma de Barcelona; Timothy Kehoe, of the University of Minnesota; and Robert M. Solow, of the Massachusetts Institute of Technology, deserve special thanks. Among other things, Jordi Caballé showed me that I could not prove what *he* already knew could *not* be proven (this happened while writing Chapter 5), thus reminding me of the old saying, attributed to a famous Spanish bullfighter, that "What cannot be, cannot be and, besides ... it is impossible." Dr. Caballé read the entire first draft of the book and pointed out to me many ideas which have greatly improved the final output. Since, perhaps mistakenly, I have not followed his suggestions entirely, he is by no means responsible for any errors that may remain. However, much of what is good in this book is due to his friendly advice.

Tim Kehoe, whose devotion to Spain and to her new vintage of young economics scholars I hope my country will officially acknowledge, read through the manuscript, and called my attention to, and guided me on, some very important issues. It will be all my fault if I have not reached his standards.

Robert Solow kindly encouraged me to round the first version of the book, which he saw as "lecture notes" for my students, and take them to the publishers. I have tried to make good use of his suggestions and I hope I have done the rounding properly, so that neither his thoughts nor those of the other contributors to the subject of economic growth quoted in the text, have been mistreated. It goes without saying that I am the only one to blame if I have failed to do my duty.

The people at Edward Elgar Publishing who helped me on this project: Dymphna Evans, Julie Leppard, Fiona Peacock and Emma Gribbon, were consistently gracious and efficient, as was the anonymous proofreader of the manuscript, and I am very grateful to them.

A grant from the Marc Rich Foundation help me cover some of the expenses needed to keep the research "on the march" and it is gratefully acknowledged.

Finally, and foremost, I thank my family, to whom I owe eternal gratitude. They took some punishment from my writing the book; but they know that compared with them nothing, not even this book, is of real value to me.

Grindenwal (Switzerland)

Part I
Introduction:
The "Stylized Facts" of
Economic Growth

"The primary economic goal ... is to achieve the highest possible
rate of sustainable economic growth ... Growth is the key
to raising living standards, to leaving a legacy of
prosperity for our children, to uplifting those most in need."
(George Bush)

Chapter 1

The "Stylized Facts" of Economic Growth

1.1 Introduction

Understanding "the nature and causes of the wealth of nations," the reasons why some countries are rich and others poor, was the main purpose of inquiry for economic science in the early days of its existence. But with the passing of time, that aim was slowly abandoned in favor of other subjects. To the economists' disclaimer, this was partly the result of a serious lack of data on which to ground their theories (and "theory without measurement" doesn't really do). The publication in recent years of two major data banks for a large number of countries has eased the situation, hence the "main questions" are back. In fact, they have become once again the center of economic research. In this revival there are new ideas and new tools. There is also some confusion, but this can be hardly avoided: it appears to be in the nature of the sediment of knowledge.

There is no doubt, therefore, that more time will have to pass before we can separate robust results from "intellectual white noise" in this new flow of research. However, on some very important issues a consensus has been reached that new ideas (such as the importance of human capital accumulation, the process of "learning-by-doing," and the existence of externalities from technical innovation) will remain with us and are likely to be fruitful. This book is about those new issues.

1.2   Trend and Cycles in the Macroeconomic Time Series

Before we move into the proper topic of this book (the long-run behavior of the macroeconomy), it is convenient to clarify the fact that most macro-economic time series, such as the real gross national product (Y), the stock of physical capital (K), the level of employment (L), or series which result from certain combination of them, such as the level of per capita output $(y = Y/L)$, the capital–labor ratio $(k = K/L)$, and so on, share a number of common features. The main point here is how to distinguish between their *long-run* and *short-run* behavior. The former constitutes the *trend* (or *tendency*) of the series; the latter, its *cycle*. How to separate one from the other is an unresolved issue. However, for our purpose it will be sufficient to plot the relevant series against time and look at it with "common sense."

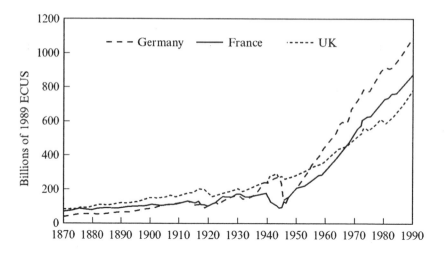

Figure 1.1: Germany, France and UK Real GDPs, 1870–1990. *Source*: Adapted from M. Burda and C. Wyplosz (1993)

For instance, Figure 1.1 depicts the performance of Germany, France and the UK real gross domestic product over the period 1870 to 1990 (a period long enough to be treated as "the long run"). The mere look at these series shows that, in conjunction (that is, observing the entire 1870–1990 period and avoiding fixing our attention on any one shorter period), the real GDP *has been growing* in all three cases. We thus say that it exhibits a *rising trend*, which means that, over the long run, the real GDP has grown. A second look, this time abstracting from the entire long-run behavior and fixing our attention on much shorter periods shows that, in all cases, although exhibiting a *long-run* increase, this has not been *smooth*: sometimes the level of real GNP accelerates, sometimes it slows down. In sum, the real GNP moves *cyclically*, but exhibits a *long-run* rising *trend*.

This (the existence of trend and cycles) is not a characteristic of the real GNP only, but of virtually all macroeconomic time series. The trend, though, is not always rising, as with the real GNP examples. It can be decreasing or even flat. For instance, Figure 1.2 represents the behavior of the US ratio of labor income to capital income (that is, the ratio of wages to profits, W/Π, known as the "functional distribution of income"). The short-

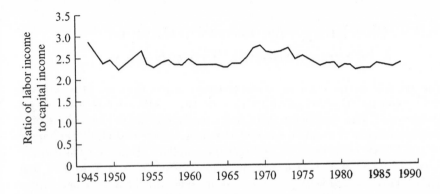

Figure 1.2: US Ratio of Labor Income to Capital Income, 1945–1990. *Source*: US Department of Commerce

run cyclical behavior of this series is clear; but it is also clear that in the long run the series exhibits no perceptible trend: it behaved cyclically, but around a constant value (no trend, or absence of any *perceptible tendency*), of approximately 7 to 3 (which means that, regardless of the many short-run variations, over the long run, that is, on average, labor receives about 70 percent, and capital 30 percent, of the US real GNP).

1.2.1 Separating "Trend" and "Cycles" in a Macroeconomic Time Series

The big question is: How are we to separate the trend from the cycles in a macroeconomic time series? We have suggested the use of "common sense." This is but a confession of the little agreement among economists about how to proceed in this matter.[1] Hopefully, the "common sense" method will have allowed the reader to obtain an idea of what really matters for the topics covered at the level of this book, namely, that almost all macroeconomic time series exhibit long-run tendencies (upwards, downwards, or simply no perceptible tendency at all), and that, over the short run, the same series move up and down once and again.

Differentiating between the trend and the cycles of a macroeconomic time series is important because the reasons that determine the trend of a series are not the same as those that determine its cycles.[2] Thus, economists divide the subject of macroeconomics into two different (albeit related) parts, namely, the *theory of the business cycle* and the *theory of economic growth.* This book is about the latter.

1.3   The Long-run Growth Rate of a Macroeconomic Time Series

For the most part, we will focus on the *long-run growth rates* of the relevant macroeconomic time series rather than on the *absolute levels* of the series themselves. The reason for this can be easily understood by means of a simple example. Imagine a country, the USA, whose real GDP per capita $(y = Y/L)$ in 1870 was US$2209 (constant dollars of 1985). The annual average rate of growth of y over the whole period from 1870 to date was 1.75. This has made it possible that in 1990 the USA real per capita income was US$18200, making the USA the richest country in the world (as measured by the level of per capita income). Now imagine that, instead of having grown, in per capita terms, at the annual average rate of 1.75, it had grown at 0.75. Then, its per capita income in 1990 would have been US$5500 and it would be enjoying the same per capita income as Mexico. (All figures in this example are measured in constant US$ of 1985.) And the only difference is but one percentage point in the growth rate. This

---

[1] It may be convenient to know, however, that although the profession has not yet agreed upon *one* specific method, we *do* have sophisticated ways of separating the trend from the cycles of a time series. But since this does not appear to be really essential for our present purpose, we refer the interested reader to, for instance, Turner (1993), Chapter 1, and she may proceed from there, should she find the story interesting.

[2] A branch of the profession, known as the "Real Business Cycle" theorists, would disagree with this statement. To them, there are "causes" for the economy's behavior, period, although distinguishing the cycles from the trend is still meaningful statistically to establish, for instance, "stylized facts" about them, as we will do in Section 1.5 below. (Luckily, we need not go into this dispute to answer the questions that we will be addressing in this book, at least not so far as we see the matter today, so happily for us we may be permitted to quietly move on.)

means that we ought to be looking for ways to raise the *rates of growth*.

With this in mind, let us look back to Figure 1.1 (the 1870–1990 real GNPs of Germany, France and the UK). This figure shows, as we already know, that these series exhibit rising trends. However, they also *seem* to show that in each case the real GNP *grows at an increasing rate*. This, however, might be a deceptive impression, although a very common one. It happens because, unconsciously, one tends to identify the *slope* of the time-series variable with the variable's rate of growth. Note, however, that the slope is given by (in our example) $\dot{Y} = dY/dt$ whereas the rate of growth is given by[3] $\overset{o}{Y} = (dY/dt)/Y = \dot{Y}/Y$ or:

$$\overset{o}{Y} = \frac{d \log Y}{dt} \tag{1.1}$$

In other words, it is the slope of $\log Y$, and *not* the slope of the *levels* of Y (or for that matter, of any macroeconomic time series) which provides the growth rate of the variable. Hence, if we want to obtain a rough idea of the growth rate of an economic time series we must plot against time

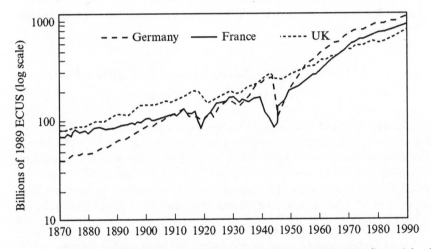

Figure 1.3: Germany, France and UK Real GDPs, 1870–1990 (logarithmic scale). *Source*: Adapted from M. Burda and C. Wyplosz (1993)

the *logarithm* of the corresponding variable, *not* the variable itself. Thus

---

[3] About notation: let x be a variable that evolves through time, $x = x(t)$ or x_t, for short. In mathematics, it is customary to represent $dx(t)/dt$ with the symbol $\dot{x}$. However, there is no clear consensus on how to represent the *growth rate* of the variable, $\dot{x}/x$. Since it will be burdensome to write this all the time, we will represent the growth rate of x by $\overset{o}{x}$. That is to say: $\dot{x} = dx/dt$ and $\overset{o}{x} = \dot{x}/x$.

for instance, Figure 1.3 graphs the logarithm, not the levels, of Germany, France and the UK real GNPs (that is, $\log Y$ instead of Y itself) against time. One property of the logarithmic transformation of a time series is that it conserves all the properties of the series, thus we see that the logarithm of the reported real GNPs exhibit (as before) cyclical rising trends. It does not seem at first glance, however, that the growth rate is increasing. Rather, since the trend of $\log Y$ is roughly a straight line, and the growth rate of a straight line is constant, the first-glance impression that emerges from Figure 1.3 is that the long-run growth rate of the real GNPs is roughly constant (that is, $\overset{o}{Y} = d \log Y / dt \approx$ constant). It might be actually increasing, however, for this is only "eye inspection." But the point is made that, by looking at the time-series graph of a variable we may obtain a very wrong idea of the variable's rate of growth. In sum, the mere "eye inspection" of the logarithmic graph provides an idea of the rate of growth that is still not entirely reliable ("rough"), but clearly much better than the one obtained from the graph of the time-series itself. Thus, since for the most part we will be interested in the growth rates rather than in the *absolute levels* of most macroeconomic time series, very often we will directly graph the logarithm of the relevant series.

1.4   Methodology: Sherlock Holmes' Four Rules of Scientific Inquiry

We acknowledge that the title of this section may sound funny, for we are supposed to quote from such authors on methodology as Popper, Kuhn, Lakatos, and Feyerabend, to mention only a few of the masters. But after years of study, we believe that Sherlock Holmes (in truth, of course, Sir Arthur Conan Doyle, only the character has devoured its author) made it simpler. As McAleer (1994, p. 317) has commented, Mr. Sherlock Holmes' detection methods

> may be interpreted as accommodating the relationship between data and theory, modeling, specification and respecification of theories, testing, re-evaluation and reformulation of theories, and finally reaching a solution to the problem at hand.

Thus, here we have "the method" of scientific inquiry as far as our preference is concerned. From Sir Arthur Conan Doyle's *A Scandal in Bohemia*:

> Dr. Watson: "This is indeed a mystery. What do you imagine that it means?"
> Sherlock Holmes: "I have no data yet. It is a capital mistake

to theorise before one has data. Insensibly one begins to twist facts to suit theories, instead of theories to suit facts."

Hence, **RULE 1:** *Begin with data.*

From *The Adventure of the Yellow Face*:

Sherlock Holmes: "What do you think of my theory?"
Dr. Watson: "It is all surmise."
Sherlock Holmes: "But at least it covers all the facts."

Hence, **RULE 2:** *Build a theory (or theories, for there may be many) that is (are) capable of covering the facts that are known to us.*

From *The Adventure of the Copper Beeches*:

Sherlock Holmes: "I have devised seven separate explanations, each of which would cover the facts as we know them. But which of these is correct can only be determined by the fresh information waiting for us."

Similarly, from *The Adventure of the Sussex Vampire*:

Sherlock Holmes: "One forms provisional theories and waits for fuller knowledge to explode them."

And from *The Adventure of Wisteria Ledge*:

Sherlock Holmes: "If the fresh facts which come to our knowledge all fit themselves into the scheme, then our hypothesis may gradually become a solution."

Hence, **RULE 3:** *Do not take for granted that your theory, or any competing one, is correct because it covers all the facts so far known to us. With time, new facts will come to our knowledge. Then it may be the case that one or more of the existing theories will also cover the new facts, in which case those theories will live on for the time being.*

But what will happen if none of them do? From *The Adventure of the Yellow Face*:

Sherlock Holmes: "When new facts come to our knowledge, which cannot be covered by [the existing theory(ies)], it will be time to reconsider [the existing theory(ies)]"

Hence, **RULE 4:** *If new evidence comes to our knowledge and it cannot be accommodated within the existing theory(ies), the latter must be re-constructed, so that we twist the theory to accommodate the facts, not the facts to accommodate the theory.*

Do not take these "rules of scientific inquiry" too strongly. Many philosophers of science would not agree with them. But we think they express the general philosophy of this book, hence we will (more or less, as always happens in science) follow them.

1.5   Kaldor's "Stylized Facts" of Economic Growth

The "facts" with which we are concerned were laid down by Kaldor (1961). He had at the time fewer data than we have available today, but nonetheless was able to identify a number of "empirical regularities" of economic growth which we now regard as a *benchmark*, the minimum requirement any model of economic growth must satisfy. They are the following:

Stylized Fact (1) In the long-run, per capita output grows at a positive rate which shows no tendency to diminish (that is, there might be some discussion as to whether it is constant or increasing, but is definitely non-decreasing). This fact can be rephrased in a number of ways. For instance, it is often indicated by saying that the real world shows *unceasing per capita income growth*. On the other hand, if we can use per capita output as an indicator of the living standard of countries (as economists usually do), this "stylized fact" can be phrased as follows: the standard of living always increases from one generation to the next. Finally, since $y = Y/L$ is a measure of labor productivity, we can say that the productivity of labor exhibits a rising trend. In sum, we have $\overset{\circ}{y} = (\overset{\circ}{Y/L}) > 0$.

Stylized Fact (2) The capital–output ratio shows no perceptible upward or downward trend, that is, in the long-run it remains roughly constant. Thus it is $K/Y \approx constant$.

Stylized Fact (3) The return to physical capital (that is, the profit rate, ρ) shows no perceptible upward or downward trend, that is, in the long run it remains roughly constant (although it does exhibit sharp changes in the short run). Thus we have $\rho = \Pi/K \approx constant$ (Π is the mass of profits).

Stylized Fact (4) There is a great variety of growth rates of per capita income ($\overset{\circ}{y}$) world-wide, that is, the rate of growth of per capita output differs substantially across countries.

From these facts many others follow (and they have also been observed in the real world). For instance, facts (1) and (2) together imply that in the long run the capital–labor ratio grows at a positive rate which shows no tendency to diminish. Moreover, it (roughly) coincides with the growth rate of per capita output. This is simple to show. From the "stylized fact (2)" we have (see Mathematical Appendix A.1):

$$\frac{K}{Y} = \text{constant} \Leftrightarrow (\overset{\circ}{K/Y})=0 \Rightarrow \left[\left(\frac{K}{L}\right)^{\!\!\circ} \!\! / \left(\frac{Y}{L}\right)\right]=0 \qquad (1.2)$$
$$\Rightarrow (\overset{\circ}{K/L}) - (\overset{\circ}{Y/L})=0 \Rightarrow \overset{\circ}{k}=\overset{\circ}{y}.$$

Facts (2) and (3) together imply that the income shares of labor and physical capital (W/Y and Π/Y, respectively) remain constant in the long run; and this, in turn, implies that the wage rate (ω) exhibits a rising trend: moreover, its rate of growth is the same as the growth rate of per capita output (that is, in the long run the real wage grows at the rate of labor productivity). This is also easy to show. By definition we have:

$$\rho = \frac{\Pi}{K} = \frac{\Pi}{Y} \cdot \frac{Y}{K} \Rightarrow \frac{\Pi}{Y} = \rho \cdot \frac{K}{Y}, \qquad (1.3)$$

hence, since K/Y is constant by the "Stylized Fact (2)" and $\rho = \Pi/K$ is also constant by the "stylized fact (3)," the income share of physical capital (Π/Y) must also be constant. Furthermore, $\Pi + W = Y$ by definition, hence it is $(\Pi/Y) + (W/Y)=1$, from which it follows $(W/Y)=1 - (\Pi/Y)$, therefore W/Y is also constant. Thus, the functional distribution of income (the ratio W/Π) is trendless. In light of the many political, social and economic changes that have taken place in the capitalist world (particularly during the second half of this century) this "fact" is surprising; but a *fact* it is: Figure 1.2 shows that it applies to the USA economy, and data from other western economies show that this fact also fits them, even with similar percentages to those of the USA economy. (Approximately 70 percent of real income goes to wages and 30 percent to profits. See Christensen *et al.*, 1980, and Dougherty, 1991, for the cases of Canada, France, Germany, Italy, Japan and the UK.) The long-run stability of factor shares also applies to Latin American countries, although there the capital share tends to be higher (thus the labor share lower) than in the advanced capitalist economies (Elias, 1990).[4] Young (1994) obtains the same result for Hong-Kong, Singapore, South Korea and Taiwan. An *economic explanation* for this fact is still lacking. Now for the rising trend in real wages. By definition we have $\omega = W/L = (W/Y)(Y/L)$, thus it is:

$$\overset{\circ}{\omega} = (\overset{\circ}{W/Y}) + (\overset{\circ}{Y/L}) = \overset{\circ}{y} \qquad (1.4)$$

because W/Y is constant, hence $(\overset{\circ}{W/Y}) = 0$.

Therefore, many empirical regularities of economic growth are known to us, but they are not all independent of each other. Thus, in the end, they can be summarized in the "Stylized Facts (1) to (4)." These are the facts any acceptable model of the long-run behavior of the macroeconomy must *satisfy*. This list is not unique, for it is possible to combine "all the facts known to us" in other ways. We have chosen this particular combination for convenience.

Suggested Reading

Solow, R. (1970). From Chapter 1, specifically the analysis on the "stylized facts" of economic growth.
Turner, P. (1993). Chapter 1.
Romer, P. (1989). Section 2.1.

---

[4] We may want to be careful, though, with *differences* in capital and labor shares reported across countries. Many less developed countries do appear to have lower labor shares than do the more advanced capitalist economies. Even Spain, a fairly developed country, does. But it is not clear that this is not just the reflection of a difference in national income accounting procedures and industrial structure. A major problem is the treatment of the income of self-employed persons, which is usually counted as purely capital income. In a country like the United States this does not make a big difference; in Spain, for instance, it does. When we divide income of self-employed persons proportionally into labor and capital income, the labor shares in the United States and Spain are very similar. Poor data prevent us from making sweeping statements about developing countries in general, but it seems that this sort of problem is common. Another problem, of course, is the presence of additional factors like land.

Part II
The Theory of Economic Growth with "Exogenous" Technical Progress

"To say that the rate of technological progress is exogenous
is not to say that it is ... always mysterious."
(Robert M. Solow)

Chapter 2

The Neoclassical Model of Economic Growth

2.1 Introduction

We thus have "the facts" and the methodology. What we need now is the theory (or theories) capable of accommodating the facts, and the first problem to be addressed is where to start because the theory of economic growth is as old as economics itself. Since it is not our intention to write a history of the ideas on the topic, most practitioners of our discipline will agree that the proper place to start is the Neoclassical Model. This was originally developed by Solow (1956) and Swan (1956). The same year, then, but independently of each other and published in different journals: one (Solow's version) American, the other (Swan's) Australian. This may explain why for many years the neoclassical model was popularly known as "the Solow model." In truth, and justice is being done lately, it is now known as "the Solow–Swan model," as we will refer to it in this book (or, at times, the S&S model, for short).

2.2 The Structure of the Model

The economy has a supply and a demand side. In each year, t, the supply side produces an amount of the single aggregative commodity *real* GNP, Y_t, using three factors of production: the existing stock of physical capital, K_t; the existing labor force, L_t, and the available technology, Θ_t. This output is then sold to (the demand side of the economy) families (consumption, C_t);

firms (investment, I_t), and the government (the public sector purchases, G_t). In truth, some of it is also exported (exports, X_t) and some of C_t, I_t and G_t is not entirely bought from the national production, but imported (imports, M_t). However, since this is a model of the long run, nothing is really lost by operating with a closed economy, as we shall see.

2.2.1   The Supply Side of the Economy

On the supply side of the economy we thus have the following:

$$Y_t = F(K_t, L_t, \Theta_t). \tag{2.1}$$

Hence, there are three sources of growth: $\Delta K, \Delta L$ and $\Delta \Theta$. It is easy to describe the meaning of ΔK (the country's stock of physical capital increases) and the meaning of ΔL (an increase in the country's labor force). It is quite another story to describe the meaning of $\Delta \Theta$, beyond the point of saying that there is an improvement in the country's available technology (or "technical progress," or "technological change") which, to begin with, it is difficult to define. In the Solow–Swan model it is defined as *anything* that allows us to produce more output even with the same amounts of capital and labor and occurs "smoothly" (that is, the level of technology grows at a *constant rate*). Therefore, "technical progress" is analytically equivalent (in the sense that it produces the same effect on output) to an increase in the capital stock, in the labor force, or in both. For that reason, in the early literature on economic growth technical progress was called "factor augmenting." Thus understood, technical progress can be captured by redefining Equation (2.1) as follows:

$$Y_t = F(B_t K_t, A_t L_t), \tag{2.2}$$

where the basic inputs K_t and L_t appear multiplied by, respectively, the index numbers B_t and A_t, which represent technical change (Θ) and are variable in time. The expressions $B_t K_t$ and $A_t L_t$ are called *capital efficiency* and *labor efficiency*, respectively. The idea is very simple: if, as time goes by, $\overset{o}{B} > 0$, production will increase even though K and L remain constant and $\overset{o}{A} = 0$. Why? Because technical change has occurred that has made the stock of physical capital "more efficient." This kind of technical change, with $\overset{o}{B} > 0$ and $\overset{o}{A} = 0$, is called *purely capital augmenting* because, analytically, it produces on output the same effect as an increase in K. Similarly, if $\overset{o}{A} > 0$, production will increase even though K and L remain constant and $\overset{o}{B} = 0$. Why? Because technical change has occurred which has made the existing labor force more efficient. This kind of technical change, with $\overset{o}{B} = 0$ and $\overset{o}{A} > 0$, is called *purely labor augmenting* because, analytically, it produces on output the same effect as an increase in L. Finally, for obvious reasons, if both $\overset{o}{B} > 0$ and $\overset{o}{A} > 0$, technical change is called *capital-and-labor augmenting*.

Given these definitions, the most logical form of dealing with technical change may seem to be to use Equation (2.2) because there is no reason to assume that technical progress will be capital biased or labor biased systematically. However, a curious thing happens, namely the relative income shares will remain constant as technical progress takes place *only* when it is *purely labor-augmenting* or, as it is usually called, "Harrod-neutral." Let us go slowly on this. Harrod (1937) defined technical progress as "neutral" when, as it takes place, the capital–output ratio and the marginal product of capital remain constant. Now of course, in a competitive economy (where factor inputs are paid their marginal products) saying that K_t/Y_t and MPK remain constant amounts to saying that the relative income shares Π_t/Y_t and W_t/Y_t remain constant (because $\Pi_t/Y_t = MPK \cdot K_t/Y_t$ and $W_t/Y_t = 1 - \Pi_t/Y_t$), hence that the functional distribution of income Π_t/W_t remains constant. Now, we are obliged to respect the "stylized facts" of Chapter 1, among which we have, in the long run, a constant capital–output ratio and a constant rate of profit ("stylized facts 2 and 3," respectively) or, equivalently, a constant functional distribution of income. By definition, if technical progress is Harrod-neutral these facts will be satisfied, thus we want technical progress to be Harrod-neutral *at the least*. However, only the purely labor-augmenting technical progress happens to be Harrod-neutral. Why this is so, we *do not know:* It is an indisputable mathematical result proved by Robinson (1938) and Uzawa (1961), but an *economic intuition* for it is still lacking. Despite the unquestionable mathematics of the case, having to accept this result without an appropriate economic story is very unpleasant, of course. But so the matter stands.[1] We

---

[1]Perhaps (but this is only a speculation) the reason is that if we were to use Equation (2.2) as the aggregate production function, we might be counting the same episode of technical progress twice. Why? Because it is important to realize that the purely labor-augmenting technical change implies that the existing labor force becomes more efficient, but not necessarily because the labor force itself has experienced any *qualitative* change due to the technical progress. In fact the qualitative change may have occurred in the capital factor, and yet we could still represent the technical progress episode as "labor augmenting." For instance, a secretary may produce more (that is, increase the output of typewritten pages) either because a new method has been developed to write faster and she has learned it (that is, a purely labor-augmenting episode of technical change), or because a new keyboard has been invented which, by itself, allows the secretary to write faster and has replaced the old one (thus leaving the capital stock K unaltered, that is, a "purely capital-augmenting" episode of technical progress). In either case, labor appears to be more efficient, hence both episodes of technical change can be represented as "purely labor augmenting." To use Solow's (1970) words, it may well be a better design

are therefore compelled to use purely labor-augmenting technical progress, hence the production function will not be Equation (2.2) but the following:

$$Y_t = F(K_t, A_t L_t) = F(K_t, E_t), \qquad (2.3)$$

where $E_t = A_t L_t$ is "labor efficiency," that is, E_t measures the labor factor, not in physical units (as could be the number of workers or the number of hours worked), but in terms of the efficiency of those physical units of labor (and A_t is, of course, an index of technology). This production function is characterized by the following assumptions: **(a)** The law of positive and diminishing marginal productivities applies, that is

$$MPK_t = \frac{\partial Y_t}{\partial K_t} > 0, \quad \frac{dMPK_t}{dK_t} = \frac{\partial^2 Y_t}{\partial K_t^2} < 0 \qquad (2.4)$$

$$MPE_t = \frac{\partial Y_t}{\partial E_t} > 0, \quad \frac{dMPE_t}{dE_t} = \frac{\partial^2 Y_t}{\partial E_t^2} < 0, \qquad (2.5)$$

and **(b)**, production exhibits constant returns to scale (CRTS), that is, if we were able to reproduce, mirror fashion, the economic structure of the country, the level of output would also be reproduced by exactly as many times. This assumption is known as "the replication argument." From the mathematical point of view it means that the aggregate production function (Equation [2.3]) is homogeneous of degree one, that is, that if K and E are both multiplied by a scalar λ, the level of output will multiply by the same scalar, that is:

$$F(\lambda K_t, \lambda E_t) = \lambda Y_t. \qquad (2.6)$$

Furthermore, we are assuming that technical change takes place "smoothly," that is, that the level of technology A_t grows at a *given constant rate*, say g, so that $A_t = A_0 e^{gt}$ (or, in discrete time terms, $A_t = A_0[1+g]^t$), where A_0 is the "initial" level of A. Thus, at any particular time t the level of technology A_t is a *given* number. This implies that the aggregate production function (Equation [2.3]), which exhibits CRTS in K_t and E_t by "assumption **(b)**," *also* exhibits CRTS in K_t and L_t. It also implies that, since by "assumption **(a)**" the law of positive and diminishing marginal productivity applies to E_t, the same law must apply to L_t. In other words, under the assumption that the level of technology grows at a given constant rate g, we have, in addition to "assumptions **(a)** and **(b)**," the following:

$$MPL_t = \frac{\partial Y_t}{\partial L_t} > 0, \quad \frac{dMPL}{dL} = \frac{\partial^2 Y_t}{\partial L_t^2} < 0, \qquad (2.7)$$

of the typewriter machine what gives the secretary the capacity of 1.04 secretaries of the previous year. (Anyway, there is something awkward in the mere thought of "machines becoming more efficient." How? By themselves? Must not there be always a person behind the fabrication of a "more efficient machine"?)

that is, the marginal productivity of labor is positive and diminishing, and:

$$F[\lambda K_t, A_t(\lambda L_t)] = \lambda Y_t, \tag{2.8}$$

that is to say, the production function (Equation [2.3]) exhibits CRTS in K_t and L_t (that is, it is homogeneous of degree one in capital and labor). The importance of these assumptions will become clear later on.

An Example: The Cobb–Douglas Production Function

The requirement of these assumptions (Equations [2.4], [2.5], [2.6], [2.7] and [2.8]) is not capricious. First, it has an element of common sense; and second, it also has an empirical basis: in 1927, Paul Douglas, an economist and later US senator from Illinois, observed that the distribution of national product between capital and labor (the "functional distribution of income," W/Π) had, as a tendency, remained constant. This was a great surprise to him, so he asked Charles Cobb, a mathematician, if he could find an aggregate production function such that rewarding each input, capital and labor, according to their marginal products (as the retribution to capital and labor is supposed to take place in a market economy), the ratio W/Π remained constant. Charles Cobb found that a production function of the following type:

$$Y_t = F(K_t, E_t) = K_t^{\alpha}(A_t L_t)^{1-\alpha}, \quad 0 < \alpha < 1, \tag{2.9}$$

where A_t is an index of the available technology, satisfied the conditions posed by Douglas. Ever since, this type of production functions have been known as "Cobb–Douglas."[2] It is easy to show that Equation (2.9) satisfies the constancy of the W/Π ratio under the requirement that the capital and labor factors be paid their marginal products. We have:

$$MPK_t = \frac{\partial Y_t}{\partial K_t} = \alpha K_t^{\alpha-1}(A_t L_t)^{1-\alpha} = \alpha \frac{K_t^{\alpha}(A_t L_t)^{1-\alpha}}{K_t} = \alpha \frac{Y_t}{K_t} \tag{2.10}$$

$$MPL_t = \frac{\partial Y_t}{\partial L_t} = (1 - \alpha)K_t^{\alpha} A_t^{1-\alpha} L_t^{1-\alpha-1} = (1 - \alpha)\frac{Y_t}{L_t}. \tag{2.11}$$

---

[2] The Cobb–Douglas production function was earlier used by Wicksell, a Swedish economist. Pasinetti (1977, p. 29) comments on this as follows: "[I]n a work written toward the end of his life, Wicksell uses the special production function: $Y = cK^{\alpha}L^{1-\alpha}$. It later became known as the Cobb–Douglas production function, after the names of two American economists who took it up." It seems as if in Pasinetti's mind Charles Cobb and Paul Douglas had deprived Wicksell of the invention of this function. However, to some degree Wicksteed (1894) preceded Wicksell (1901) and there might be still earlier predecessors. The Cobb–Douglas production function is a good example of "Stigler's law," according to which the person after whom an invention is named seldom coincides with the one who made the invention.

If capital and labor are paid according to their marginal products, the mass of wages and the mass of profits are, respectively:

$$W_t = MPL_t \cdot L_t = (1-\alpha)\frac{Y_t}{L_t} \cdot L_t = (1-\alpha)Y_t \qquad (2.12)$$

$$\Pi_t = MPK_t \cdot K_t = \alpha\frac{Y_t}{K_t} \cdot K_t = \alpha Y_t, \qquad (2.13)$$

therefore:

$$\frac{W_t}{\Pi_t} = \frac{(1-\alpha)Y_t}{\alpha Y_t} = \frac{1-\alpha}{\alpha}, \qquad (2.14)$$

which is constant. Thus, the Cobb–Douglas production function is capable of generating the fact observed by Paul Douglas, a fact which, judging by Figure 1.2 is still valid. As pointed out in Section 1.5, despite the many political, social and economic changes which have occurred in the USA since Paul Douglas made his observation, the ratio W/Π has been kept within the narrow band of 2 to 3 (that is, on average, approximately 30 percent of the USA real GNP goes to profits and 70 percent to wages), and this fact is captured by the Cobb–Douglas production function with $\alpha = 0.3$ and $1 - \alpha = 0.7$.

Now the Cobb–Douglas production function satisfies assumptions **(a)** and **(b)**, that is, it exhibits positive but decreasing marginal productivities of the main inputs K_t and E_t and is homogeneous of degree one (exhibits CRTS). (We leave this as an exercise.) Hence, our assumptions about the production function (Equation [2.3]) are reasonable. On the other hand, since the Cobb–Douglas production function (Equation [2.9]) seems to be a good representation of the generic aggregate production function (Equation [2.3]), we will often use the Cobb–Douglas representation. This will allow us to obtain "closed solutions" to many problems (no mystery is involved here: working with the generic function is often burdensome; working with specific forms of the generic function makes things easier).

Interestingly, with the Cobb–Douglas production function it does not matter whether technical change is capital augmenting, labor augmenting, or *both* at the same time. This is easy to show, and since we will use this property of the Cobb–Douglas production function in Chapter 8, we will do the proof. Consider the production function Equation (2.9), that is:

$$Y_t = F(K_t, E_t) = K_t^\alpha (A_t L_t)^{1-\alpha}, \quad 0 < \alpha < 1,$$

where A_t grows at the constant rate g, thus it can be written as $A_t = A_0 e^{gt}$. Since A_t is an *index number* and A_0 is its value at the (initial) time we choose to begin the counting, A_0 can be any number we like. Economists have a preference for setting the initial value of index numbers at 100, but this is merely a convention. It is as well to set the initial value at 1 (and matters will be simplified.) Hence we have:

$$Y_t = e^{g(1-\alpha)t} K_t^\alpha L_t^{1-\alpha} = \left(e^{\gamma t} K_t\right)^\alpha L_t^{1-\alpha},$$

where $\gamma = g(1 - \alpha)/\alpha$, a constant. Clearly, $e^{\gamma t}$ is an index number B_t which, starting off at the value $B_0 = 1$, grows at the constant rate γ, thus we have:

$$Y_t = (B_t K_t)^\alpha L_t^{1-\alpha},$$

that is, the production function is purely capital augmenting. Similarly, the production function (2.9) can also be written as both, capital-and-labor augmenting, as follows:

$$Y_t = \left(e^{\mu t} K_t\right)^\alpha \left(e^{\eta t} L_t\right)^{1-\alpha} = (B_t^* K_t)^\alpha (A_t^* L_t)^{1-\alpha},$$

where B_t^* and A_t^* are index numbers which, starting at the initial values $B_0^* = 1$ and $A_0^* = 1$, respectively, grow at the constant rates μ and η, respectively, and where μ and η are any two positive constants which satisfy the following condition:

$$\frac{\mu\alpha + \eta(1 - \alpha)}{1 - \alpha} = g.$$

Thus, if we carried out our analysis in terms of a Cobb–Douglas production function, we would not have to worry about the form of technical progress because all forms of it (capital augmenting, labor augmenting, or capital-and-labor augmenting) can be accommodated. Since, as already pointed out, the Cobb–Douglas production function seems to be a good representation of production in the real world, economists do in practice use mostly this specific production function. It is always better, of course, to carry out the analysis in terms of a generic production function. But it seems that adopting the specific Cobb–Douglas form for the production function is *not* a big theoretical sin (and it gives us some relief from the embarrassment of being forced to use only *purely labor-augmenting* technical change without really knowing the reason).

Graphical Representation of the Supply Side

Note that our production function (Equation [2.3]) comprises three variables: Y_t, K_t and E_t. This means that its graphical representation requires a three dimensional space (a big practical difficulty with that, of course). Hence, we have to manage to reduce our three-variable production function to one containing only two variables, so that its graphical representation will require a simple two dimensional space. This can be done using the assumption of CRTS, as follows:

$$\frac{Y_t}{E_t} = F\left(\frac{K_t}{E_t}, 1\right) = \frac{Y_t}{A_t L_t} = F\left(\frac{K_t}{A_t L_t}, 1\right). \tag{2.15}$$

Note that $Y_t/E_t = Y_t/(A_t L_t)$ is a new variable: it measures national output neither in absolute levels (Y_t) nor in per capita levels $(y_t = Y_t/L_t)$ but in "labor-efficiency units." Similarly, $K_t/E_t = K_t/(A_t L_t)$ measures the capital stock neither in absolute levels (K_t) nor in per capita levels $(k_t = K_t/L_t)$ but in labor-efficiency units. Thus we need to provide a symbol for variables that are measured in those units, and for that we will use lower case letters with a tilde above. For instance, $\tilde{y}_t = Y_t/E_t = Y_t/(A_t L_t)$ measures the national product in labor-efficiency units, and so does $\tilde{k}_t = K_t/E_t = K_t/(A_t L_t)$ for the capital stock, and so on. Thus the rule is: capital letters (that is, Y_t, K_t, and so on) are the absolute levels of the corresponding variable; lower case letters (that is, y_t, k_t, and so on) are per capita levels; and lower case letters with a tilde above (that is, $\tilde{y}_t, \tilde{k}_t$, and so on) are the variables expressed in labor efficiency units.

Regarding the labor-efficiency variables, note two things: first, they are not measured in practice, hence they are purely "theoretical constructs" (do not worry about this; it happens in all sciences). Second, they are *not* the variables in which we are really interested: remember that we look for theories capable of accommodating the "stylized facts" of Chapter 1, and those facts refer to variables that are measured either in absolute or in per capita levels. Do not worry about this, either. We will have a theory in terms of $\tilde{y}_t, \tilde{k}_t$, and so on, but note that it is easy to revert from those variables to y_t, k_t, and so on, as follows:

(1) From $\tilde{y}_t = \dfrac{Y_t}{A_t L_t}$ we have $\tilde{y}_t = \dfrac{1}{A_t} \cdot y_t$, so that $y_t = A_t \tilde{y}_t$, $\qquad$ (2.16)

(2) From $\tilde{k}_t = \dfrac{K_t}{A_t L_t}$ we have $\tilde{k}_t = \dfrac{1}{A_t} \cdot k_t$, so that $k_t = A_t \tilde{k}_t$, $\qquad$ (2.17)

and so on. With this in mind, the aggregate production function (Equation [2.3]) can be expressed in labor-efficiency units as follows:

$$\tilde{y}_t = F(\tilde{k}_t, 1) = f(\tilde{k}_t). \tag{2.18}$$

Now this is a two-variable function with labor-efficiency output depending on labor-efficiency capital, therefore easy to represent graphically. For that, all we need to know is its shape, that is, the signs of $f'(\tilde{k}_t)$ and $f''(\tilde{k}_t)$. We have:

$$MPK = \frac{\partial Y_t}{\partial K_t} = \frac{\partial \left[A_t L_t f(\tilde{k}_t) \right]}{\partial K_t} = A_t L_t f'(\tilde{k}_t) \frac{1}{A_t L_t} = f'(\tilde{k}_t). \qquad (2.19)$$

Thus, $d\tilde{y}/d\tilde{k} = f'(\tilde{k})$ happens to be the MPK which, by assumption (a), is positive, that is, $f'(\tilde{k}) > 0$, hence we already know that $\tilde{y}_t$ is an increasing function of $\tilde{k}_t$. On the other hand, we have:

$$\frac{dMPK_t}{dK_t} = \frac{\partial^2 Y_t}{\partial K_t^2} = \frac{\partial f'(\tilde{k}_t)}{\partial K_t} = f''(\tilde{k}_t) \cdot \frac{1}{A_t L_t}, \qquad (2.20)$$

which, also by assumption (a), is negative, and since $A_t L_t > 0$, it must be $f''(\tilde{k}_t) < 0$. Therefore, the labor-efficiency production function (Equation [2.16]) has the shape depicted in Figure 2.1.

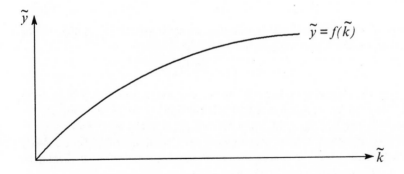

Figure 2.1: The Supply Side of the Economy (labor-efficiency units)

2.2.2 The Demand Side of the Economy

On the demand side we have that the absolute level of real demand (Y^D) is the following:

$$Y_t^D = C_t + I_t + G_t + X_t - M_t. \qquad (2.21)$$

Since this is a long-run model of the economy, classical full employment equilibrium must hold, therefore we have $Y = Y^D$, that is:

$$Y_t = C_t + I_t + G_t + X_t - M_t. \qquad (2.22)$$

Subtracting taxes (T) from both sides of this equation and rearranging, we obtain:

$$Y_t - T_t = C_t + I_t + (G_t - T_t) + (X_t - M_t). \qquad (2.23)$$

In the short run the government can have deficits $(G-T>0)$ or superavits $(G-T<0)$, but in the long run neither of these is sustainable; thus, as a tendency, $G-T=0$.[3] It similarly happens with the balance of trade, $X-M$. In the short run a country may be a net borrower $(X-M<0)$ or a net lender $(X-M>0)$, but neither situation is sustainable in the long run; hence, as a tendency, $X-M=0$. We thus have:

$$Y_t - T_t = C_t + I_t. \qquad (2.24)$$

The left-hand side of this equation is the disposable income of persons, which is either consumed (C_t) or saved (S_t), that is: $Y_t - T_t = C_t + S_t$, hence Equation (2.24) becomes:

$$C_t + S_t = C_t + I_t, \qquad (2.25)$$

and canceling out C_t from both sides of the equation we obtain:

$$S_t = I_t. \qquad (2.26)$$

Now we need a theory of the determination of savings, S. The Solow–Swan model incorporates a very simple one, namely:

$$S_t = sY_t \quad (0 < s < 1), \qquad (2.27)$$

that is, over the long run savings (S) are a constant proportion s of income (Y). Simple as it is, this is not a bad assumption as far as the long run is concerned. It implies that the long-run marginal propensity to consume, $1 - s$, is also constant, which goes against the "secular stagnation thesis" of the early Keynesian, but supported by the empirical record (Kuznets [1946]). Replacing Equation (2.27) into Equation (2.26) we obtain:

$$I_t = sY_t. \qquad (2.28)$$

Since we have expressed the supply side of the economy in terms of labor-efficiency units, we ought to do the same with the demand side. We have:

$$\frac{I_t}{E_t} = \frac{I_t}{A_t L_t} = s\frac{Y_t}{E_t} = s\frac{Y_t}{A_t L_t}, \qquad (2.29)$$

---

[3]How long is the "long run?" We ask this question because some countries (never mind which ones: they are too numerous) have been running a domestic deficit (that is, $G-T>0$) for as long as *we* can remember. Perhaps *our* existence is not long enough to represent the long run ... Or perhaps it will be better to say, not that "as a tendency, $G-T=0$," but that $G-T$ is *trendless*. If so, we will have $G-T = constant$ instead of $G-T=0$, which clearly will not make any difference for the analysis.

that is to say:

$$\tilde{i}_t = s\tilde{y}_t = sf(\tilde{k}_t). \tag{2.30}$$

Going back to Figure 2.1, the above labor-efficiency investment function can be represented as indicated in Figure 2.2 below. (Clearly, the distance that separates $\tilde{i}_t$ from $\tilde{y}_t$ is $\tilde{c}_t$. In this way, logically, the equilibrium equation $\tilde{c}_t + \tilde{i}_t = \tilde{y}_t$ holds.)

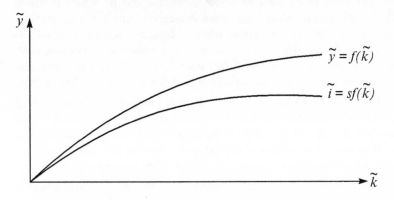

Figure 2.2: Output and Investment (labor-efficiency units)

2.2.3 The Link between the Supply and the Demand Sides of the Economy

The link between the supply and demand sides of the economy is provided by the *net* investment, which each year adds to the capital stock. Hence, assuming that the capital stock depreciates annually at the rate δ ($0 < \delta < 1$), *net* investment is given by:

$$\dot{K}_t = \frac{dK_t}{dt} = I_t - \delta K_t. \tag{2.31}$$

Once again, we need to express this equation in terms of "labor-efficiency" so that all the variables in the model are measured in the same units. From Equation (2.17) we obtain (time subindices are suppressed for convenience):

$$\dot{\tilde{k}} = \frac{d\tilde{k}}{dt} = \frac{\frac{dK}{dt}AL - \left(\frac{dA}{dt}L + \frac{dL}{dt}A\right)K}{A^2L^2} = \frac{\frac{dK}{dt}}{AL} - \overset{\circ}{A}\tilde{k} - \overset{\circ}{L}\tilde{k} \tag{2.32}$$

and using Equation (2.31) we have:

$$\dot{\tilde{k}} = \frac{d\tilde{k}}{dt} = \frac{I - \delta K}{AL} - \overset{\circ}{A}\tilde{k} - \overset{\circ}{L}\tilde{k} = \tilde{i} - (\delta + \overset{\circ}{A} + \overset{\circ}{L})\tilde{k} \tag{2.33}$$

and since $\tilde{i} = sf(\tilde{k})$ we obtain:

$$\dot{\tilde{k}} = \frac{d\tilde{k}}{dt} = sf(\tilde{k}) - (\delta + \overset{\circ}{A} + \overset{\circ}{L})\tilde{k}. \tag{2.34}$$

Now we face the *second* problem with the Solow–Swan model. The first, you will remember, had to do with technical progress: We identified it analytically, but aside from that, we know nothing about it: where it comes from, what motivates it, what retribution it receives, and how that retribution comes about. In sum, we know what it *does*, but ignore all about its *nature*. In the S&S model we circumvent this problem by assuming that, somewhere and somehow, someone "produces" the technical progress and gives it to us in a continual, smooth dose and free of charge, that is, that technical progress takes place at a constant, exogenously given rate, $\overset{\circ}{A}_t = g$. (In Chapters 6, 7 and 8 we will reconsider this assumption, for it is the main concern of very recent research in growth theory.) The problem we face now (the second problem) is similar and concerns the labor force: we know that it grows (because we see it), but at what rate and why?

This question is *not* rhetorical: we need to know $\overset{\circ}{L}$ and the truth is that in the Solow–Swan model no theory of population exists to tell us. Hence, what we do is basically the same we did with technical progress, namely, we assume that over time the population grows "smoothly" at an exogenously given rate, say $\overset{\circ}{L}_t = n$. With these assumptions, Equation (2.34) becomes (time subindices are recouped):

$$\dot{\tilde{k}}_t = \frac{d\tilde{k}_t}{dt} = sf(\tilde{k}_t) - (\delta + n + g)\tilde{k}_t. \tag{2.35}$$

This is called the *fundamental growth (or accumulation) equation*. Note that since we assume g and n to be constant in the long run, the whole term $(\delta + n + g)$ is also constant, and therefore $(\delta + n + g)\tilde{k}_t$ is a straight line with slope $(\delta + n + g.)$

It is important to understand $(\delta + n + g)$ as the rate of depreciation of $\tilde{k}$. This is as follows. Note, first, that $\tilde{k} = K/(AL)$. Thus, a higher δ reduces $\tilde{k}$ by making the *physical* stock of capital, K, to wear out faster. Second, a higher n lowers $\tilde{k}$ because it forces K to be spread more thinly among a larger labor force, L. Finally, the higher g, the higher AL (the number of labor efficiency units), hence $\tilde{k}$ tends to fall. In other words, $(\delta + n + g)$ tends to diminish (that is, it "depreciates") the *accumulation* of the labor-efficient capital stock, $\tilde{k}$. Thus, much in the same way as δ alone is the rate of depreciation of the physical capital stock, K, $(\delta + n + g)$ is to be interpreted as the rate of depreciation of $\tilde{k}$. Therefore, the incorporation of the depreciation line $(\delta + n + g)\tilde{k}_t$ yields the graphical representation for the complete Solow–Swan model given in Figure 2.3.

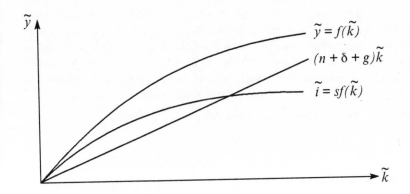

Figure 2.3: The Entire Solow–Swan Model (all variables are expressed in labor-efficiency units)

2.3 The Dynamics of the Solow–Swan Model

The *accumulation Equation* (2.35) is the "engine of growth." It is a differential equation in $\tilde{k}_t$ whose graphical solution is depicted in Figure 2.4. Imagine that the economy starts out with a level $\tilde{k}_0$. (This, as we know, implies a level K_0 of the capital stock, L_0 of the labor force, and a certain level of technological knowledge, A_0. Thus, in a way, $\tilde{k}_0$ measures the "general" starting point of the economy in terms of capital stock and labor efficiency.) With $\tilde{k}_0$, a level of (labor-efficiency units) output, $\tilde{y}_0$, is produced, of which $\tilde{i}_0 = s\tilde{y}_0$ is saved and invested, and an amount $\tilde{c}_0$ is consumed. Now, to produce $\tilde{y}_0$ with $\tilde{k}_0$ some of the (labor-efficient) capital stock is "depreciated" in the amount $(\delta + n + g)\tilde{k}_0$. However, since at this level gross investment $\tilde{i}_0$ exceeds depreciation (that is, $\tilde{i}_0 > [\delta + n + g]\tilde{k}_0$), Equation (2.35) implies $\dot{\tilde{k}}_0 > 0$, that is, in the current period (year $t = 0$) *net* investment is positive, hence for the following year $(t = 1)$ the economy will have a higher $\tilde{k}$, $\tilde{k}_1 > \tilde{k}_0$. Following the same steps, we will find that, in year $t = 1$, $\tilde{y}_1$ will be produced with $\tilde{k}_1$, and so on. Moreover, also in that year *net investment* will be positive (that is, $\dot{\tilde{k}}_1 > 0$), hence the economy will start year $t = 2$ with a higher $\tilde{k}$, and so on. Thus the economy "moves forward." It is clear, though, that the moment will come in which savings (therefore investment) will be just sufficient to cover "depreciation," and in that year $\overset{.}{\tilde{k}} = 0$, that is, *net* investment is zero, $\tilde{k}$ does not grow any further, and the "forward movement" will cease. That point, represented by $\tilde{k}^*, \tilde{y}^*, \tilde{c}^*$, and so on, is called the *steady state*. It does not mean that the economy itself will "stop moving" (or "be paralyzed") but only that it will *reproduce*, year after year, the same conditions as regards $\tilde{k}, \tilde{y}, \tilde{c}$, and so on, which will remain constant at the levels $\tilde{k}^*, \tilde{y}^*, \tilde{c}^*$, and so on. Similarly, if the economy's starting point had been $\tilde{k}'_0$ depreciation would have exceeded investment (that is, *net* investment would have been negative), the labor-efficient capital stock would have diminished (that is, $\overset{.}{\tilde{k}}'_0 < 0$), and so

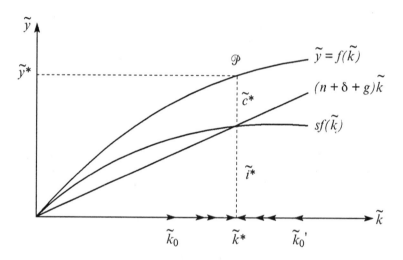

Figure 2.4: The Dynamics of the Solow–Swan Model.

on, and the economy would also have reached the same steady state, this time moving backwards. Therefore, regardless of where an economy starts in terms of $\tilde{k}$, it is pushed towards a steady state position in which, *so long as* the parameters δ, n and g *do not change*, it will continue for ever, reproducing the same levels $\tilde{k}^*, \tilde{y}^*, \tilde{c}^*$, and so on.

Now, we really do not care about the levels of $\tilde{k}, \tilde{y}, \tilde{c}$, and so on, which are "artificial constructs." What we care to know is what happens to the variables actually measured in the real world (Y, y, K, k, C, c, I, i, and so on; that is to say, the absolute and per capita levels of the macro-variables to which the "stylized facts" of Chapter 1 refer and the model must accommodate). Hence, we now turn to this question.

2.4 The Solow–Swan Model and the "Stylized Facts of Economic Growth"

As indicated in the previous section, the economy moves towards its long-run, steady-state equilibrium (represented by point $\mathcal{P}$, in Figure 2.4). In that position, $\tilde{k}$, $\tilde{y}$, and so on, cease to grow (for they take constant values $\tilde{k}^*$, $\tilde{y}^*$, and so on, respectively) but k and y, and so on, do *not*. This can be shown as follows. From:

$$\tilde{y} = \tilde{y}^*(constant) \Rightarrow \overset{\circ}{\tilde{y}} = 0 \Leftrightarrow [Y/(\overset{\circ}{AL})] = 0 \Leftrightarrow \overset{\circ}{Y} - \overset{\circ}{A} - \overset{\circ}{L} = 0 \Leftrightarrow \overset{\circ}{Y} - \overset{\circ}{L} = \overset{\circ}{A}$$

$$\Leftrightarrow (Y\overset{\circ}{/}L) = \overset{\circ}{A} \Leftrightarrow \overset{\circ}{y} = g > 0,$$

that is, once the economy reaches its steady state, per capita income will grow at a positive rate, which happens to be the same as that of the (purely labor-augmenting) technical change. Thus, the Solow–Swan model is consistent with the "stylized fact (1)." Similarly, from:

$$\tilde{k} = \tilde{k}^*(constant) \Rightarrow \overset{\circ}{\tilde{k}} = 0 \Leftrightarrow [K/(\overset{\circ}{AL})] = 0 \Leftrightarrow \overset{\circ}{K} - \overset{\circ}{A} - \overset{\circ}{L} = 0 \Leftrightarrow \overset{\circ}{K} - \overset{\circ}{L} = \overset{\circ}{A},$$

which implies $\overset{\circ}{k} = g > 0$, that is, k will also grow at the same rate as technical change. We thus have the following:

$$K\overset{\circ}{/}Y = \left[\left(\frac{K}{L} \right)\overset{\circ}{/} \left(\frac{Y}{L} \right) \right] = (K\overset{\circ}{/}L) - (Y\overset{\circ}{/}L) = \overset{\circ}{k} - \overset{\circ}{y} = g - g = 0,$$

which implies that the ratio K/Y is constant, therefore the model also accommodates the "stylized fact (2)." Also, we know from Equation (2.19) that $MPK = f'(\tilde{k})$ and that in a competitive economy factor inputs are paid their marginal products, hence:

$$\rho = MPK = f'(\tilde{k}). \tag{2.36}$$

But, in the long-run, steady-state equilibrium, $\tilde{k}_t = \tilde{k}^* = constant$, therefore $f'(k^*) = constant$, thus in the long run ρ is also constant, hence the Solow–Swan model also satisfies the "stylized fact (3)."

Whether the S&S model also satisfies the "stylized fact (4)" is a more complicated matter (a big problem in itself), and we leave this entire question (that is, the great dispersion of per capita income growth rates around the world and the problem of convergence between poor and rich countries) for the next chapter. For now, it takes a little algebra to show that the Solow–Swan model also leads to the following results (we leave the proof as an exercise):

$$\overset{\circ}{c} = g, \quad \overset{\circ}{C} = g + n, \quad \overset{\circ}{i} = g, \quad \overset{\circ}{I} = g + n, \tag{2.37}$$

that is to say, over the long-run, steady-state equilibrium path, the *per capita* variables (y, k, c, i) all grow at the same rate g (the growth rate of the purely labor-augmenting technical progress); whereas the *absolute levels* of those variables (Y, K, C, I) also grow at an equal rate, $g + n$ (that is, at the sum of the growth rates of the labor-augmenting technical progress and the labor force). Given this symmetry in growth rates, the steady-state (long-run) equilibrium path is called the *balanced growth path*. Note that along this path all variables grow at *constant* rates.

2.5   The Solow–Swan Model without Technical Progress

Imagine that there is no technical progress, that is, that we have a situation in which there are increases in the stock of physical capital or/and the labor force but $\overset{o}{A} = g = 0$. It is clear from our previous discussion that in that case $\overset{o}{y} = \overset{o}{k} = 0$. Hence, the neoclassical Solow–Swan model predicts that *sustained growth* of the kind that we observe in reality (that is, economic growth that satisfies the "stylized facts" of Chapter 1) is possible only if there is technical progress. In other words, accumulation of physical capital and increases in the labor force are *not* sufficient, either each one alone or both together, to generate *unceasing economic growth* as we see it in the real world.[4]

The economic reason behind this result is simple. First, imagine that there is only physical capital accumulation and nothing else. Since the Solow–Swan model assumes decreasing MPK, each new bit of physical capital will increase total output Y by an ever-decreasing amount; thus, with a fixed labor force, $y = Y/L$ will grow at a decreasing rate, hence $\overset{o}{y}$ will eventually come to a halt. Now imagine that there are only increases in the labor force. Since, by assumption, the MPL is also decreasing, the same result will follow, and more evidently, in this case.

Finally, consider the case in which there are *both* accumulation of physical capital and increases in the labor force. Since, also by assumption, there are CRTS in K and L, doubling both, for instance, will double Y, but the ratio $y = Y/L$ will not grow at all. Hence, either there are continual infusions of technical progress, or economic growth as we see it in reality is impossible within the neoclassical Solow–Swan model. In the end, therefore, technical progress is the true engine of growth in this model. (We will

---

[4]The interested reader may want to derive this result by herself: the procedure is analytically similar to the one we followed to this point, the only difference being the assumption that there is no technical progress.

come back to this issue later, for it is an important feature of the model.)

2.6 Policy Experiments and Empirics

2.6.1 Changes in the Saving Rate

Imagine that the savings rate increases from its current value, s_0, to s_1. Consequently, the labor-efficient investment function $\tilde{i} = s_0 f(\tilde{k})$ shifts to $\tilde{i} = s_1 f(\tilde{k})$ and the current steady state position, represented by $\mathcal{P} = \{\tilde{k}^*, \tilde{y}^*, etc.\}$ in Figure 2.5, is lost. As a result of this, at the current steady state value of the labor-efficient capital stock, $\tilde{k}^*$, investment is greater than "depreciation," that is, $\tilde{i}^* = s_1 f(\tilde{k}^*) > (n+\delta+g)\tilde{k}^*$, therefore *net* investment is positive, hence for the next period the economy's labor-efficient capital stock will grow, thus moving the economy towards a new steady state position, represented by $\mathcal{P}' = \{\tilde{k}'^*, \tilde{y}'^*, etc.\}$. The transition to the new

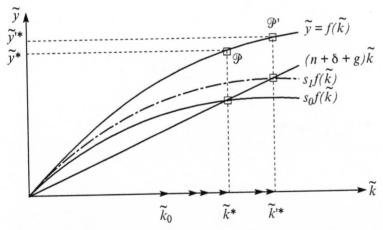

Figure 2.5: Transition to the New Steady State Following an Increase in the Rate of Savings

steady state has taken T years (say from the current period, t, to $t + T$), after which the economy settles at the (once again) constant *labor-efficient* values $\tilde{y}'^*, \tilde{k}'^*$, and so on. Given that $\tilde{k}'^* > \tilde{k}^*$, we have $\tilde{y}'^* > \tilde{y}^*$. Since, on the other hand, y and $\tilde{y}$ are linked one for one by $y = A\tilde{y}$, and A grows exogenously at the rate g, the steady state path of y after the increase in s, $\{y^*\} = \{y^*_{t+T}, y^*_{t+T+1}, etc.\}$, must be *above* the previous steady state path of y, $\{..., y^*_{t-2}, y^*_{t-1}, y^*_t\}$, but *parallel* to it when measured in logarithmic scale, for y grows at the rate g on whatever the steady state path. Now the question is, what path does y follow *during the transition* from the old to the new steady state, that is, from period t to period $t+T$? The situation is depicted in Figure 2.6, of which panel (a) shows the evolution of s and panel (b) the evolution of the logarithm of y. Prior to period t the rate of savings is s_0 and the economy's corresponding steady state path of y is $\{..., y_{t-2}^*, y_{t-1}^*, y_t^*\}$ (per capita income grows at the rate g, hence $\log y$ follows the trajectory $\{..., \mathcal{A}_{t-2} = \log y_{t-2}^*, \mathcal{A}_{t-1} = \log y_{t-1}^*, \mathcal{A}_t = \log y_t^*\}$). Then the savings rate is raised to $s_1 > s_0$, the economy's steady state is lost and a new one reached

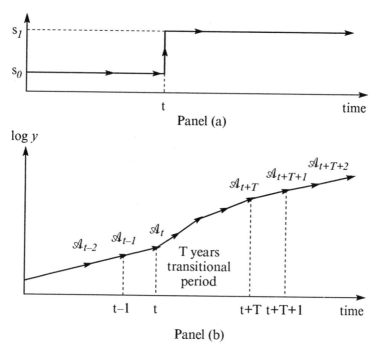

Panel (a)

Panel (b)

Figure 2.6: Per Capita Income Trajectory Following an Increase in the Rate of Savings (Panel [b] is drawn in logarithmic scale)

after a transitional period of T years. We know that in the new steady state $\log y$ will follow the trajectory $\{\mathcal{A}_{t+T} = \log y_{t+T}^*, \mathcal{A}_{t+T+1} = \log y_{t+T+1}^*, ...\}$, which is above and parallel to the previous steady state trajectory of $\log y$. Clearly, this implies that in the transitional period (that is, during the T years from period t to period $t+T$) the *slope* of $\log y$ must be *greater* than in either steady state trajectories. In other words, during the transitional period per capita income grows at a rate higher than g, as represented in

Figure 2.6, panel (b). (The reason why, in this particular example [that is, an *increase* in the rate of savings] the *transitional* trajectory of log y is *concave* will become clear in Chapter 3.)

Empirics

The S&S model thus predicts that countries with a higher rate of savings (therefore a higher proportion of real GNP devoted to investment), should tend to also have a higher level of per capita income. How well does this prediction fair against the actual data? The international evidence on the relationship between savings (therefore investment) rates and per capita income is depicted in Figure 2.7, which relates those two variables for a

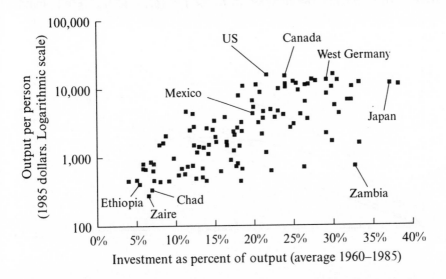

Figure 2.7: International Evidence on Savings (therefore Investment) Rates and Per Capita Income. *Source:* N. Gregory Mankiw, *Macroeconomics*, 1992, p. 88

sample of 112 countries. Clearly, the data do not reject the prediction of the S&S model.

2.6.2 Changes in the Rate of Population Growth

Imagine that the rate of population growth, n, increases from its current value, n_0, to n_1. Consequently, the labor-efficiency depreciation line,

$(n_0+\delta+g)\tilde{k}$ rotates upwards to $(n_1+\delta+g)\tilde{k}$ and the current steady state position, represented by $\mathcal{P}=\{\tilde{k}^*, \tilde{y}^*, \textit{ etc.}\}$ in Figure 2.8, is lost. As a result of this, at the current steady state value of the labor-efficient capital stock, $\tilde{k}^*$, investment is lower than "depreciation," that is, $\tilde{i}^* = sf(\tilde{k}^*) < (n_1+\delta+g)\tilde{k}^*$, therefore *net* investment is negative, hence for the next period the economy's labor-efficient capital stock will diminish, thus moving the economy towards a new steady state position, represented by $\mathcal{P}' = \{\tilde{k}'^*, \tilde{y}'^*, \textit{ etc.}\}$. The transition to the new steady state has taken T years (say from the current period, t, to $t+T$), after which the economy settles at the (once again) constant *labor-efficient* values $\tilde{y}'^*, \tilde{k}'^*$, and so on. Given that $\tilde{k}'^* < \tilde{k}^*$, we have $\tilde{y}'^* < \tilde{y}^*$. Since, on the other hand, y and $\tilde{y}$ are linked one for one by $y = A\tilde{y}$, and A grows exogenously at the rate g, the steady state path of y after the increase in n, $\{y^*\} = \{y^*_{t+T}, y^*_{t+T+1}, \textit{etc.}\}$, must

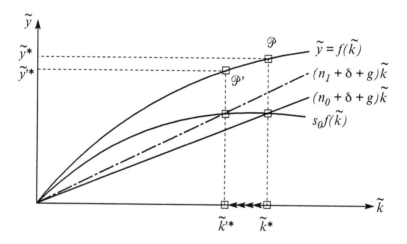

Figure 2.8: Transition to the New Steady State Following an Increase in the Rate of Population Growth

be *below* the previous steady state path of y, $\{..., y^*_{t-2}, y^*_{t-1}, y^*_t\}$, but *parallel* to it when measured in logarithmic scale, for y grows at the rate g on whatever the steady state path. Now the question is, what path does y follow *during the transition* from the old to the new steady state, that is, from period t to period $t + T$? The situation is depicted in Figure 2.9, of which panel (a) shows the evolution of n and panel (b) the evolution of the logarithm of y. Prior to period t the rate of population growth is n_0 and the economy's corresponding steady state path of y is $\{..., y^*_{t-2}, y^*_{t-1}, y^*_t\}$ (per capita income grows at the rate g, hence log y

follows the trajectory $\{..., \mathcal{A}_{t-2} = \log y^*_{t-2}, \mathcal{A}_{t-1} = \log y^*_{t-1}, \mathcal{A}_t = \log y^*_t\}$).
Then the rate of population growth is raised to $n_1 > n_0$, the economy's
steady state is lost and a new one reached after a transitional period of T
years. We know that in the new steady state $\log y$ will follow the trajectory
$\{\mathcal{A}_{t+T} = \log y^*_{t+T}, \mathcal{A}_{t+T+1} = \log y^*_{t+T+1}, ...\}$, which is below and parallel to
the previous steady state trajectory of $\log y$. Clearly, this implies that in
the transitional period (that is, during the T years from period t to period

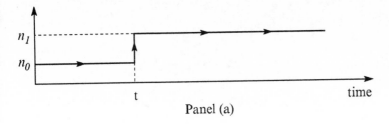

Panel (a)

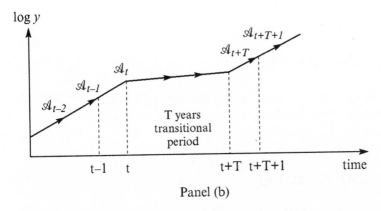

Panel (b)

Figure 2.9: Per Capita Income Trajectory Following an Increase in the Rate
of Population Growth. (Panel [b] in is drawn in log scale)

$t + T$) the *slope* of $\log y$ must be *lower* than in either steady state trajectories. In other words, during the transitional period per capita income grows
at a rate lower than g, as represented in Figure 2.9, panel (b). (The reason
why in this case the *transitional* trajectory of $\log y$ is *convex* will become
clear in Chapter 3.)

Empirics

The Solow–Swan model thus predicts that countries with higher rates of
population growth should tend to have lower levels of per capita income.

Figure 2.10 shows that this prediction is consistent with the international evidence.

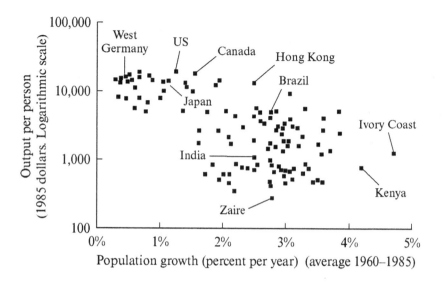

Figure 2.10: International Evidence on Population Growth and Per Capita Income. *Source:* N.G. Mankiw, *Macroeconomics*, 1992, p.99

Suggested Reading

Mankiw, N. Gregory (1992). Ch. 4, Case Studies 4.2, 4.3 and 4.5.

Problems

Problem 2.1. Imagine that a country's capital stock is devastated by a regretful event, such as an earthquake or a war. When reconstruction begins, what would the Solow–Swan model predict as regards the country's rate of growth? Can you find any historical example(s) consistent with your explanation?

Problem 2.2. Two countries, i and j, whose economies are well represented by the Cobb–Douglas production function $Y_t = K_t^\alpha (A_t L_t)^{1-\alpha}$ and behave according to the Solow–Swan model, have the same parameters

s, n, δ and g but differ in their levels of technology, $A_{it} > A_{jt}$. They are both in steady state but, as a result of their difference in the level of technology, output in country i is twice as large as output in country j, that is, $Y_{it} = 2Y_{jt}$.

(a) Represent the current situation of these two countries in a graph.
(b) By what factor do the two countries' capital stock differ?
(c) By what factor do the two countries' level of technology differ?
(d) Assuming that factor inputs (K and L) are paid their marginal productivities (as the S&S model assumes) and that they are free to migrate without cost, will they (either, K or L, or both) have any incentive to move from one country to the other? Why (or why not)?

Problem 2.3. (This question needs not have a clear cut answer. Thus, it is proposed mainly for discussion; whatever you conclude, provide arguments.) The country of Solowandia has a publicly run *fully funded* social security system. However, when the system was created in the late 1950s, the government did not make it mandatory for all citizens to participate in it: the workers were obliged, but self-employed persons (such as peasants, retail traders, and so on) were left at liberty — they could join in or stay out, whatever they wished to do. As it happened, many did not, and quite a few among them, besides, did not save on their own in the years that followed. Thus they now find themselves with no pension and no savings, and because of this, social turmoil is in sight. To avoid the otherwise inevitable, the government has called upon a team of experts for counsel. They all agree that the state will have to pay a pension to these individuals even though they never contributed to the existing social security fund; there is disagreement among the experts, however, as to how implement this policy. Two courses of action are being considered:

(a) Obtain the required revenue from the existing capitalized fund (even though it rightfully belongs only to those who have made contributions to it), and give the social security system a mandatory *pay-as-you-go* structure from now on;

(b) Obtain the revenue needed to pay the additional pensions by levying an earn-marked tax on everyone so as to increase the existing social security fund by the amount required, and make the current *fully funded* system mandatory for everyone from now on — so that the same problem does not repeate itself in the future.

The government chooses (a), and a professor of economics warns that by doing so the party in government will surely avoid political trouble for itself, but the measure chosen may have a serious negative growth impact on the economy. Now you choose sides.

Chapter 3

The Hypothesis of Convergence (I): Economies with the Same Steady State

3.1 Introduction

The level of per capita income is often used as an indicator for the degree of poverty (or richness) of the different countries (see the Appendix at the end of this chapter). Now, on that basis we need only look at the data

Table 3.1: *Real* Per Capita Income Around the World ($US1990)

Country	*Real* GDP Per Capita, 1990
USA	21,360
Japan	16,950
Korea	7,910
Mexico	5,980
Brazil	4,780
India	1,150

Source: The World Bank, *World Development Report, 1992.*

sample provided in Table 3.1 to realize the enormity of the gap between rich and poor countries today (thus, for instance, the USA is nineteen times richer than India). Hence, the following questions arise: Is there any theoretical and (or) empirical reason to believe that the "automatic forces" of the market economy will reduce this gap, or will they tend to widen it instead? What could the poor countries do to overcome their poverty? Which policies are adequate to that end and which are *not*? These questions have long attracted the attention of economists, but in the past the lack of reliable data on which to test their theories rendered much of their valuable effort quite frustrating for them. However, the situation has improved with the publication in recent years of two sets of international historical statistics, one by Maddison (1982, 1989 and 1991), the other by Summers and Heston (1991 and 1995 for the latest update). The ensuing debate, known as the "catching-up" controversy, is currently at the forefront of the economics research agenda.

The present chapter, and the next one, recap some results on this topic. They are derived from the Solow–Swan model developed in Chapter 2. They are also far from being definite (the literature in this area is evolving *by the day*). The content of these two chapters must, therefore, be taken as an "introduction" to the topic. Quite likely, in a few years (and surely *very* few) they will be needing revision. But this should not be discouraging; on the contrary, since new scientific results *never* spring from the vacuum, the "innovations" in this area will be easier to follow up in light of what is mentioned in these two chapters.

3.2 The Hypothesis of Convergence

The theoretical foundations of the "catching-up" controversy are easily traced in the neoclassical Solow–Swan model of economic growth. Since $\tilde{k}_t = K_t/A_t L_t = (1/A_t)k_t$ and $\tilde{y}_t = Y_t/A_t L_t = (1/A_t)y_t$, we have $k_t = A_t \tilde{k}_t$ and $y_t = A_t \tilde{y}_t$, therefore we obtain $\overset{o}{k} = g + \overset{o}{\tilde{k}}$ and $\overset{o}{y} = g + \overset{o}{\tilde{y}}$. In steady state $\overset{o}{\tilde{k}} = 0$ and $\overset{o}{\tilde{y}} = 0$, hence k and y both grow at the same rate as technical progress, g (a result we already knew). However, outside the steady state neither $\overset{o}{\tilde{k}}$ nor $\overset{o}{\tilde{y}}$ are zero, thus we need to know their value in order to determine $\overset{o}{k}$ and $\overset{o}{y}$. We have (see Mathematical Appendix B.1):

$$\overset{o}{\tilde{y}}_t = \mathrm{Sh}_K \cdot \overset{o}{\tilde{k}}_t, \qquad (3.1)$$

where Sh_K stands for "capital share" (Π/Y). Thus it is:

$$\overset{o}{y}_t = g + \overset{o}{\tilde{y}} = g + \mathrm{Sh}_K \cdot \overset{o}{\tilde{k}}_t . \qquad (3.2)$$

Dividing the *fundamental growth equation* (Equation [2.35]) by $\tilde{k}_t$, we obtain $\overset{o}{\tilde{k}}$, and substituting the result into Equation (3.2), we have:

$$\overset{o}{y}_t = g + \text{Sh}_K \left[s \frac{f(\tilde{k}_t)}{\tilde{k}_t} - (\delta + n + g) \right]. \tag{3.3}$$

For simplicity, assume that the production function is Cobb–Douglas in capital and effective labor, that is, $Y_t = F(K_t, E_t) = K_t^\alpha E_t^{1-\alpha} = K_t^\alpha (A_t L_t)^{1-\alpha}$. In this case $K_t = Y_t^{1/\alpha}(A_t L_t)^{(\alpha-1)/\alpha}$, therefore we have:

$$s \frac{f(\tilde{k}_t)}{\tilde{k}_t} = s A_t^{(1-\alpha)/\alpha} y_t^{(\alpha-1)/\alpha}. \tag{3.4}$$

From the Cobb–Douglas production function we also obtain:

$$\text{Sh}_K = \frac{\Pi}{Y} = \frac{K \cdot PMK}{Y} = \frac{K(\partial Y / \partial K)}{Y} = \alpha. \tag{3.5}$$

Substituting Equations (3.5) and (3.4) into Equation (3.2), and considering the fact that $y^{(\alpha-1)/\alpha} = \exp(\frac{\alpha-1}{\alpha} \log y)$, we have:

$$\overset{o}{y}_t = g + \alpha \left[s A_t^{(1-\alpha)/\alpha} e^{\log y_t \cdot (\alpha-1)/\alpha} - (\delta + n + g) \right], \tag{3.6}$$

which can be further developed by means of a Taylor expansion around the steady state value of $\overset{o}{y}$ (that is, around $y = y^*$ or $\log y = \log y^*$). This yields (see Mathematical Appendix B.2):

$$\overset{o}{y}_t = g + (\alpha-1) \left[s A_t^{(1-\alpha)/\alpha} y_t^{(\alpha-1)/\alpha} \right]_{y=y^*} (\log y_t - \log y_t^*). \tag{3.7}$$

From Equation (3.4) we have:

$$\left[s A_t^{(1-\alpha)/\alpha} y_t^{(\alpha-1)/\alpha} \right]_{y=y^*} = s \frac{f(\tilde{k}^*)}{\tilde{k}^*}, \tag{3.8}$$

and since $\overset{o}{\tilde{k}} = 0$ in the steady state, from the fundamental growth equation (Equation [2.35]) results:

$$s \frac{f(\tilde{k}^*)}{\tilde{k}^*} = \delta + n + g. \tag{3.9}$$

Thus, using Equations (3.9) and (3.8), Equation (3.7) can be written as follows:

$$\overset{o}{y}_t = g + (\alpha - 1)(\delta + n + g)(\log y_t - \log y_t^*), \tag{3.10}$$

and letting:

$$(\alpha - 1)(\delta + n + g) = \lambda, \tag{3.11}$$

we have:

$$\overset{\circ}{y_t} = g + \lambda(\log y_t - \log y_t^*). \tag{3.12}$$

This result must be carefully interpreted. In the first place, note that $\log y - \log y^*$ measures the (per capita income) distance which currently separates the economy from its steady state. Thus, the larger the absolute value of $\log y - \log y^*$, the further away the economy is from its long-run (steady state) position. Obviously, the following cases are possible:

(1) $\log y - \log y^* = 0$, that is, the economy is on its long-run (steady-state) position. In this case, $\overset{\circ}{y} = g$, that is to say, per capita income grows at the rate g (the rate of technological progress).

(2) $\log y - \log y^* < 0$, that is, current per capita income is *below* the long-run (steady state) level. In this case, $\overset{\circ}{y} > g$ because $\lambda < 0$, that is to say, the economy grows in per capita terms at a *higher* rate than the long-run (steady state) per capita growth rate, g.

(3) $\log y - \log y^* > 0$, that is, current per capita income is *above* the long-run (steady state) level. In this case, $\overset{\circ}{y} < g$ because $\lambda < 0$, that is to say, the economy grows in per capita terms at a *lower* rate than the long-run (steady state) per capita growth rate, g.

Figure 3.1 depicts what each of these cases implies. First, consider a situation in which currently (period $t = 0$) the economy is in steady state (case [1] above). We have: $\log y_0 = \log y_0^*$, and this is represented by point $\mathcal{A}_0$. In this situation per capita income grows at the rate g, hence for the next period ($t = 1$) its value will be $y_1 = y_0(1+g)$, thus moving along the steady state trajectory from point $\mathcal{A}_0$ to point $\mathcal{A}_1$. Similarly, for period $t = 2$ it will move from point $\mathcal{A}_1$ to point $\mathcal{A}_2$, and so on. Now consider a situation in which per capita income is initially *below* the steady state level (case [2] above). We have: $\log y_0 < \log y_0^*$, and this is represented by point $\mathcal{B}_0$. If starting at this position per capita income grew at the rate g, its value in period $t = 1$ would be $y_0(1+g)$, thus moving from point $\mathcal{B}_0$ to $\mathcal{B}_1$. However, we know that at levels below the steady state value per capita income grows at a rate *higher* than g, hence its value in period $t = 1$ will be higher than $y_0(1+g)$, thus moving from point $\mathcal{B}_0$ to some point *above* $\mathcal{B}_1$, such as $\mathcal{B}_1'$. Similarly, for period $t = 2$ it will *not* move to point $\mathcal{B}_2$, but to some point above it. Which point, exactly? If y grew at the same rate as in the previous period, that point would be $\mathcal{B}_2'$; however, since $\lambda < 0$, $\overset{\circ}{y}$ falls as the distance to the steady state decreases (that is, as $\log y - \log y^*$ becomes smaller in absolute value), hence the new position is neither B_2 nor B_2', but some point in between, such us B_2'', and so on. Thus clearly, per capita income approaches its steady state level "as time goes by." (Moreover, it does so following a concave trajectory, that is to say, asymptotically.) Case [3] above is entirely similar to this, hence the same result applies (the trajectory in this case is convex, of course). Thus the following conclusion is obtained: regardless of its initial value, per capita income *converges* to its steady state level. This is logical because Equation (3.12) tells us that $\overset{o}{y}$ is higher than g (that is, y grows faster than y^*) as long as $\log y < \log y^*$, therefore the former must eventually catch-up with the latter.

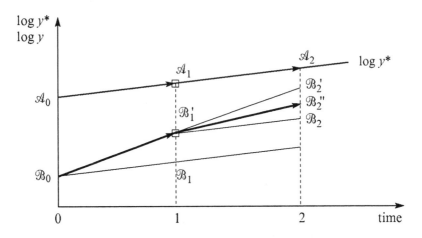

Figure 3.1: Convergence Towards the Steady State

In a way, this result only restates what we already knew, namely that there is a long-run, steady-state equilibrium towards which the economy tends regardless of its initial position. However, as presented here it allows us to provide an answer to the question of whether the "automatic forces" of a market economy will tend to reduce the gap of per capita income between countries (that is, whether the different economies tend to converge *among* themselves). To see this, consider the case of two economies, i and j, with the *same* steady state but *different* initial levels of per capita income, that is, $y_{i,t}^* = y_{j,t}^*$ and $y_{i,0} \neq y_{j,0}$. Specifically, assume that both economies are initially below their *common* steady state level, and also that economy j has a lower per capita income than economy i. (This is only for convenience. Other initial positions in relation to the common steady state level will produce the same theoretical result.) Figure 3.2 depicts the situation. The initial positions are represented by points B_0 (for economy i) and C_0 (for economy

j). Since $y_{i,0} < y_0^*$, economy i will grow in per capita terms at a rate higher than g; hence, for period $t = 1$ it will move to a point such as B_1', and so on, thus reducing its distance to the steady state. Now, since $y_{j,0} < y_{i,0} < y_0^*$, economy j will grow in per capita terms at a rate higher than g and *also* higher than the per capita growth rate of economy i. Hence, for period $t = 1$ it will move to neither point C_1 nor point C_1', but to some point above them, such as C_1'', etc. Clearly, this process implies a reduction of the per capita income gap between the two economies, that is, economy j is "catching-up" with economy i in terms of per capita income. Therefore, the Solow–Swan model predicts that economies with the *same* steady state will converge in per capita income terms. This prediction applies to economies with the *same* steady state, and is known as the "Hypothesis of Convergence."

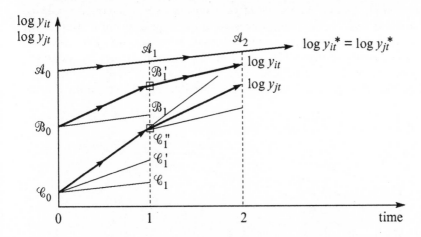

Figure 3.2: Per Capita Income Convergence

Now the steady state is determined by A, s, n, δ and g. This is clear from Figure 2.4 (in Chapter 2) and can also be seen as follows: From the labor-augmented aggregate production function $Y = K^\alpha (AL)^{1-\alpha}$ we have $\tilde{y} = \tilde{k}^\alpha$. In steady state $d\tilde{k}/dt = 0$; hence, from the fundamental growth equation (Equation [2.35]) we obtain $s\tilde{y}^* = (n+\delta+g)\tilde{k}^*$, which yields:

$$\tilde{k}_t^* = \left(\frac{s}{n + \delta + g} \right) \tilde{y}_t^*. \tag{3.13}$$

Substituting this result into $\tilde{y} = \tilde{k}^\alpha$, noting that $\tilde{y}_t = y_t / A_t$, and taking logarithms, we have:

$$\log y_t^* = \log A_t + \frac{\alpha}{1-\alpha} \log s - \frac{\alpha}{1-\alpha} \log(n + \delta + g). \tag{3.14}$$

Clearly, the steady state level of y depends positively on the level of technology and the rate of saving (therefore of investment), and negatively on "depreciation" $(n+\delta+g)$. Therefore, the hypothesis of convergence refers only to economies with the *same* values of those variables *only*. We now turn to the testing of this prediction.

3.3   Tests of the Convergence Hypothesis

3.3.1   The "Collapsing Distribution of Per Capita Incomes" (or σ-convergence) Test

Figure 3.3 depicts the per capita income paths of three equal-steady-state economies (1, 2 and 3) in process of per capita income convergence. Clearly, this process implies that the dispersion of per capita incomes (that is, the distance that separates per capita incomes from one another) decreases with the passing of time. Thus, we can test for convergence by measuring the dispersion of per capita incomes at successive periods and seeing if it falls "as time goes by" (that is, the distribution of per capita incomes

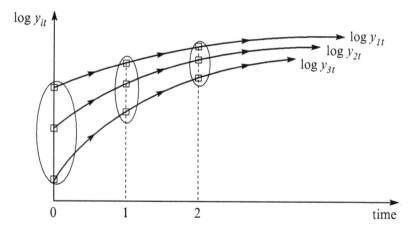

Figure 3.3: Falling Dispersion of y's in Convergence

"tends to collapse"). Now, the usual measure of dispersion is the *sample variance*. Hence, let σ_t^2 be the variance of per capita incomes (or, since we usually work with data in logarithmic terms, the variance of $\log y_i$) at time t $(t=0,1,2,\ldots,T)$. Convergence will occur if:

$$\sigma_0^2 > \sigma_1^2 > \sigma_2^2 > \ldots > \sigma_T^2. \tag{3.15}$$

When applying this test, however, care must be taken to compute σ_t^2 for a large number of successive periods. The reason is that the different economies are often deviated from their longer-term trajectories by short-term shocks; hence, unless we consider a large number of successive periods the results can be very misleading.

3.3.2 The "Barro Regressions" (or β-convergence) Test

A number of authors (notably Barro, 1991a, 1991b, and Barro and Sala-i-Martín, 1991, 1992, among others) have developed an alternative test of the convergence hypothesis. The test, popularly known as β-convergence or "Barro regressions," is very simple to use in practice. However, it takes a long journey to derive its mathematical structure. We begin from Equation (3.12), where the story starts (as it should be). Since $\overset{o}{y} = (dy_t/dt)/y_t$ and this is the same as $d \log y_t/dt$, this equation can be written as follows:

$$\frac{d \log y_t}{dt} = (g - \lambda \log y_t^*) + \lambda \log y_t, \tag{3.16}$$

which (moving from continuous to discrete time terms) can be approximated by:

$$\log y_{t+1} - \log y_t = (g - \lambda \log y_t^*) + \lambda \log y_t, \tag{3.17}$$

that is to say:

$$\log y_{t+1} = (g - \lambda \log y_t^*) + (1 + \lambda) \log y_t. \tag{3.18}$$

This is a first-order difference equation in $\log y_t$, but of a complicated nature because the independent term $(g - \lambda \log y_t^*)$ is *not* constant, for y_t^* grows at the rate g, hence it is convenient to write the equation in a simpler form. Since $y_t = A_t \tilde{y}_t$ for all t, we have:

$$\log(A_{t+1}\tilde{y}_{t+1}) = g - \lambda \log(A_t \tilde{y}_t^*) + (1 + \lambda) \log(A_t \tilde{y}_t), \tag{3.19}$$

that is to say:

$$\begin{aligned}
\log \tilde{y}_{t+1} &= g - \lambda \log \tilde{y}_t^* + (1+\lambda) \log \tilde{y}_t + \log A_t - \log[A_t(1+g)] \\
&= -\lambda \log \tilde{y}_t^* + (1 + \lambda) \log \tilde{y}_t,
\end{aligned} \tag{3.20}$$

where use has been made of the fact that $A_{t+1} = A_t(1+g)$ and also that $\log(1+g) \approx g$ (this approximation is obtained by means of a Taylor expansion of $\log[1+g]$ around the value of $1+g=1$). Now, $\tilde{y}_t^*$ is the steady state level of $\tilde{y}_t$, which is constant (note that whereas y_t^* is *not* constant, which was the trouble with Equation [3.18], $\tilde{y}_t^*$ *is*), that is, $\tilde{y}_t^* = \tilde{y}^*$. Therefore we have:

$$\log \tilde{y}_{t+1} = (1 + \lambda) \log \tilde{y}_t - \lambda \log \tilde{y}^*. \tag{3.21}$$

This is a first-order difference equation in $\log \tilde{y}_t$, but of constant independent term $(-\lambda \log \tilde{y}^*)$, therefore easy to solve (see Mathematical Appendix B.3[1]). We have:

$$\log \tilde{y}_T = e^{\lambda T} \log \tilde{y}_0 + (1 - e^{\lambda T}) \log \tilde{y}^*. \tag{3.22}$$

Since $\tilde{y}^*$ is constant, it makes no difference at which period it is evaluated. For convenience, we evaluate it at the initial period $t = 0$. We have:

$$\log \tilde{y}_T = e^{\lambda T} \log \tilde{y}_0 + (1 - e^{\lambda T}) \log \tilde{y}_0^*. \tag{3.23}$$

As it stands, this equation is of no empirical use because data on labor-effective per capita income ($\tilde{y}$) are not available, hence we have to write the equation in terms of per capita income (y). Since $\tilde{y}_t = y_t/A_t$, we have:

$$\log \frac{y_T}{A_T} = e^{\lambda T} \log \frac{y_0}{A_0} + (1 - e^{\lambda T}) \log \frac{y_0^*}{A_0}, \tag{3.24}$$

that is to say:

$$\log y_T = gT + (1 - e^{\lambda T}) \log y_0^* + e^{\lambda T} \log y_0 \tag{3.25}$$

where use has been made of the fact that $A_T = (1+g)^T A_0$ and therefore $\log A_T = T \log(1+g) + \log A_0 \approx Tg + \log A_0$. Subtracting $\log y_0$ from both sides of this equation, we obtain:

$$\log \frac{y_T}{y_0} = Tg + (1 - e^{\lambda T}) \log y_0^* + (e^{\lambda T} - 1) \log y_0. \tag{3.26}$$

The left-hand side of this equation is the growth rate of per capita income over the entire $[0, T]$ period (see Mathematical Appendix B.4). Hence, if we divide it by T (the number of years in the period) the result, $\frac{1}{T} \cdot \log(y_T/y_0)$, is the average *annual* growth rate of per capita income during that period, that is:

$$\frac{1}{T} \log \left(\frac{y_T}{y_0} \right) = g + \frac{1 - e^{\lambda T}}{T} \log y_0^* + \frac{e^{\lambda T} - 1}{T} \log y_0. \tag{3.27}$$

---

[1] Readers acquainted with the theory of differential equations will notice that we will be taking a mathematical detour on the solution of this equation. However, this book is written with the aim of being accessible to as many readers as possible, therefore the mathematical level must be kept to a minimum. (On the other hand, not much time is saved by solving Equation [3.21] by alternative means.)

Since $g + [(1 - e^{\lambda T})/T] \log y_0^*$ and $(e^{\lambda T} - 1)/T$ are both constant, let:

$$g + \frac{1 - e^{\lambda T}}{T} \log y_0^* = a \qquad (3.28)$$

$$\frac{e^{\lambda T} - 1}{T} = \beta < 0, \qquad (3.29)$$

therefore we have:

$$\frac{1}{T} \log \left(\frac{y_T}{y_0} \right) = a + \beta \log y_0; \quad \beta < 0. \qquad (3.30)$$

Thus, for a cross-section of N countries i $(i = 1, 2, \ldots, N)$ with the *same* steady state, the regression:

$$\frac{1}{T} \log \left(\frac{y_{i,T}}{y_{i,0}} \right) = a + \beta \log y_{i,0} + \xi_{i,[0,T]}, \qquad (3.31)$$

where $\xi_{i,[0,T]} \sim \mathcal{N}(0, \sigma_\xi^2)$, should produce an estimated $\widehat{\beta} < 0$. Since data on real per capita income for a large (over one hundred) number of countries are available from the data banks mentioned in the "Introduction," the regression Equation (3.31) can be run, thus providing a simple test for the convergence hypothesis, and the reason why the test is known as "Barro regressions" or β-convergence is now obvious. (How reliable this test is, will be discussed below.)

3.3.3 σ-convergence *vs.* β-convergence: The Galton Fallacy

We thus have two alternative ways of testing the hypothesis of convergence. Which one is better? This is a difficult question because both tests have advantages and inconveniences. On the one hand, σ-convergence is a single purpose test in the sense that it *only* allows us to know whether the convergence hypothesis holds for a given sample of economies. The β-convergence test goes beyond this single purpose since it *also* allows us to know the *speed* of the actual process of convergence. On the other hand, σ-convergence is a *more robust* test of convergence, for it is a statistical property that whereas the distribution of per capita income cannot collapse without having $\widehat{\beta} < 0$ in the regression Equation (3.31), we can have $\widehat{\beta} < 0$ in this regression without a collapsing distribution of per capita income (in other words, σ-convergence implies β-convergence but β-convergence does *not* imply σ-convergence. In fact, we may have β-convergence and σ-*divergence* for the same sample of countries). Let us consider each of these issues in turn.

(a) Determining the Speed of Convergence.

Equation (3.12) and the subsequent explanation of it make clear that, the higher λ, the more rapidly the economy approaches the steady state. Thus, the parameter λ provides a measure of the speed of convergence. For instance, if $\lambda = -0.05$ per year, then 5 percent of the gap between y_t and y_t^* disappears in one year (hence, it would take 14 years to eliminate one half of the initial gap, 28 years to eliminate three quarters of it, and so on). Also, we know from Equation (3.29) that the coefficient β in the "Barro regression" Equation (3.31) is $\beta = (e^{\lambda T} - 1)/T$, hence the speed of convergence, λ, is readily obtained from the estimate of the coefficient β in a "Barro regression."[2]

---

[2] We could go the other way round, estimating λ directly from the *non*-linear form of regression Equation (3.31), that is:

$$\frac{1}{T} \log \left(\frac{y_{i,T}}{y_{i,0}} \right) = a + \left(\frac{e^{\lambda T} - 1}{T} \right) \log y_{i,0} + \xi_{i,0}, \qquad (3.32)$$

and computing $\widehat{\beta}$ from the estimate of λ. In practice, it is actually more convenient to run the non-linear regression, obtain an estimate of λ and, from this estimate, compute the value of β. This does not have as much to do with the theory behind the hypothesis of convergence as it does with the econometrics of it (that is to say, with the statistical "tricks" we have developed to test the convergence hypothesis). To see this, note that in Equation (3.31) we regress the *average* rate of growth of per capita income over the period $[0, T]$ on the initial level of per capita income, that is, we use as dependent variable an average of the actual rates of growth of per capita income in each year of the $[0, T]$ interval. In other words, we have managed to replace the actual rates of growth of per capita income in each year $(\overset{\circ}{y}_0, \overset{\circ}{y}_1, \overset{\circ}{y}_2, \ldots, \overset{\circ}{y}_T)$ with an average of them $(\frac{1}{T} \overset{\circ}{y}_{[0,T]})$ Now, over the $[0, T]$ interval the actual growth rate of per capita . income in each year falls as the economy moves from time 0 to time T (that is, $\overset{\circ}{y}_0 > \overset{\circ}{y}_1 > \overset{\circ}{y}_2 \ldots$) because $\overset{\circ}{y}_t$ decreases as the economy approaches the steady state. Hence, the longer the period of estimation $([0, T])$, the smaller the *average* rate of growth we use, for it combines a larger number of the smaller future rates of per capita income growth with the same higher initial rates. This means that the raw data for the dependent variable $\frac{1}{T} \overset{\circ}{y}_{[0,T]}$ are *not* the same for the period 1960–1980, to give an example, than for the longer period 1960–1990; in fact, they are smaller. Hence, the linear regression Equation (3.31) will produce a lower (in absolute value) $\widehat{\beta}$ for the larger 1960–1990 period than for the shorter period 1960–1980. Therefore, due to our econometric set-up (and *only* because of it) the linear regression Equation (3.31) produces a lower (in absolute value) estimate $\widehat{\beta}$ the larger the period of estimation $[0, T]$. This creates a problem, for it forces the estimated speed of convergence, λ, to also vary with the length of the estimation interval, and it makes a big difference whether the speed of convergence is -0.01 or -0.04, for example. Since we do not want the speed of convergence to (artificially) take different values depending on the length of the estimation interval, it is better to run the non-linear regression. In this case, the dependent variable still suffers from the same problem, that is, it changes with the length of the interval $[0, T]$, but this should not bias the estimate of λ because the non-linear form takes the length of the interval, T, into consideration (that is, the estimate of λ is "corrected" for the value of T). Thus, the non-linear regression is necessary when we seek to *compare* results obtained from different samples of economies for which the periods of estimation are not exactly the same.

(b) β-convergence and the Galton Fallacy. To show that σ-convergence implies β-convergence but β-convergence does *not* imply σ-convergence, we return to regression Equation (3.31). Since the term T in this equation scales down the regression line without affecting the slope β, we can remove it from the equation with no loss, and the best way of doing this is to let $T=1$ so that we have:

$$\log y_{i,1} - \log y_{i,0} = a + \beta \log y_{i,0} + \xi_{i,[0,1]} \tag{3.33}$$

or, in general:

$$\log y_{i,t} - \log y_{i,t-1} = a + \beta \log y_{i,t-1} + \xi_{i,t}, \tag{3.34}$$

which can be written as follows:

$$\log y_{i,t} = a + (1 + \beta) \log y_{i,t-1} + \xi_{i,t}, \tag{3.35}$$

and from this we have:

$$\text{var}(\log y_{i,t}) = (1 + \beta)^2 \text{var}(\log y_{i,t-1}) + \text{var}(\xi_t), \tag{3.36}$$

that is to say:

$$\sigma_t^2 = (1 + \beta)^2 \sigma_{t-1}^2 + \sigma_{\xi_t}^2. \tag{3.37}$$

Since $\sigma_{\xi_t}^2 > 0$ it follows from this equation that:

$$\sigma_t^2 < \sigma_{t-1}^2 \Rightarrow \beta < 0$$
$$\beta < 0 \not\Rightarrow \sigma_t^2 < \sigma_{t-1}^2, \tag{3.38}$$

and note, in particular, that $\beta < 0$ is compatible with $\sigma_t^2 \geq \sigma_{t-1}^2$.

It is worthwhile to explore the statistical origin of this property a bit further (Quah [1993]). From Equation (3.35) we have that the OLS estimate of $(1 + \beta)$ is:

$$1 + \hat{\beta} = \frac{\text{cov}(\log y_{i,t}, \log y_{i,t-1})}{\text{var}(\log y_{i,t-1})} = \frac{\text{cov}(\log y_{i,t}, \log y_{i,t-1})}{\sigma_{t-1}^2}. \tag{3.39}$$

Now assume that, for the sample at hand, the distribution of per capita income is *not* collapsing, that is, the per capita income variance does *not* decrease over time; for instance, assume that it remains constant, that is, $\sigma_{t-1}^2 = \sigma_t^2$ (the argument is entirely similar if $\sigma_{t-1}^2 < \sigma_t^2$). Thus, Equation (3.39) can be written as follows:

$$1 + \hat{\beta} = \frac{\text{cov}(\log y_{i,t}, \log y_{i,t-1})}{\sqrt{\sigma_t^2} \cdot \sqrt{\sigma_{t-1}^2}} = r_{\log y_{i,t}, \log y_{i,t-1}}, \tag{3.40}$$

where $r_{\log y_{i,t}, \log y_{i,t-1}}$ is the correlation coefficient between $\log y_{i,t-1}$ and $\log y_{i,t}$ which, by definition, takes values from -1 to $+1$. Hence we have:

$$-1 \leq 1 + \widehat{\beta} \leq 1, \tag{3.41}$$

that is to say:

$$-2 \leq \widehat{\beta} \leq 0. \tag{3.42}$$

This means that the regression Equation (3.31) might produce an estimate $\widehat{\beta} < 0$ even when the distribution of per capita incomes is *not* falling (as in our case, in which, by principle, it remains constant). This result, which applies to (and is relevant for) many issues in economics besides the one at hand, is known as "Galton's fallacy" (in "honor" of Francis Galton, the nineteenth century British scientist and first writer known to have been trapped by it,[3] though many more followed him on that [see Friedman, 1993]). Thus, clearly, we cannot rely blindly on Barro regressions to test the hypothesis of convergence. On the other hand, we need this test to determine the speed of convergence. The solution, it seems, is to run the σ-convergence test whenever the β-convergence one produces an estimate $\widehat{\beta} < 0$. Short of this, we cannot be sure that Galton's fallacy is not at work.

3.4   Empirical Results on Convergence

The S&S model predicts convergence among equal-steady-state economies, that is, that if N economies i ($i = 1, 2, \ldots, N$) have the *same* steady state (that is, they share the same values of A, s, n, δ, and g, which are the variables that determine the steady state position), then those economies tend to converge in per capita income terms. Thus, in purity, to test this prediction we should *not* include in the same sample such countries as India

---

[3] Galton, Sir Francis (1822–1911). "English scientist, explorer, and anthropologist. A cousin of Charles Darwin, he was among the first to recognize the implications for mankind of Darwin's theory of evolution. He coined the word eugenics to denote scientific endeavors to increase the proportion of persons with better than average genetic endowment through selective mating of marriage partners ... He wrote 9 books and some 200 papers, some of them related to correlational calculus as a branch of applied statistics, in which he was a pioneer" (from the *Encyclopaedia Britannica*). In one of those papers, Galton (1886) invented regression analysis, but he fell victim of the "regression trap." He measured the heights in a sample of fathers and their sons, and found that taller than average fathers had sons who were not above average by as much as their fathers. Specifically, sons were above average by only 2/3 of an inch for every inch their fathers exceeded the average. He thus concluded that the population was "regressing toward mediocrity" in height: with the passage of time heights would tend toward equality. He therefore expected the variance of heights to collapse with the passing of time, but he waited for that in vain.

and the USA (for instance), for they do *not* have the same steady state. If we ignore this fact, the results of the test will not bear upon the convergence hypothesis *proper* (hence, they will not be usable to *falsify* the Solow–Swan model). Of course, there are no two literally equal-steady-state economies, this is obvious. In practice, by economies with "the same steady state" we mean economies with *similar* values of A, s, n, δ, and g. Hence, while it is incorrect to include in the same sample countries as different as India and the USA (to use the previous example), it is reasonable to test the hypothesis of convergence among the economies of the G-7 group, or the USA States (each state taken as a separate country), and so on, for each of these groups have *similar* values of A, s, n, δ, and g.

Using this criterion, the σ-convergence and β-convergence tests have been applied to a large number of samples in recent years. However, the seminal work in this area belongs to Barro and Sala-i-Martín (1995 for a compilation), from whom we quote results for three different sets of economies, namely, the USA States, the European regions, and the Japanese prefectures. Table 3.2 shows the results of the β-convergence test.[4] Since, according to the standard errors reported, the (logarithm of

Table 3.2: β-convergence Around the World

Sample (Period of Estimation)	λ (s.e.)	Coefficient of $\log y_{i,0}$ $\beta = \frac{e^{\lambda T}-1}{T}$
48 USA States (1880–1990)	-0.0174 (0.0026)	[.]
47 Japanese Prefectures (1930–1990)	-0.0279 (0.0033)	[.]
90 European Regions (1950–1990)	-0.019 (0.002)	[.]

Source : Robert J. Barro and Xavier Sala-i-Martín (1995), Ch.11

the) initial level of per capita income is statistically significant in each case and $\widehat{\beta} < 0$, we conclude that the data in these three samples are consistent with the convergence hypothesis as stated by the Solow–Swan model (that is, economies with the same steady state tend to converge in per capita income terms). One striking feature of these results is the similarity of the speed of convergence *across* samples, which is closely around the value $\lambda = -0.0226$, or 2 percent per year (specifically, it is -0.0174 for the USA

[4] The estimation was done using the non-linear regression Equation (3.32) (see footnote 2). (But if you found it too hard to follow, do *not* worry about either that footnote or this one: they relate to an econometric matter which, though important, is unessential at the level of this book.)

States at one end of the spectrum, and −0.0279 for the Japanese prefectures at the other; following the statistical tradition, the mid-way value chosen here is appropriate). This implies that, for the samples considered, between two and three per cent of an initial gap in per capita income is eliminated in one year (thus, it would take 35 years to eliminate one-half of the initial gap, 70 years to eliminate three quarters of it, and so on). Hence, convergence takes place among "equal-steady-state" economies, but at *very low* pace. Figure 3.4 shows the results of the σ-convergence test for the same

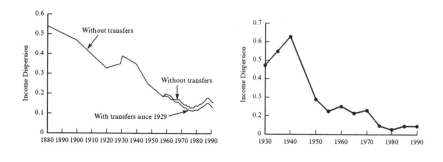

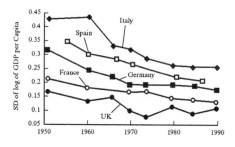

Figure 3.4: σ-convergence Around the World

samples of economies. This, as we know, is needed to check the goodness of the β-convergence results. The three panels are from Barro and Sala-i-Martín (1995); we have, from left to right and bottom, σ-convergence for the USA States, the Japanese prefectures and regions within several European countries. Clearly, convergence is not rejected in all three cases.

3.5 An Obstacle in the Way...

In the previous section we saw that the empirical studies yield an estimated value for the speed of convergence of $\lambda = -0.0226$, or around. Now, this poses a problem. To see why, recall from Equation (3.11) that $\lambda = (\alpha-1)(n+g+\delta)$. Thus, using the benchmark values of $n+g = \overset{o}{Y} = 0.032$ and $\delta = 0.04$, which are quite realistic (they are, in fact, the *actual* values for the USA economy), we have:

$$\alpha = \frac{\lambda + (n + g + \delta)}{n + g + \delta} = \frac{-0.0226 + 0.032 + 0.04}{0.032 + 0.04} = 0.68,$$

that is, to accord with the estimated speed of convergence of $\lambda = -0.0226$, the parameter α must be equal to 0.68. But α *is* the relative share of capital, which is around 0.3 (or 30 percent) for the USA and most industrialized economies (Maddison, 1987). Hence, this is what we have: to accord with the estimated speed of converge of $\lambda = -0.0226$, the share of capital in national income must be as high as 68 percent; however, neither in the USA nor anywhere else we find a capital share of that magnitude. What is happening here?

3.5.1 ...and an Ingenious Solution: The "Broad" Concept of K

Mankiw, Romer and Weil (1992) have suggested a simple (but also logical) explanation for this puzzle. They argue that we are not thinking of K in the right way. Recall that, so far, by K we mean *physical* capital, that is to say, structures and equipment. Accordingly, when we speak of (gross) investment we mean physical capital replacement plus additions to the stock of physical capital. At the same time, however, we refer to (gross) investment as output that is not *consumed*. Now, it is a reality of life that not all the output "not consumed" is used to either replace or increase the existing stock of physical capital, for we know that some of it is devoted to maintain and increase the stock of *human* capital (health, education, and so on). It is simply not fitting to divide output into consumption and physical capital investment *alone*. More accurately, the division is into consumption, investment in physical capital, *and* investment in *human* capital. In terms of the aggregate production function this means that we should extend the traditional two-factor function $Y_t = F(K_t, L_t; \text{Technology})$ to $Y_t = F(K_t, L_t, H_t; \text{Technology})$, to emphasize the fact that the output level also depends on the stock of human capital, H. Another way to think of this is to say that much of what we call "labor" is actually human capital.

The implication is that in the traditional Cobb–Douglas specification of the aggregate production function, the share of labor in national income, $1 - \alpha$, is *overestimated*, for it includes *both* the labor share as such *and* the share of human capital; whereas the share of "capital," α, is underestimated because it includes *only* the share of physical capital and should include *both* this share and the share of human capital.

To see the implications of this idea for the problem at hand, consider the following "human capital–augmented" aggregate production function that is Cobb–Douglas in physical capital K, human capital H, and effective labor $\Theta_t L_t$, that is:

$$Y_t = K_t^{\alpha_0} H_t^{\alpha_1} (\Theta_t L_t)^{1-\alpha_0-\alpha_1}, \tag{3.43}$$

where Θ_t is an index of technology. Assuming that resources (output) are efficiently allocated to K and H, investment in each of these inputs will take place up to the levels where the marginal products are equal, that is, $MPK = MPH$. Since:

$$MPK = \partial Y_t / \partial K_t = \alpha_0 \cdot (Y_t / K_t)$$
$$MPH = \partial Y_t / \partial H_t = \alpha_1 \cdot (Y_t / H_t), \tag{3.44}$$

we have:

$$\alpha_0 \cdot \frac{Y_t}{K_t} = \alpha_1 \cdot \frac{Y_t}{H_t}, \tag{3.45}$$

therefore:

$$H_t = \frac{\alpha_1}{\alpha_0} \cdot K_t. \tag{3.46}$$

Substituting this equation into the aggregate production function, we obtain:

$$Y_t = \Theta_t^{1-(\alpha_0+\alpha_1)} \cdot \left(\frac{\alpha_1}{\alpha_0}\right)^{\alpha_1} K_t^{\alpha_0+\alpha_1} L_t^{1-(\alpha_0+\alpha_1)}, \tag{3.47}$$

which can be written in the form:

$$Y_t = K_t^{\alpha_0+\alpha_1} (A_t L_t)^{1-(\alpha_0+\alpha_1)}, \tag{3.48}$$

where:

$$A_t = \Theta_t \cdot \left(\frac{\alpha_1}{\alpha_0}\right)^{\alpha_1/(1-\alpha_0-\alpha_1)}$$

is the index of technology. Thus, if we want to use the traditional Cobb–Douglas specification for the aggregate production function, we need to bear in mind that the income share of the single measure of capital K is $\alpha = \alpha_0 + \alpha_1 = 0.3 + \alpha_1$, that is, the sum of the shares of physical capital

($\alpha_0 = 0.3$) and human capital (α_1). This means that the correct expression for the speed of convergence λ is: $\lambda = (\alpha_0 + \alpha_1 - 1)(n + g + \delta)$. Hence, the figures will square if the share of human capital in national income, α_1, is equal to 0.38. But is it? In their study, Mankiw, Romer and Weil (1992) conclude from cross-country regressions that a reasonable specification for the aggregate production function is the following (therefore, the figures match remarkably well):

$$Y_t = K_t^{0.33} H_t^{0.33} (\Theta_t L_t)^{0.33}.$$

Note that Θ_t is merely a direct transformation of A_t; besides, since α_0 and α_1 turn out to be statistically similar (≈ 0.33), we can replace Θ with A in Equation (3.43), so that we do not need to use different symbols for the level of technology, that is, we will write the Cobb–Douglas "human capital-augmented" production function thus:

$$Y_t = K_t^{\alpha_0} H_t^{\alpha_1} (A_t L_t)^{1-\alpha_0-\alpha_1}. \tag{3.49}$$

3.5.2   ...which Calls for a "Readjustment" of the Solow–Swan Model: The Human Capital Augmented Neoclassical Model

An interesting question is the following: Since we know that the adequate aggregate production function is the one containing the stock of human capital as an argument, that is, in general: $Y_t = F(K_t, H_t, L_t, A_t)$, should we not start all over? The answer is that it depends on whether our specific purpose requires that physical and human capital be clearly separated. In some cases, as with the questions so far addressed in this chapter, the separation is not necessary: simply interpret K as a composite commodity, the aggregate of physical and human capital, and bear in mind that when we specify the "traditional" production function as a Cobb–Douglas the parameter α represents the income share of capital in general, that is, physical and human capital together, and that, therefore, its observed value is 0.68 instead of 0.3 (consequently, $1-\alpha$ is 0.32 instead of 0.7). However, in other cases it *is* convenient to have physical and human capital separated. One such case is provided in the next chapter; hence, it is appropriate to "adjust" some pieces of the Solow–Swan model now. We begin by writing the "human capital-augmented" production function (Equation [3.49]) in terms of labor-efficiency units:

$$\tilde{y}_t = \tilde{k}_t^{\alpha_0} \tilde{h}_t^{\alpha_1}. \tag{3.50}$$

Since savings are allocated to both investment in physical capital and investment in human capital, instead of the single fundamental growth Equation

(2.35) of Chapter 2 we have the following pair of accumulation equations (for simplicity, we assume that physical and human capital depreciate at the same rate, δ):

$$\frac{d\tilde{k}_t}{dt} = s_K \tilde{y}_t - (\delta + n + g)\tilde{k}_t$$

$$\frac{d\tilde{h}_t}{dt} = s_H \tilde{y}_t - (\delta + n + g)\tilde{h}_t. \tag{3.51}$$

In steady state $d\tilde{k}/dt = 0$ and $d\tilde{h}/dt = 0$, and $\tilde{k}$, $\tilde{h}$ and $\tilde{y}$ take constant values $\tilde{k} = \tilde{k}^*$, $\tilde{h} = \tilde{h}^*$ and $\tilde{y} = \tilde{y}^*$, respectively. Thus we have:

$$s_K \tilde{y}^* = (n + \delta + g)\tilde{k}^*$$
$$s_H \tilde{y}^* = (n + \delta + g)\tilde{h}^* \tag{3.52}$$

The solution of this system of equations yields:

$$\tilde{k}^* = \left(\frac{s_K^{1-\alpha_1} s_H^{\alpha_1}}{n + \delta + g} \right)^{1/(1-\alpha_0-\alpha_1)}$$

$$\tilde{h}^* = \left(\frac{s_K^{\alpha_0} s_H^{1-\alpha_0}}{n + \delta + g} \right)^{1/(1-\alpha_0-\alpha_1)} \tag{3.53}$$

Substituting these expressions into Equation (3.50), noting that $\tilde{y}_t = y_t/A_t$, and taking logarithms, we obtain:

$$\log y_t^* = \log A_t + \frac{\alpha_0}{1-\alpha_0-\alpha_1} \log s_K + \frac{\alpha_1}{1-\alpha_0-\alpha_1} \log s_H$$

$$- \frac{\alpha_0+\alpha_1}{1-\alpha_0-\alpha_1} \log(n + \delta + g), \tag{3.54}$$

which is the "human capital-augmented" counterpart of Equation (3.14). Since physical and human capital are now separated, quite logically the new equation adds the fact that y_t^*, the steady state level of per capita income, also depends on the rate of human capital investment, s_H.

Appendix: Per Capita Income as an Indicator of Living Standards

As mentioned in the "Introduction" to this chapter, the level of per capita income is often used as an indicator for the degree of poverty (or richness) of the different countries (that is to say, it is used as a measure of living standards). Care must be taken, however, to express the level of per capita income in the appropriate units, so that sound comparisons between different countries can be made. To see this, imagine that we want to compare the living standards of the USA and Japan on the basis of their levels of income per capita. To that end, we need to express both levels of per capita income in the same units, and a common practice is to proceed as follows: let e be the dollar–yen *nominal* exchange rate defined as the number of US dollars needed to buy one yen, that is:

$$e = \frac{x \text{ US dollars}}{1 \text{ yen}}.$$

Thus, we can transform the (yen-denominated) per capita income of Japan, y_J^Y, into US dollars as follows: $y_J^\$ = y_J^Y \cdot e$. Once this operation is done, we compare $y_J^\$$ with $y_{US}^\$$ (the USA level of per capita income). However, this procedure ignores the fact that one \$US does not buy in Japan the same amount of goods one dollar buys in the USA. Hence, the (*nominal*) exchange rate, e, is *not* the appropriate factor to transform yens into dollars (at least, not when it comes to discussing relative living standards). Now consider the following alternative procedure: let $P_{US}^\$$ be the price of a given basket of consumer goods in the USA, and P_J^Y the price of the same basket in Japan. Thus with the (yen-denominated) Japanese per capita income of y_J^Y, a number y_J^Y/P_J^Y of *that* basket of consumer goods can be bought in Japan, and *this* is the Japanese standard of living. Now, to buy the same amount of goods in the USA, a dollar-denominated income of $(y_J^Y/P_J^Y) \cdot P_{US}^\$$ is needed, hence *this* is the true dollar equivalent of the Japanese per capita income. Therefore, the $y_J^\$$ we must compare with $y_{US}^\$$ is the following:

$$y_J^\$ = y_J^Y \cdot \frac{P_{US}^\$}{P_J^Y},$$

hence the appropriate factor to transform yens into US dollars is the relative price ratio $P_{US}^\$/P_J^Y$. This ratio is called the *purchasing parity power* (PPP) exchange rate between the two countries, $e_{J,\text{US}}^{\text{PPP}}$. Thus in general, the appropriate method to transform the own-currency denominated per capita income of country i, y_i^{oc}, into US dollars is:

$$y_i^\$ = y_i^{oc} \cdot \frac{P_{US}^\$}{P_i^{oc}} = y_i^{oc} \cdot e_{i,\text{US}}^{\text{PPP}}.$$

Table 3.1 was constructed using the PPP method. Table 3.3 shows how dramatically the results can change when using the alternative, nominal exchange rate method: not only the relative difference in poverty changes (thus for instance the USA appears to be 62 times richer than India while in reality it is only [!] 19 times richer), but also the ranking changes. For instance, Japan appears to be richer than the USA; in reality, the opposite is true.

Table 3.3: *Nominal* Per Capita Income Around the World

Country	*Real* GDP Per Capita, 1990 $US
USA	21,360
Japan	25,340
Korea	5,400
Mexico	2,490
Brazil	2,680
India	350

Source: The World Bank, *World Development Report, 1992.*

Chapter 4

The Hypothesis of Convergence (II): Economies with Different Steady States

4.1 Introduction

We saw in the previous chapter that the Solow–Swan model predicts convergence among equal-steady-state economies and that this prediction is *not* rejected by the data. Now, however important a question like "Do the living standards of the US States, and so on, tend to converge?" may be, it is even more important to know whether the living standards of Mexico and the USA or, more generally, today's rich and poor countries, can be expected to converge. In fact, that is *the* question we intended to answer in the first place. Hence, what does the S&S model *predict* about this? The short answer is, "*Nothing*; but whatever actually happens in reality (that is, whether convergence between the poor and rich countries occurs or not) the model provides *valuable information* as to *why*." To see this, we return to Equation (3.12) and consider the case of two economies, i and j, with different steady state parameterizations. We have:

$$\overset{\circ}{y}_{i,t} = g_i + \lambda(\log y_{i,t} - \log y_{i,t}^*) \tag{4.1}$$

$$\overset{\circ}{y}_{j,t} = g_j + \lambda(\log y_{j,t} - \log y_{j,t}^*). \tag{4.2}$$

59

In these equations we assume λ to be the same for both economies because, as shown in the previous section, it is a striking empirical regularity that the speed of convergence towards the own steady state shows little variation across samples. (We ignore the reason for this, that is, *why* economies that are different in their steady-state parameterization share this property, we do not know; but since it appears to be a robust empirical finding, we assume that all economies converge towards their own steady states at roughly the same speed.) From these two equations follows that whether $\overset{o}{y_i}$ is lower, equal, or higher than $\overset{o}{y_j}$, depends on the rates of technical progress and on how distant the economies are from their own steady states. Clearly, those factors can combine in so many different ways that nothing can be predicted as to which economy will grow faster. In theory, it is possible that the richer economy grows faster, at the same rate, or more slowly than the poorer one. Hence, the model can accommodate whatever actually occurs in reality. As it happens, the gap between the rich and poor countries is actually *widening*, as Figure 4.1 (which is self-explanatory)

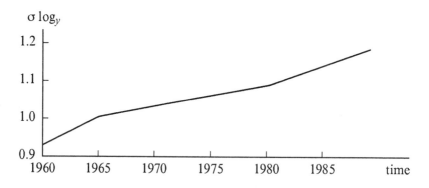

Figure 4.1: Divergence of Per Capita Incomes (114 Countries)

clearly shows. In any event, the Solow–Swan model is *consistent* with this fact. However, consistency alone is a poor merit: a model that says nothing about anything is consistent with everything, yet that does not make it a good model. Hence, why is there no convergence between the poor and rich countries? Is it that the very fact of being poor is a hindrance to economic growth? Or is it something else that impedes poor countries from growing faster than rich ones, and if so, *what*, exactly, is it? Or is it *both*? Fortunately, the Solow–Swan model provides a framework to investigate these questions. The method (a reformulation of the "Barro-regression test") is often called "*conditional β-convergence*," that is, "conditional" to the fact that we *control for differences in steady states.*[1]

4.2 Controlling for Differences in Steady States

To see how this can be done, we return to Equation (3.27). In this equation we took $g + [(1 - e^{\lambda T})/T] \log y_0^*$ as a constant because for any individual economy y_0^* is a datum; thus, since homogeneous economies are assumed to have the same g and y_0^*, we were able to move from Equation (3.27) to regression Equation (3.31) taking $a = g + [(1 - e^{\lambda T})/T] \log y_0^*$ as the intercept (therefore a *common* constant) in the regression line. However, when we have a sample of "heterogeneous" economies this step cannot be taken, for neither y_0^* is the same for all of them nor can we assume (at least not without an appropriate explanation) that g is. Thus, in principle, for each economy i $(i = 1, 2, \dots, N)$ we have:

$$\frac{1}{T} \log \left(\frac{y_{i,T}}{y_{i,0}} \right) = g_i + \frac{1 - e^{\lambda T}}{T} \log y_{i,0}^* + \frac{e^{\lambda T} - 1}{T} \log y_{i,0}. \qquad (4.3)$$

Now $\log y_{i,0}^*$ is not directly observable, but Equation (3.54) gives the appropriate expression for it. Using this equation we obtain:

$$
\begin{aligned}
\frac{1}{T} \log \left(\frac{y_{i,T}}{y_{i,0}} \right) = {} & g_i + \frac{1 - e^{\lambda T}}{T} \log A_{i,0} + \left(\frac{1 - e^{\lambda T}}{T} \right) \left(\frac{\alpha_{0i}}{1 - \alpha_{0i} - \alpha_{1i}} \right) \log s_{Ki} \\[2mm]
& + \left(\frac{1 - e^{\lambda T}}{T} \right) \left(\frac{\alpha_{1i}}{1 - \alpha_{0i} - \alpha_{1i}} \right) \log s_{Hi} \qquad (4.4) \\[2mm]
& - \left(\frac{1 - e^{\lambda T}}{T} \right) \left(\frac{\alpha_{0i} + \alpha_{1i}}{1 - \alpha_{0i} - \alpha_{1i}} \right) \log(n_i + \delta_i + g_i) + \beta \log y_{i,0}
\end{aligned}
$$

The simple inspection of this equation shows that too many country-specific "parameters" $(g_i, \alpha_{0i}, \alpha_{1i}, \delta_i, n_i, A_{0i})$ are present to be able to run a standard OLS regression on it. Moreover, in some cases (as with the

---

[1] We are not altogether convinced of the necessity for this name. To be sure, we (the economics profession) may well be having too many names attached to the S&S model convergence hypothesis. For one thing, there is only one hypothesis of convergence coming out of the *standard* S&S model, and it is always conditional in one sense, namely: it predicts convergence among economies on the "condition" that they have the same steady state. However, since the name "conditional convergence" to refer to the hypothesis of convergence being used to deal with samples of *different-steady-state* economies *after such differences are controlled for* is widely utilized, we obey by it. (But there is no real problem here. We only call the reader's attention to be careful when reading this literature so that she avoids to be confused by names.)

rates of technical progress and physical and human capital depreciation) we cannot know their values because no reliable data exist on which they can be computed. (If one is willing to assume that factor shares α_0 and α_1 are invariant across countries, g_is could be computed as total factor productivity growth from growth accounting exercises [see Chapter 6 below]; however, given the degree of non-competitive arrangements in labor markets, it is unlikely that those estimates would be any good.) Therefore, it is necessary to cut down on the number of independent variables to make empirical use of Equation (4.4).

In their seminal paper, Mankiw, Romer and Weil (1992) simply take capital shares, depreciation rates and rates of technical progress as constant. As for the initial level of technology, $A_{i,0}$, they argue (appropriately) that it "reflects not just technology but resource endowments, climate, institutions, and so on," therefore it has a country specific component. On this basis they model the initial level of technology as follows:

$$\log A_{i,0} = a + \varepsilon_{i,0}, \qquad (4.5)$$

where a is a constant and ε is the country-specific deviation from it. This is really a clever trick, but it could create a problem of wrong specification, for it gives away with $\log A_{i0}$ by simply "transforming" it into an error-regression term. There are other potentially troubling problems with the above-mentioned assumptions. In the first place, if $\delta + g$ and $\alpha_0 + \alpha_1$ are both constant, and n is *not*, then λ *could* turn out to be *not* constant statistically because $\lambda = -(\alpha_0 + \alpha_1 - 1)(n_i + \delta + g)$; hence we have a varying parameter (β) on the main variable $\log y_{i0}$. If, alternatively, λ and $\delta + g$ are both constant, then $\alpha_0 + \alpha_1$ is *not*, in which case we have varying parameters on the other variables of the model (that is, $\log s_{Ki}, \log s_{Hi}$ and $\log n_i$).

Assuming g to be the same for all countries is also problematic; for, as Grossman and Helpman (1994, p.29) remark, "the rate at which producers in Japan have acquired new technologies, be they technologies that were new to the global economy or those that were new only to the local economy or the individual firm, has been remarkedly different from the rate of technology acquisition in Chad, for example." From the econometric point of view, if there are differences in the rates of technological progress and we ignore them, those differences are dumped into the error term of any econometric counterpart of Equation (4.4); if, at the same time, the rate of technical progress happens to be correlated with the rates of investment in physical and (or) human capital, then $\log s_{Ki}$ and (or) $\log s_{Hi}$ will be correlated with the error term, thus the OLS estimates will be biased. Hence the question is, are the rates of physical and (or) human capital investment correlated with the rate of technical progress? This question cannot be analyzed within the Solow–Swan model because it takes technological change as *exogenous* (that is, the model does specify how *g comes about*); but even simple models of *endogenous* technical change make clear that *g* depends on the rates of physical (as in the "learning-by-doing" version of Arrow, 1962, and Romer, 1986, see Chapter 7 below) or human capital investment (as in the theory of "technological diffusion" proposed by Nelson and Phelps, 1966, which, quite reasonably, assumes that more human capital increases the ability to absorb new technologies).

There may also be a problem in using the rate of population growth as an explanatory variable for the rate of per capita income growth. True, it "comes in the package" of the Solow–Swan model (which, besides, takes *n* as exogenously determined). But the empirical observation that population growth falls as per capita incomes rise (that is, poor countries tend to have higher rates of population growth than rich ones), casts doubts on the validity of the Solow–Swan assumption. For, if *n* is determined endogenously by living standards, then Equation (4.4) postulates the wrong causation as regards *n*. Consequently, a negative coefficient on this variable from a regression based on Equation (4.4) may mean *either* that high rates of population growth cause low rates of per capita income growth (as stated by the Solow–Swan model), *or* (here is the trouble) the opposite.

The list of "complaints" could continue. But are these not "small matters" in an area in which we are willing to accept that an aggregate production function exists, or that the data on which we validate or reject our theories are correct in the first place? At some point, researchers must stop quarreling about the "econometric ballistics" and ask themselves the question (long ago forgotten in economics, but fortunately coming back into the picture) of whether the results derived from a set of informal ("first-approximation") assumptions really *make sense*. Therefore, we had better move to that stage. Equation (4.4) becomes:

$$\frac{1}{T} \log \left(\frac{y_{i,T}}{y_{i,0}} \right) = \gamma_0 + \gamma_1 \log s_{Ki} + \gamma_2 \log s_{Hi}$$

$$+ \ \gamma_3 \log n_i + \beta \log y_{i,0} + \xi_{i,[0,T]}, \tag{4.6}$$

where it is assumed that $\xi_{i,t} \sim \mathcal{N}(0, \sigma_\xi^2)$. Since, by construction, the coefficient of each explanatory variable in this regression tells us the *net* effect of that variable upon the (annual average) rate of growth of per capita income over the $[0, T]$ period, the coefficient β tells us the *net* effect of y_0. Therefore, an estimate $\widehat{\beta} < 0$ in this regression means that, *caeteris paribus*, economies should grow faster in per capita terms the lower their initial per capita income level. In this regard, note that it is possible to have $\widehat{\beta} < 0$ from regression Equation (4.6) and still observe in the real world that the low per capita income countries are *not* "catching-up" with the high per capita income ones (that is, that, as is the actual case, the per capita income gap between them is *not* decreasing). But then we would conclude that this happens because (some of) the other explanatory variables work so as to *counteract* the tendency for poor countries to grow faster in per capita terms than rich ones, thus we can concentrate our attention in those variables. Therefore, the potential of this "augmented Barro regression" (as it is called) to provide useful information about the actual process of convergence is enormous.

4.3   Empirical Results on Conditional β-convergence

Mankiw, Romer and Weil (MR&W) (1992) estimate regression Equation (4.6) using data from the Real National Accounts constructed by Summers and Heston (S&H) (1988). The estimation extends over the period 1960–1985, and the explanatory variables are measured as follows: n is the average (of the $1960-1985$ interval) rate of growth of the working-age population, working age defined as 15 to 64; s_K is the average share of total (that is, private and public) real investment in real GDP; $\log y_0$ is real GDP in 1960 divided by the working-age population in that year; and s_H is proxied by the percentage of the working-age population that is in secondary school (this is surely an imperfect measure of s_H but one has to bear in mind that measuring human capital is complicated; besides, MR&W's was a "first approximation" to the problem). As usual, the dependent variable, $(1/T)\,\overset{\circ}{y}_{i,[0,T]}$, is the 1960–1985 average of the growth rate of per capita income. Table 4.1 shows the results of this estimation for a sample containing 75 countries (the full sample provided by S&H, 1988, save for the oil-producing nations [which are basically rent-seeking economies, hence one should not expect them to conform to the Solow–Swan model] and a second list of countries for which S&H themselves graded the data as unreliable).

The immediate conclusion from these estimates is that more investment in physical and human capital *is* good for growth and a more rapid expansion of the population is *not*, all in accordance with the predictions of the Solow–Swan model. But how are we to interpret the estimate $\hat{\beta} = -0.366$? Surely one is not entitled to say that poverty is "good for growth," or, even milder, that it is "no hindrance" to it. To grow faster, it appears, countries should invest more in physical and human capital, and this conforms to common sense. However, whereas it is possible, even easy, to save 25 percent of an annual real income of \$US21,360 (actual figures for the USA,

1990), it is not so easy to save an equal percentage of an income of $US1,339 (actual figure for India, 1990, real PPP). Poverty *is* a hindrance to saving, hence to investment, therefore to growth. The estimate $\widehat{\beta} = -0.366$ means ... simply that if the poor countries parameterized their economies in a mirror-fashion of the rich ones, then the fact of being poor would not restrict their growth; on the contrary, they would begin to grow faster than their rich partners. Now this, of course, we already knew; for if all countries, the rich and the poor, had the same growth parameters (that is, the same steady state), then the hypothesis of convergence would apply.

Table 4.1: Growth Determinants, 1960–1985

Basic regression Dependent variable: $\overset{o}{y}_{[1960-1985]}$ (annual average) Sample size: 75 Countries	
Constant	3.69
	(0.91)
$\log y_{1960}$	−0.366
	(0.067)
$\log s_K$	0.538
	(0.102)
$\log s_H$	0.271
	(0.081)
$\log n$	−0.551
	(0.288)
$\bar{R}^2$	0.43
s.e.e	0.3
Implied λ	0.0182

Source: N. Gregory Mankiw *et al.* (1992)

4.4 Adding Variables to the "Basic Conditional Barro Regression"

Thus the main conclusion to this point is that the poor countries are not catching up with the rich ones because: (1) their population is expanding too fast; and (2) they do not have enough savings to invest in physical and human capital. Moreover, there seems to be little hope that they will ever obtain the necessary savings out of their own incomes, for these are already too low. But surely there is a catch here: since the stocks of physical and human capital are relatively low in the poor countries, the returns to those factors should be relatively high. Prima facie, this should attract physical and human capital from abroad. In fact, that is what the very foundation of the Solow–Swan model, namely that factor inputs exhibit decreasing marginal productivities, suggests. Why, then, are the poor countries lacking the necessary resources to grow faster? Perhaps the problem is that foreign investments are not secure in poor countries; or that, in those countries where they would be, they do not flow in because barriers to foreign investment exist; or that, if they would be secure and are not impeded to move in, there might be political unrest which makes running a business in those countries a painful experience, and so on. Perhaps the "founding father" had it right:

> In all countries where there is tolerable security, every man of common understanding will endeavor to employ whatever stock he can command ... A man must be perfectly crazy who, where there is tolerable security, does not employ all the stock which he commands, whether it be his own or borrowed of other people ... In those unfortunate countries, indeed, where men are continually afraid of the violence of their superiors, they frequently conceal a great part of their stock, in order to have it always at hand to carry with them to some place of safety, in case of their being threatened with any of those disasters to which they consider themselves as at all times exposed. This ... seems to have been a common practice among our ancestors during the violence of the feudal government. (Smith, 1776, p. 268)

Hence, why not expand the "basic regression" Equation (4.6) with such variables as "promotion of property rights," "degree of international openness," "political stability," and so on? To be sure, the Solow–Swan model provides some ground to do that, for we still have to recoup "A" from its unnatural place in the error term of the basic regression Equation (4.6). In other words, we are suggesting that instead of dumping the initial level of technology $\log A_{i,0}$ into the error term of the basic regression Equation (4.6) (the method used by Mankiw, Romer and Weil, 1992), we proxy it by an appropriate combination of such variables as those mentioned above. This raises the obvious question of how those variables relate to the level of technology. Pack (1994, 67) provides an account of reasons, for instance:

> (a) Diffusion of technological know-how occurs through direct foreign investment, licensing, consultants, and informal knowledge transfers. Each of these is facilitated by international trade.

(b) Where knowledge becomes available, costly local adaptation is often required to achieve levels of total factor productivity realized in industrialized countries with the same machinery. Moreover, the reward to such effort is not always appropriable by private firms. For example, the increased use of high-yield seeds known as the Green Revolution, which increased productivity of agriculture in developing countries, required publicly provided research on adaptation.

(c) Protectionist policies allow firms to avoid a commitment of resources in activities such as quality control and product specialization. Although firms shielded from rivals could increase their profits by such activities, the absence of competitive pressures allows the indulgence of a preference for an easy life.

Therefore, trade barriers (and protectionism in general), the lack of appropriate public support to private investment be it domestic or foreign (let alone political corruption [see Shleifer and Vishny, 1993]), either impede technological diffusion or deter technological adaptation or both; in sum, they favor technological backwardness.

With this in mind, adding variables to the basic regression Equation (4.6) has become almost a fashion in recent years. The results from this exercise show that promotion of property rights, openness to international trade, political stability, law enforcement, public incentives to investment and a low level of taxation, all favor economic growth (Barro, 1991; Sachs and Warner, 1995); too much government intervention and a high level of inflation do not (Fisher, 1993); and the evidence is inconclusive as regards the type of political regime (democracy, dictatorship) (Przeworski and Limongi, 1994). (For a complete survey, see Barro, 1997.)

Reflecting on this empirical literature, the editors of *The Economist* (May 25 1996, p. 16) put together a compact explanation for "why poor countries stay poor" (this explanation needs not be shared by all, but it surely deserves careful consideration, hence we quote it at length):

> The enormous wealth of the world's rich countries is due to nothing more than advanced technology and accumulated capital. Yet both of these, it seems, are available to all. Technology is more readily transferable across borders than ever before. Indeed, much of the innovation of the past 20 years has been directed at the very task of shrinking distance. Progress in transport, telecommunications and computers has made it easier for poor countries to take part in the global economy. And it is often a feature of the newest technologies that they are easier

for poor countries to adopt than the techniques they are replacing (compare satellite telephony with wire-based systems). In short, there is nothing about being poor, as such, that denies a country access to either capital or technology.

What then is the problem? One plausible answer is skills. What use is modern technology if a poor country's workers cannot read the instructions on a bag of fertiliser? Studies of the East Asian tigers agree that heavy investments in education paid off handsomely. Yet it is important not to press this explanation too far. Remember that skills, too, can be bought and sold across borders. If lack of skills were the only thing holding poor countries back from spectacular growth, then the returns to possessing skills in such countries would be staggeringly high. Foreigners with skills would migrate to poor countries, in a flood rather than the present trickle. And far few educated citizens of India, Mexico and Nigeria would be found working in London or Washington, DC.

This point is of broader relevance. The recent debate about Asia's growth 'miracle' has made popular the view that, to grow, countries need merely to invest: in equipment, in roads, in human capital (i.e. in skills). This is misleading: there is no 'merely' about it. True, East Asia accumulated lots of capital; given that, its growth is unsurprising. But one also needs to ask, under what conditions will the right sort of investment happen? The simplest answer is, under conditions that grant the investor —a firm buying a new machine, a family sending its children to school— an adequate return. In much of the third world, such conditions are absent, and that is why poor countries stay poor.

Establishing those conditions is the task of economic policy. The past ten years have witnessed a resurgence of academic interest in growth, a subject oddly neglected hitherto. The thrust of the newest work, which has a refreshingly empirical flavour, is that policy is what matters above all. Many studies now show that secure property rights, reliable enforcement of contracts, a liberal trade regime, low taxes and public spending, a welcome for foreign investors, etc. work best. The tigers' rapid growth, [by and large based on those policies], is impressive. There is no reason why other poor countries should not aspire [to it].

Not everyone, though, agrees with the exercise of (endlessly?) expanding the basic "*conditional* Barro-regression." For, as Solow (1994, p. 51) remarks, adding explanatory variables to the basic growth regression may help avoid the danger of misspecification, but it may also contribute to blur the fundamental growth determinants:

> As the range of explanatory variables broadens, it becomes harder and harder to believe in an underlying structural relation that amounts to more than a sly way of saying that Japan grew rapidly and the United Kingdom grew slowly ...

What Solow seems to imply is that we have two ways of dealing with A (which the Solow–Swan model takes as exogenously given): one is Mankiw, Romer and Weil's method, that is, to dump A into the error regression term and take the risk of econometric bias due to omitted variable; the other is to replace A with its determinants, but then we ought to be serious about it: some *theory* concerning the determination of A is necessary; and, as a theory, it must contain few and *fundamental* variables. Simply adding an unlimited number of determinants, although based on good common sense grounds, does *not* seem to be the right way of dealing with A. (Moreover, many of the "additional" variables considered in this literature do not appear to be robust [Levine and Renelt, 1992], which makes Solow's case even more valuable.)

4.5   Summary of Results and a "Second Pass" on Convergence

In Chapter 3 we addressed the question of whether the automatic forces of a market economy should be expected to drive *equal-steady-state* economies into convergence in per capita income terms. We said that according to the standard version of the Solow–Swan model, the answer is *yes;* moreover, we found that this prediction, which we called "the hypothesis of convergence," passes the "σ test," which we took as the appropriate statistical tool to falsify this hypothesis. We also used another statistical tool in Chapter 3, namely the "Barro regression" or "β-convergence test," but not really to falsify the convergence hypothesis, for it was shown not to be a reliable tool for that; we used it only to determine the *speed of convergence* among equal-steady-state economies once we knew, through the σ test, that the "convergence hypothesis" does hold in the real world.

In the present chapter we are again addressing the question of convergence, but in relation to *different-steady-state* economies. Thus far, we have found that in this case the S&S model does not predict anything: it simply cannot tell whether different-steady-state economies are bound to converge, diverge, or remain in the same relative position to each other. This is a misfortune; a definite prediction is essential to know whether we ought to expect the poor countries to "catch-up" with the rich ones. However, as if compensating for this shortcoming, the S&S model allows us to look at the issue of worldwide economic convergence from a different angle, as follows: If s, n, δ, g and A were the same everywhere, the world's different economies would converge; hence, if they actually do not, the *reason* must be exclusively that s's, n's, δ's, g's and A's are not all the same everywhere. Trivial? Surely, but also very informative: it has directed us to a new and significant task, namely to investigate *how* different s's, n's, and so on, *matter for convergence*.

On this, we have been lucky: the S&S model provides a suitable *method* to know how different s's, n's, and so on, *shape* the process of economic growth. This method, known as "*conditional β-convergence*" or "*conditional* Barro regression," works as follows. First, we apply the σ test to the worldwide per capita incomes data just to find out what, exactly, has been happening to the world's per capita income dispersion. We find that for the past few decades it has been widening, so we conclude that (at least since the 1960s) there has been per capita income *divergence* worldwide. Second, once we know this, we try to find what *reasons* might explain it, for which we use worldwide cross-country "Barro-regressions" (or "*conditional β-convergence*"). This method allows us to uncover a number of reasons (the ones explained in Sections 4.3 and 4.4) why the world's per capita incomes dispersion has been increasing since at least (as far as the data goes) the 1960s. Now those findings, besides giving us a plausible explanation for the empirically observed worldwide per capita income divergence, also give us valuable information as to *what* the poor economies may do to grow faster. Thus, we have obtained no little from our endeavor.

Any problem with this knowledge? Well ... no, if we give it its real meaning; yes, if we do not use it properly. Consider, for instance, the following examples:

(a) "Since the worldwide dispersion of per capita incomes has been increasing, we conclude that *the capitalist process* of economic growth is *characterized* by worldwide divergence."

This conclusion is unwarranted: it does not follow from the premise. Why? Because all we know is that *over the last few decades* the variance of the worldwide per capita income distribution has been increasing and that this can be accommodated and given a plausible explanation within the Solow–Swan model. Now, nothing in this knowledge allows us to conclude that the market mechanism is intrinsically *bound* to generate worldwide divergence of per capita incomes (so that it must bring more worldwide divergence in the future). For one thing, the theory on which our knowledge is based (the standard version of the S&S model) gives us no clue to that effect — hence, no help coming from this side; for another thing, our empirical ancillary (that is, the σ test) only tells us what it can, namely what the world *has been* like, not what it *will be* like.

So the question arises as to whether a world that up to now has been diverging (or, for that matter, converging) can be empirically and/or theoretically consistent with it *not* doing the same in the future. The answer is *yes*. To see why, consider the situation depicted in Figure 4.2. It represents a world with four (only to make the figure tractable; they could be as many

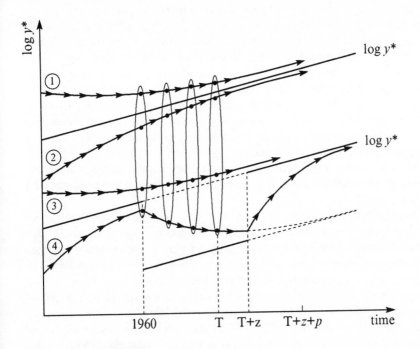

Figure 4.2: The "σ Test" and the Process of Worldwide Per Capita Incomes Convergence (Divergence)

as we liked) economies, 1, 2, 3, and 4, each converging to its own steady state, as predicted in the S&S model. Now imagine that a researcher living in 1960 had applied the σ test to the data, had these been available to him: he would have found *conditional σ-convergence*. (Since this researcher never existed and, besides, we never had worldwide per capita income data before 1960, we actually don't know whether the world was really like this at the time. Probably not, but it doesn't matter; this is only an example.) Now (just imagine) something happened in 1960, namely, country 4's steady state jumped to a lower level because, say, a revolution brought the country to economic isolation and so its physical and human capital investment rates fell sharply. Thus, starting in 1960 this country began to move (downwards) to its new steady-state path. To be sure, by the *current period*, T in the figure, it has not yet reached its new steady state and is still moving towards it. Now imagine that *today* (period T in the figure) a researcher has per capita income data on the four countries only *since* 1960 (as is the actual case). So she applies the σ test to her data: she finds that the per capita income variance *has been* increasing (hence *conditional* σ-divergence) *from 1960 to date*. Now imagine that z year from today, that is, in period T+z, this country 4 will witness a counter-revolution that puts everything back to what it was prior to 1960 (including foreign investment: hence, the physical and human capital investment rates return to their pre–1960 levels). So the country then begins to move (upwards) to the new (which is its "old") steady state. Clearly, if a researcher living at (future) time T+z + p were to apply the σ test to the per capita income data collected since 1960, she could well find *anything*: "conditional" σ-divergence, convergence, or neither.

(b) "Since the worldwide dispersion of per capita incomes *has been* increasing, we conclude that the 'poor countries' are not *catching-up* with the 'rich' ones."

This conclusion, too, is unwarranted: it does not follow from the premise and, to a large extent, is mere word playing. Why? Because even though the variance of the worldwide distribution of per capita incomes has been increasing, the *ordinal* position of countries *within* the distribution has been changing, with some (but not all) of the countries that were poor in 1960 becoming rich (think of the "South Koreas") and some (but not all) of the countries that were rich, becoming poor (think of the "Venezuelas"). The fact that (not only since 1960 but all through history) there are South Koreas (the so-called *economic miracles*) as well as Venezuelas (the so-called *economic disasters*), indicates that we cannot go straightforward from the premise "the world dispersion of per capita incomes is increasing" to the conclusion "the poor countries are not catching up with the rich ones."

Thus, in modesty, we have to recognize that our current statistical and theoretical tools (the σ test, the convergence hypothesis) are unsuited to tackle these "big questions" (Quah, 1993, 1996). Thus, while the appropriate tools to address them are being developed (Quah, 1996, for a complete reference), we can concentrate our attention in matters for which we appear to be better armed. For instance: we want to have "South Koreas," that is to say *growth miracles*, do we not? So we want the poor countries to start moving towards ever-higher steady state paths (as Solow, 1997, puts it, what the poor countries need is "trend-lifting"). This, according to the knowledge we now have, will require that they increase their investment rates in physical and human capital, their levels of technology, and so on (all that we have come up with in the analysis of *conditional* convergence). So the question is, how can they do that? Aside from *The Economist*'s recipe, which to some does not appear as sufficient but (perhaps?) only necessary infrastructure, we may be able to learn from the experience of the "South Koreas." How have they done it? What sort of *specific policies* (not only economic but also political, social, educational, cultural, etc.) *have* they *implemented* in the past which may have contributed to their success?

The answers to these questions are likely to be found in the writings of the economic historians, the social and political analysts,[2] and even the "casual observers." So perhaps, we should "come to working terms" with them, difficult as this may be. Why difficult? Because as Solow (1994) says, "it takes two to tango," and there is a long history of mutual disdain (when not overt opposition) between the "institutional" and the "theoretical" minded economists. The former do not like to see their work encapsulated in *models* (which they often regard as "molds"), and the latter consider these as essential for scientific progress. Who is to take the first step?

4.6 Conclusion

Knowing if there are any theoretically and (or) empirically based reasons to expect that today's world economies will be moving towards convergence in per capita income terms is an all-time question in economics. The literature surveyed in this chapter shows how well economists are performing at this task. We are not doing too badly: We know that since the 1960s the worldwide dispersion of per capita incomes has been increasing, and we also know a few plausible reasons to explain it. We do not think, however, that this is all that is important to know about the process of economic growth and development; most likely, it is only a piece of it. However, we ought to be optimistic: as mentioned in Chapter 3, research is booming on this topic, and this is no little thing after so long a silence in mainstream economics.

---

[2] The reader will find George Mikes's *The Land of the Rising Yen* (Penguin Books, 1986) amusing and informative of Japanese idiosyncrasy, which surely has something to do with Japan's so rapid economic expansion.

Chapter 5

Economic Growth and Social Welfare: The "Golden Rules" of Accumulation

5.1 Introduction

The neoclassical Solow–Swan model provides a suitable framework for the analysis of long-run social welfare issues. In this chapter we explore these possibilities with regard to the problem of *intergenerational generosity*. It relates to the question, first posed by Ramsey (1928), of "How much should a nation save?" Now, this is an open-ended question because the answer depends on the *purpose* for which the nation saves, that is, "how much should it save *to* ..." Consequently, there are as many questions (therefore also as many answers) as there are purposes for the *act of saving*. The analysis presented here is based upon the work of Ramsey himself and, more recently, Phelps (1961, 1966), Cass (1965) and Koopmans (1965).[1]

---

[1] F. Ramsey was a Cambridge (England) mathematician and philosopher. He died at the age of twenty six and by then he had already written several articles we now regard as "classics," some of them steaming from his undergraduate essays. Keynes (1930) eulogizes him.

5.2 The "Golden Rule" of Accumulation

We saw in Chapter 2 that changes in the rate of savings cannot affect the steady state *growth rates* of K, k, Y, y, I, i, C and c, but they do affect the steady state *levels* of those variables. Hence, the following question is appropriate: "What savings rate gives rise to the steady state path with highest levels of c?"[2] The answer is simple: since $c_t = A_t\tilde{c}_t$ and A_t always grows by assumption, the highest steady state *path* for $c_t, \{c_t\}$, is the one that corresponds to the highest steady state *value* of $\tilde{c}_t$. Thus, we have to find the rate of savings that generates the highest steady state value of $\tilde{c}$ for *given values* of n, δ, and g. This amounts to solving the following program:

$$\left. \begin{array}{l} \max.\{\tilde{c}_t = \tilde{y}_t - \tilde{i}_t = f(\tilde{k}_t) - sf(\tilde{k}_t)\} \\ \text{s.to: } \dot{\tilde{k}}_t = 0 \end{array} \right\}. \qquad (5.1)$$

Since the restriction equation $\dot{\tilde{k}}_t = 0$ (which is imposed by the steady state condition) can be written as $sf(\tilde{k}_t) = (n + \delta + g)\tilde{k}_t$, we have:

$$\left. \begin{array}{l} \max.\{\tilde{c}_t = f(\tilde{k}_t) - sf(\tilde{k}_t)\} \\ \text{s.to: } sf(\tilde{k}_t) = (n + \delta + g)\tilde{k}_t \end{array} \right\}. \qquad (5.2)$$

Substituting the restriction into the objective function the maximization problem becomes:

$$\max.\{\tilde{c}_t = f(\tilde{k}_t) - (n + \delta + g)\tilde{k}_t\} \qquad (5.3)$$

The first order condition for the solution of this problem is:

$$\frac{d\tilde{c}_t}{d\tilde{k}_t} = f'(\tilde{k}_t) - (n + \delta + g) = 0, \qquad (5.4)$$

which implies:

$$f'(\tilde{k}_t) = n + \delta + g. \qquad (5.5)$$

Equation (5.5) is known as the "Golden Rule of Capital Accumulation" (Phelps [1961]). Its solution gives the steady state value of $\tilde{k}$ (call it $\tilde{k}^*_{gold}$) whose corresponding steady state *path* for $c_t, \{c_t\}_{gold}$, is the highest attainable given n, δ and g. Once $\tilde{k}^*_{gold}$ is known, it may be substituted into the restriction equation. This yields $sf(\tilde{k}^*_{gold}) = (n+\delta+g)\tilde{k}^*_{gold}$, from which we can obtain s_{gold}, the savings rate we are trying to find. Figure 5.1 describes the situation. Given n, δ and g, $\tilde{c}$ is maximum where $f'(\tilde{k}_t) = n + \delta + g$,

---

[2]Related questions, such as "What savings rate gives rise to the steady state path with highest levels of y, or k, and so on?" have a trivial answer, namely: $s = 100$ percent.

that is to say, where the slope of $\tilde{y}_t = f(\tilde{k}_t)$ equals the slope of $(n + \delta + g)\tilde{k}_t$. This happens for $\tilde{k}_t = \tilde{k}_{gold}^*$, which is the steady state level of $\tilde{k}$ only with $s = s_{gold}$.

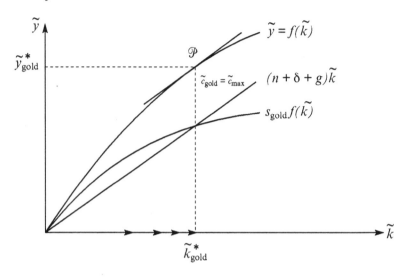

Figure 5.1: The "Golden Rule" of Accumulation

The "Golden Rule" of Accumulation takes its name from the Biblical "Golden Rule of Conduct" (St Luke, Ch. 7, Verse 31), which states the following: "Do unto others as you would have others do unto you." The reason for the analogy can be explained thus: If past generations (beginning with our parents, grandparents, and so on, this depending on the time it takes the economy to move from one steady state to another) had saved a proportion s_{gold} of their income, the economy would be currently positioned on its "Golden Rule" steady state and we would enjoy the highest level of consumption per capita compatible with the given rates of population growth and capital depreciation. Therefore, we would prefer that our parents had saved the proportion s_{gold} of their income. Now, if this is so we ought to behave accordingly and save s_{gold} of *our* income so that *future generations* can enjoy the highest possible levels of consumption per capita (irrespective of what our ancestors actually did). Hence, the "Golden Rule" describes a situation in which "each generation saves (for future generations) that fraction of income which it would have past generations save for it" (Phelps, 1966, p. 5).

5.3   The "Golden Rule" of Accumulation and the Actual Economies

It often happens that we do *not* do what the Bible demands from us, therefore the following question is in order: are actual economies on their *"Golden Rule" steady states?* In other words, are *we* (the current generation) saving the proportion s_{gold} of our income? To find out, note that the "Golden Rule" (Equation [5.5]) can be written as follows:

$$f'(\tilde{k}_t) - \delta = n + g. \tag{5.6}$$

Now, we know from Chapter 2 that $f'(\tilde{k}_t)$ is the MPK (also the rate of profit, $\varrho = \Pi_t/K_t$), hence $f'(\tilde{k}_t) - \delta$ is the *net-of-depreciation MPK* (therefore also the net-of-depreciation rate of profit). We also know that $n + g$ is the economy's long-run rate of output growth, $\overset{\circ}{Y}$. Hence, Equation (5.6) tells us that at the "Golden Rule" steady-state position the net-of-depreciation MPK (or what is the same thing, the net-of-depreciation rate of profit) equals the economy's long-run rate of output growth. Based on this information we can *calibrate* where an economy stands in relation to its "Golden Rule" steady state position. As an example, consider the case of the US economy for which we have the following data (period of estimation from 1950 to 1985):

(a) The national product (real GNP) grows at an average annual rate of 3.2 percent, that is, $\overset{\circ}{Y} = n + g = 0.032$;
(b) the capital stock is approximately 2.5 times the national product of one year, that is, $K_t = 2.5Y_t$;
(c) the depreciation of the capital stock is about 10 percent of national product, that is, $\delta K_t = 0.1Y_t$;
(d) the profit share is about 30 percent, that is, $\Pi_t/Y_t = 0.3$.

From (b) and (c) we obtain the rate of capital depreciation as follows:

$$\delta = \frac{\delta K}{K} = \frac{0.1Y}{2.5Y} = 0.04.$$

From (b) and (d) we derive the marginal product of capital (or rate of profit) in the following form:

$$\frac{\Pi}{Y} = \frac{MPK \cdot K}{Y} = MPK \cdot \left(\frac{K}{Y}\right) = MPK \cdot (2.5) = 0.3 \Rightarrow MPK = 0.12,$$

thus we have:

$$MPK - \delta = 0.12 - 0.04 = 0.08.$$

Since $0.08 > \overset{o}{Y} = n + g = 0.032$ we conclude that the US economy is *not* on its "Golden Rule" steady-state position. The reason is that the MPK is too high (therefore the capital stock is too low). This means that $s < s_{gold}$ (that is, the US economy is not on its "Golden Rule" steady state because its current rate of savings is too low for that purpose).

5.4   The "Modified" Golden Rule

We have seen that at present the US economy is not on its "Golden Rule" steady state because, specifically, its rate of savings is too low for that purpose. Interestingly, the same situation applies to the British, French, German and indeed all western economies. Thus, clearly, frugality is *not* ruled by Biblical advice. The question is, *Why?* This section provides a plausible answer based on the (for the time being) following "speculation": Since society is free to *choose* any savings rate she likes, the answer may be that society does not regard the "Golden Rule" as *optimal*, that is, capable of *maximizing her welfare*. Now this speculation entails the suspicion on our part that s_{gold} is *not* the optimal rate of saving for society. This is a reasonable suspicion, for the opposite, namely, that s_{gold} *is* the optimal rate of savings, leaves us with no logical answer other than to assume that actual economies are not on their "Golden Rule" steady states because people are foolish (which is hard to accept). Thus, our task in this section is to determine the rate of savings *socially optimal* (that is, capable of maximizing *social welfare*).

Of course, this task makes sense only if we are willing to assume that a *social welfare function* exists (so that it can be maximized) in the first place. But does it? This is a much debated issue in economics, particularly ever since Arrow (1963) demonstrated that, given a set of (reasonable) conditions (including no dictatorship), there is no method by which individual preferences can *always* be combined to produce an index for the social ranking of preferences. However, the Arrow theorem is less imposing than it may seem at first. For some of its "reasonable conditions" can be individually (that is, one-at-a-time) discarded without provoking an ethically unacceptable outcome (the condition of no dictatorship being saved from the killing), and this alone is sufficient in *each* case to overturn the "impossibility theorem" (Sen, 1970).

There remains to know on *what* social utility depends. To avoid an endless (though perhaps *not* irrelevant) discussion on this issue, we simply take for good Keynes's view (surely shared by many) that "consumption, to repeat the obvious, is the sole end and object of all economic activity" (Keynes, 1936). Hence we assume that, in each moment, the economic welfare of society is a function of the level of per capita consumption at *that* moment. This gives us the following *instantaneous* "felicity function:"

$$U_t = U(c_t); \quad U'_t > 0, \ U''_t < 0. \tag{5.7}$$

Now, we know that attached to each rate of savings there is a corresponding *stream* of future investment, therefore of capital stocks, production, and consumption. This implies, together with Equation (5.7), that attached to each rate of savings there is also a corresponding stream of *instantaneous utility*, $\{U_t\} = \{U_0, U_1, U_2, ...\}$. Therefore, by definition the *optimal* rate of savings is the one whose instantaneous utility path provides the highest *total* (life-cycle) felicity. The problem is, how do we measure *total* utility?

To begin with, imagine we do the following: $\mathcal{U} = U_0 + U_1 + U_2 + \ ....$ This measure of total utility, logical as it may appear to be, is unsatisfactory for various reasons: First, it assumes that society is indifferent to the timing of utility receipts, that is to say, that she attaches the same value to utility received *today* and to utility *to be received* in the future (for example, twenty years from now). However, it is possible that, if offered "to receive a candy *either* today *or* twenty years from now," society chose to have the candy *today*. To be sure, many people believe that this *time preference* behavior is akin to human nature. Now, one candy is one candy both today and tomorrow, hence it *always* produces the same *instantaneous* utility. Thus, if society prefers "to have the candy today" it means that she attaches higher value to present than to future utility receipts. Hence, we must allow for the possibility of time preference in the measurement of total utility. This is achieved by computing total utility as the present discounted value of the instantaneous utility stream, that is, $\mathcal{U} = U_0 + U_1/(1+\varrho) + U_2/(1+\varrho)^2 + \cdots$, where ϱ is the *time preference rate* at which society discounts future utility receipts.

Second, there is the problem of defining the *length* of the felicity path, that is, the life-cycle (or time horizon) for society. One solution is to use a finite number of years, T, in recognition of the fact that "society" is made up of the living individuals, whose life-cycle is finite.[3] Hence we have $\mathcal{U} = U_0 + U_1/(1+\varrho) + U_2/(1+\varrho)^2 + \cdots + U_T/(1+\varrho)^T$. This, however, requires that we add the condition $\tilde{k}_{T+1} = 0$, that is, that no resources are left after T years, for otherwise total utility is *not* maximized. The trouble is, *What if we happen to be alive after T years?* Surely it is too much of a gamble to use up resources in such way that nothing is left to survive on after a

---

[3] "What is to be avoided above all is the re-establishing of 'Society' as an abstraction *vis-à-vis* the individual" (Marx, 1898, 1977 for an English translation, p. 234).

number of years.[4] Hence, we rather use the condition $\tilde{k}_{T+1} = \bar{\tilde{k}} > 0$, so that some resources are left for period $T+1$, to be used if needed. Now, this means that T years is *not* the time horizon society wants to operate with after all. For this reason, many economists and social philosophers conclude that the only logical time horizon *for society* is infinity. Hence we have:

$$\mathcal{U} = \sum_{t=0}^{\infty} \frac{1}{(1+\varrho)^t} U(c_t). \tag{5.8}$$

Therefore, society seeks to solve the following problem: she has to choose s so that total utility, as measured by Equation (5.8), is maximized. In solving this problem, however, she operates under one constraint, namely, the level of consumption per capita in any period is bounded as follows: $c_t = y_t - i_t$ or, what is the same, $c_t = A_t(\tilde{y}_t - \tilde{i}_t)$. Hence we have the following program:

$$\left. \begin{array}{c} \max. \left\{ \mathcal{U} = \displaystyle\sum_{t=0}^{\infty} \frac{1}{(1+\varrho)^t} U(c_t) \right\} \\[2em] \text{s.to: } c_t = A_t(\tilde{y}_t - \tilde{i}_t) \end{array} \right\}. \tag{5.9}$$

From the "Fundamental Growth Equation" (Equation [2.35]) it is:

$$\tilde{i}_t = \frac{d\tilde{k}_t}{dt} + (n + \delta + g)\tilde{k}_t = \tilde{k}_{t+1} - \tilde{k}_t + (n + \delta + g)\tilde{k}_t. \tag{5.10}$$

Using this expression for $\tilde{i}_t$ and substituting the restriction equation into the objective function the maximization program becomes:

$$\max. \left\{ \mathcal{U} = \sum_{t=0}^{\infty} \frac{1}{(1+\varrho)^t} U\left(A_t \left[f(\tilde{k}_t) - (n+\delta+g-1)\tilde{k}_t - \tilde{k}_{t+1} \right] \right) \right\}. \tag{5.11}$$

Here only $\tilde{k}_t$ is a choice variable, and there is one $\tilde{k}$ for each period from $t = 1$ to $t = \infty$. (That is, an entire sequence of capital stocks $\{\tilde{k}_t\} = \{\tilde{k}_1, \tilde{k}_2, ...\}$. The sequence begins with $\tilde{k}_1$ because $\tilde{k}_0$ is *given* by inheritance). A_t, the level of technology, is *not* a choice variable because by assumption it grows at the constant rate g, and A_0, the current (therefore *initial*) level of technology is given by inheritance, so that A_t is exogenously

---

[4] Clearly, choosing T sufficiently large to ensure that no individual presently living remains alive afterwards does *not* solve the problem. For some resources will then be left unused (and total utility wouldn't be maximized).

given by $A_t = A_0 e^{gt}$ (or, in discrete time terms, $A_0[1+g]^t$). Thus we have:

$$\max_{\{\tilde{k}_t\}} \left\{ \mathcal{U} = \sum_{t=0}^{\infty} \frac{1}{(1+\varrho)^t} U\left(A_t \left[f(\tilde{k}_t) - (n+\delta+g-1)\tilde{k}_t - \tilde{k}_{t+1} \right]\right) \right\}. \quad (5.12)$$

The first order conditions for the solution of this program are the following (see Mathematical Appendix C.1):

$$f'(\tilde{k}_t) - (n+\delta+g-1) = (1+\varrho)\frac{A_{t-1}}{A_t} \cdot \frac{U'(c_{t-1})}{U'(c_t)}; \quad (t=1,2,...,\infty). \quad (5.13)$$

The left-hand side of this equation is familiar to us. As for the right-hand side of it, everything is given except for $U'(c_{t-1})$ and $U'(c_t)$, which depend upon the specific form taken by the instantaneous felicity function (Equation [5.7]). One specification of the latter that is often used in practice is the following (see Problem 5.3):

$$U_t = U(c_t) = \log c_t. \quad (5.14)$$

In this case we have:

$$U'(c_{t-1}) = \frac{1}{c_{t-1}} \quad \text{and} \quad U'(c_t) = \frac{1}{c_t}. \quad (5.15)$$

Substituting these results into Equation (5.13) we obtain:

$$f'(\tilde{k}_t) - (n+\delta+g-1) = (1+\varrho)\frac{c_t A_{t-1}}{c_{t-1} A_t}; \quad (t=1,2,...,\infty). \quad (5.16)$$

This is a differential equation in $\tilde{k}_t$ whose solution yields the sequence of capital stocks $\{\tilde{k}_{t,op}\} = \{\tilde{k}_{1,op}, \tilde{k}_{2,op}, ...\}$ that will result from choosing the optimal rate of savings. However, for our present purpose we do *not* need to solve this equation explicitly. To see why, note that since the equation must hold for all $t(t=1,2,...,\infty)$, it will hold in particular for the period in which the economy arrives to its steady state and for all subsequent periods, where (as we know) c grows at the same rate as the level of technology (i.e. it grows at the rate g). Thus, *along the steady state path* we have:

$$f'(\tilde{k}_{op}^*) - (n+\delta+g-1) = (1+\varrho)\frac{c_{t-1}(1+g)A_{t-1}}{c_{t-1}A_{t-1}(1+g)} = (1+\varrho), \quad (5.17)$$

hence:

$$f'(\tilde{k}_{op}^*) = n + \delta + g + \varrho, \quad (5.18)$$

or what is the same:

$$f'(\tilde{k}_{op}^*) - \delta = n + g + \varrho. \quad (5.19)$$

Therefore, the optimal rate of savings, s_{op}, is such that, *in the steady state to which it leads*, Equation (5.18) is satisfied (that is, such that the net-of-depreciation MPK equals the economy's long-run rate of output growth $(n+g)$ *plus* the time-preference rate at which the current generation discounts future utility, ϱ). Equation (5.18) is often called the "Modified Golden Rule." Note that if ϱ were equal to zero, that is, if the current generation valued their children's felicity as much as they value theirs,[5] k_{op}^* would equal $\tilde{k}_{gold}^*$ and the "Modified Golden Rule" would coincide with the "Golden Rule" itself. Obviously, this is not the case (for, as we know, $\tilde{k}_{actual} = \tilde{k}_{op}^* < \tilde{k}_{gold}^*$, which means $\varrho > 0$). Figure 5.2 depicts the situation.

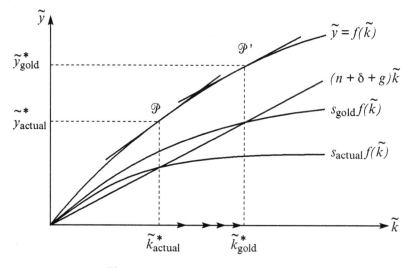

Figure 5.2: The "Modified Golden Rule"

What happens here is that raising s from its actual level to s_{gold} means a *sacrifice* for the current generation in terms of forgone consumption *today*, while the benefits of the change may never accrue to this generation. This is shown in Figure 5.3. Imagine that the savings rate is raised today (period t) from its current value s_{actual} to s_{gold}. The immediate consequence is a decrease in current consumption from $\mathcal{A}$ to $\mathcal{B}$ as the economy begins to move towards the "Golden Rule" steady state. We know that once the transition is completed (period $t+T$) consumption settles on its highest steady state path, therefore above the level that would prevail under s_{actual} (points $\mathcal{D}$ and $\mathcal{D}'$, respectively). Hence the *effective* path is $\{\mathcal{A}\to\mathcal{B}\to\mathcal{C}\to\mathcal{D}...\}$. Thus

---

[5]Trouble with this interpretation of $\varrho = 0$? If so, think of it in this way: it is *one* interpretation you are entitled to question. (On the other hand, it may be worth considering.)

the *gain* in consumption overweights the *loss* no matter how large the latter. The trouble is that the current generation is certain to incur the loss, but ignores for how long (if at all) it will enjoy the gain, so it does not raise s.

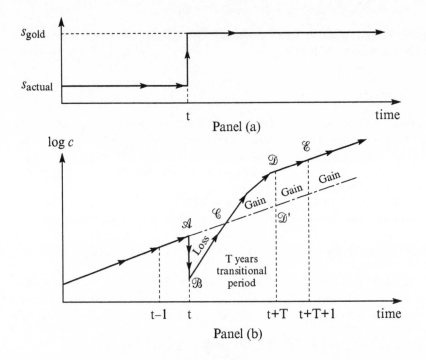

Figure 5.3: The Gain and the Loss from Saving s_{gold}

One interesting question is whether this behavior by the current generation is ethically defensible. Ramsey (1928) did not think so, and attributed the practice of discounting future consumption ($\varrho > 0$) to "the weakness of the imagination." (It is true that he was thinking of savings as a *national policy*, thus scorning the government for putting up with the public's habit of discounting the value of future consumption. But why should the government implement policies that go against the *preferences* of the people it represents?) Sir Roy F. Harrod (1948) was of the same opinion as Ramsey, only he stated it more forcefully: "time preference," he said, "[is] a polite expression for rapacity." However, other economists and social philosophers hold a different view, neatly stated by Marglin (1963, p. 97) as follows:

If I am going to play the Benthamite game ... I want to play the rest of the game of philosophical liberalism as well: In particular I want the government to reflect only the preferences of present individuals ... [And] it seems clear that many people take the view that "We are always doing something for posterity, but I would fain see posterity do something for us."

Thus in the end, whether "time preference" is ethically acceptable is entirely a matter of personal thinking.

Problems

Problem 5.1. (From Jones [1976], and based on Phelps [1961].) Imagine that the poor country of Solowandia receives an offer from the European Union of a once-and-for-all gift of capital of *any* quantity her government *chooses*. This offer has one condition attached, namely, that whatever amount of capital the island chooses *today*, it must save sufficient each year to maintain the "efficient" capital–labor ratio ($\tilde{k} = K/[AL]$) constant at the *initially chosen* level. In other words, the EU offer is the following:

Offer: *Any* quantity of capital (and, consequently, *any* $\tilde{k}$ ratio) *now* (time $t = 0$).
Condition: In the future, Solowandia must save (therefore, *invest*) sufficient to keep the "efficient" capital–labor ratio constant at the level chosen *now* (that is, the condition is $\tilde{k}_t = \tilde{k}_0$ for all $t > 0$).

What quantity of capital should Solowandia choose?

Problem 5.2. Consider an economic system that is based on the following simple rule: "Profits (that is, income accruing from capital services) are wholly invested and wages (that is, income accruing from labor services) wholly consumed."

(a) Prove that this economy will always be on its "Golden Rule" steady state position.
(b) Discuss the difficulties a government may encounter in trying to implement this rule, first, democratically (that is, by *persuasion*); and second, dictatorially (that is, by *coercion*).

Problem 5.3. Consider the following instantaneous felicity function:

$$U_t = U(c_t) = \frac{c_t^{1-\phi} - 1}{1 - \phi}; \quad (\phi > 0).$$

(a) Prove that given this specification the parameter ϕ measures the degree in which society is *willing* to *substitute consumption intertemporally* (that is, to postpone consumption from the present to the future or, reciprocally, to advance future consumption to the present). Specifically, show that the higher ϕ, the lower the willingness of society to substitute consumption intertemporally. Can you give a reason for why this is so?

(b) The empirical evidence, though variable in its results, suggests that the parameter ϕ in this instantaneous felicity function is close to unity. Using this estimate for ϕ show that U_t simply reduces to:

$$U_t = U(c_t) = \log c_t.$$

Note. This exercise is difficult but it is worth struggling with it. Try to solve it on your own, but if you fail, do not despair: it *is* really difficult. (The solution is provided below.)

Problem 5.4. (From Professor David Weil of Brown University.) Consider two economies described by the Ramsey–Cass–Koopmans model which are the same in every respect (population growth, savings rate, and so on) except their discount rates: people in country A discount the future more than people in country B. Assume that both countries start off with the same (per capita) capital stock k_0 which is below either country's steady state level. Which country will have higher initial consumption? Explain.

Solution to Problem 5.3

(a) In this specification, the parameter ϕ measures the degree in which society is *willing* to *substitute consumption intertemporally* (that is, to postpone consumption from the present to the future or, reciprocally, to advance future consumption to the present). Specifically, the higher ϕ, the lower the willingness of society to substitute consumption intertemporally. To see this, note that using this functional form for the instantaneous felicity function, total utility becomes:

$$\mathcal{U} = \sum_{t=0}^{\infty} \frac{1}{(1+\varrho)^t} \cdot \frac{c_t^{1-\phi} - 1}{1 - \phi}; \quad (\phi > 0),$$

which can be written in expanded form as follows:

$$\mathcal{U} = \frac{1}{(1+\varrho)^0} \cdot \frac{c_0^{1-\phi} - 1}{1-\phi} + \frac{1}{(1+\varrho)^1} \cdot \frac{c_1^{1-\phi} - 1}{1-\phi} + \frac{1}{(1+\varrho)^2} \cdot \frac{c_2^{1-\phi} - 1}{1-\phi}$$

$$+ \frac{1}{(1+\varrho)^3} \cdot \frac{c_3^{1-\phi} - 1}{1-\phi} + \cdots = \mathcal{U}(c_0, c_1, c_2, c_3, \cdots).$$

Society will be willing to substitute consumption intertemporally if her level of welfare is unaltered by the substitution, that is, so long as:

$$dU = \frac{\partial U}{\partial c_0}dc_0 + \frac{\partial U}{\partial c_1}dc_1 + \frac{\partial U}{\partial c_2}dc_2 + \cdots = 0.$$

Now consider two different periods, t and $t + \tau$. If consumption is shifted from one of these periods to the other, we will have $dc_t \neq 0$ and $dc_{t+\tau} \neq 0$ whereas $dc = 0$ in all the other periods. Thus it is:

$$dU = \frac{\partial U}{\partial c_t}dc_t + \frac{\partial U}{\partial c_{t+\tau}}dc_{t+\tau} = 0,$$

therefore we have:

$$\frac{dc_{t+\tau}}{dc_t} = -\frac{\partial U/\partial c_t}{\partial U/\partial c_{t+\tau}} = -\frac{c_t^{-\phi}/(1+\varrho)^t}{c_{t+\tau}^{-\phi}/(1+\varrho)^{t+\tau}} = -(1+\varrho)^{\tau}(\frac{c_{t+\tau}}{c_t})^{\phi},$$

that is to say:

$$dc_{t+\tau} = -(1+\varrho)^{\tau}(\frac{c_{t+\tau}}{c_t})^{\phi}dc_t.$$

Note that $(1 + \varrho)^{\tau}(\frac{c_{t+\tau}}{c_t})^{\phi}$ is the proportion in which society is willing to substitute consumption intertemporally. Thus for instance, if this proportion is 2 we know that society is willing to give up *one* unit of period t's consumption ($dc_t = -1$) in exchange for *two* units of additional consumption in period $t + \tau$ ($dc_{t+\tau} = 2$). Now, $(1+\varrho)^{\tau}(c_{t+\tau}/c_t)^{\phi}$ increases with ϕ because $c_{t+\tau} > c_t$ on any steady-state path. Therefore, as ϕ rises so does $dc_{t+\tau}$, that is, society demands a higher amount of additional consumption in period $t + \tau$ to give up one unit of consumption in period t. This shows that her willingness to shift consumption over time is lower the higher ϕ. One reason (*the* reason?) for this is that, since $\partial U/\partial c_t = c_t^{-\phi}/(1+\varrho)^t$, the higher ϕ, the lower the marginal utility of consumption in any one period, therefore intertemporal substitution is less appealing (for it adds less to utility) the higher is ϕ.

(b) The empirical evidence, though variable in its results, suggests that this parameter is close to unity. Using this estimate for ϕ we can reduce the proposed instantaneous felicity function to simply $U_t = \log c_t$. To do this, use l'Hôpital's rule to solve the limit's indeterminacy and recall that $d(c_t^{1-\phi})/d\phi = c_t^{1-\phi}\log c_t$. We thus have:

$$\lim_{\phi \to 1} U(c_t) = \lim_{\phi \to 1} \frac{c_t^{1-\phi} - 1}{1 - \phi} = \log c_t,$$

therefore:

$$U_t = U(c_t) = \log c_t.$$

In passing, if you wonder what the "−1" is doing in the instantaneous felicity function, note that we need it there to solve the limit. (*Why?*) Finally, note that the relatively low value of ϕ is consistent with theory, for the following reason. On the one hand, society *does* have an interest in substituting consumption intertemporally. To see why, consider a situation in which nothing is available for consumption this year and much is at our disposal for the next: obviously, we would rather move some future consumption to the present. Hence, $\phi = 0$ (that is, total indifference to the timing of consumption) is *irrational*. For this reason we *assume* $\phi > 0$. On the other hand, ϕ cannot be high, for this is *inconsistent* with the alleged interest of society in substituting consumption intertemporally. Hence the theory suggests that ϕ is positive but low.

Chapter 6

Growth Accounting and the Solow Residual

6.1 Introduction

In the previous chapters we have seen that the neoclassical Solow–Swan model explains the economic growth which we observe in reality (that is, economic growth that satisfies the "stylized facts [1] to [4]") as resulting from the combination of three elements, namely: physical and human capital, K (in an aggregate sense); labor, L, and the level of technology, A.

Now the question arises as to how much of the output growth can be attributed to each factor in particular. To answer this question we need to break down the growth in output into three components, each identifiable as the contribution of one factor of production (that is, the contributions of capital, labor and technical progress). This procedure is known as "Growth Accounting." The methodology, based on the pioneering work of Solow (1957), is presented in this chapter.

6.2 Solow's Growth Accounting Procedure

We start from the neoclassical labor-augmented production function:

$$Y_t = F(K_t, E_t) = F(K_t, A_t L_t),\tag{6.1}$$

and take time derivatives to obtain the following equation:

$$\frac{dY_t}{dt} = \frac{\partial F}{\partial K_t} \cdot \frac{dK_t}{dt} + \frac{\partial F}{\partial E_t} \cdot \frac{dE_t}{dt} = \frac{\partial F}{\partial K_t} \cdot \frac{dK_t}{dt} + \frac{\partial F}{\partial E_t} \cdot \left(A_t \cdot \frac{dL_t}{dt} + L_t \cdot \frac{dA_t}{dt} \right),$$

from which we have (with little manipulation):

$$\frac{dY_t/dt}{Y_t} = \frac{\partial F}{\partial K_t} \cdot \frac{K_t}{Y_t} \cdot \frac{dK_t/dt}{K_t} + \frac{\partial F}{\partial E_t} \cdot \frac{E_t}{Y_t} \cdot \frac{dL_t/dt}{L_t} + \frac{\partial F}{\partial E_t} \frac{E_t}{Y_t} \cdot \frac{dA_t/dt}{A_t}. \quad (6.2)$$

Now note that $E_t = A_t L_t$, and also that from Equation (6.1) we obtain:

$$\frac{\partial Y_t}{\partial L_t} = \frac{\partial F}{\partial E_t} \cdot \frac{\partial E_t}{\partial L_t} = \frac{\partial F}{\partial E_t} \cdot A_t, \quad (6.3)$$

from which it follows:

$$\frac{\partial F}{\partial E_t} = \frac{1}{A_t} \cdot \frac{\partial F}{\partial L_t}. \quad (6.4)$$

Replacing E_t and $\partial F/\partial E_t$ in Equation (6.2) with their values given by $A_t L_t$ and Equation (6.4) respectively, we have:

$$\frac{dY_t/dt}{Y_t} = \frac{\partial F}{\partial K_t} \cdot \frac{K_t}{Y_t} \cdot \frac{dK_t/dt}{K_t} + \frac{\partial Y_t}{\partial L_t} \cdot \frac{L_t}{Y_t} \cdot \frac{dL_t/dt}{L_t} + \frac{\partial Y_t}{\partial L_t} \frac{L_t}{Y_t} \frac{dA_t/dt}{A_t}, \quad (6.5)$$

that is:

$$\overset{o}{Y} = \varepsilon_K \overset{o}{K} + \varepsilon_L \overset{o}{L} + \varepsilon_L \overset{o}{A}, \quad (6.6)$$

where ε_K and ε_L stand for the elasticity of aggregate output with respect to capital and with respect to labor, respectively. Equation (6.6) is called the "Growth Accounting Equation" and it can be interpreted thus: $\varepsilon_K \overset{o}{K}$ is the contribution of physical capital to output growth, $\varepsilon_L \overset{o}{L}$ is the contribution of labor and $\varepsilon_L \overset{o}{A}$ is the contribution of technical progress.

6.3 Practical Uses of the Growth Accounting Equation

In a competitive economy factor inputs are paid their marginal products, that is, $\rho_t = MPK = \partial F/\partial K_t$ and $\omega_t = MPL = \partial F/\partial L_t$. Thus we have:

$$\varepsilon_K = \rho_t \cdot \frac{K_t}{Y_t} = \frac{\Pi_t}{Y_t} \quad (6.7)$$

and:

$$\varepsilon_L = \omega_t \cdot \frac{L_t}{Y_t} = \frac{W_t}{Y_t}, \quad (6.8)$$

that is, ε_K and ε_L coincide with the relative share of profits and the relative share of wages in total total output. Once this equivalence is made, Equation (6.6) is of great practical value because it allows us to compute the contributions of each input (capital, labor and technical progress) to output growth. As an example, we use the following data from the USA (period of estimation, 1950–1985):

(a) National output grows at an average annual rate of 3.2 percent, that is, $\overset{o}{Y} = 0.032$. Since $\overset{o}{Y} = \overset{o}{K}$ (by "stylized fact [2]"), we also have $\overset{o}{K} = 0.032$.
(b) The relative shares of profits and wages in national output are (on average) 30 and 70 percent, respectively; that is, $\Pi/Y = 0.3$ and $W/Y = 0.7$, hence $\varepsilon_K = 0.3$ and $\varepsilon_L = 0.7$.
(c) Population growth is $\overset{o}{L} = 1.5$ percent (annual average).

Thus we have: $\varepsilon_K \cdot \overset{o}{K} = (0.3)(0.032) = 0.0096 \approx 30$ percent of the 3.2 percent growth of national output (this is the contribution of capital); $\varepsilon_L \cdot \overset{o}{L} = (0.7)(0.015) = 0.0105 \approx 33$ percent of the 3.2 percent growth of national output (this is the contribution of labor). The contribution of technical progress can be obtained from Equation (6.10) as follows:

$$\varepsilon_L \cdot \overset{o}{A} = \overset{o}{Y} - (\varepsilon_K \cdot \overset{o}{K} + \varepsilon_L \cdot \overset{o}{L}), \tag{6.9}$$

therefore we have: $\varepsilon_L \cdot \overset{o}{A} = 0.032 - (0.0096 + 0.0105) = 0.0119 \approx 37$ percent of the 3.2 percent growth of national output (this is the contribution of technical progress). Note that the contribution of technical progress is obtained as a "residual" (that is, whatever is left after the contributions of capital and labor are computed). For this reason Equation (6.9) is called the *Solow residual.* The size of this residual would diminish if we used the "broad concept" of capital, thus including under K human as well as physical capital. As we know, in this case the relevant production function for the USA (to continue with the same example) is $Y_t = K_t^{0.68}(A_t L_t)^{0.32}$ instead of $Y_t = K_t^{0.3}(A_t L_t)^{0.7}$, hence the Solow residual becomes $\varepsilon_L \cdot \overset{o}{A} = 0.032 - (0.02176 + 0.0048) = 0.00544$, or 17 percent of the 3.2 percent growth of US output.

From Equation (6.9) we can compute the growth rate of the level of technology $(\overset{o}{A})$ as follows:

$$\overset{o}{A} = \frac{\overset{o}{Y} - (\varepsilon_K \cdot \overset{o}{K} + \varepsilon_L \cdot \overset{o}{L})}{\varepsilon_L}. \tag{6.10}$$

In the growth accounting literature, A_t (the index of the level of technology) is often called *total factor productivity* (TFP), thus its rate of growth $\overset{o}{A}$ is referred to as the growth rate of total factor productivity. The index

A_t is called *total factor productivity* for the following reason: we use the index Y/L to measure the productivity of labor *alone*, but if we want to measure the *joint* productivity of capital and labor (that is, the "total factor productivity") we need and index in which both L *and* K appear in the denominator. One such index is constructed from Equation (6.10) as follows:

$$\overset{o}{A} = \frac{1}{\varepsilon_L}\overset{o}{Y} - \left(\frac{\varepsilon_K}{\varepsilon_L}\overset{o}{K} + \overset{o}{L}\right) = \text{growth rate of } \left(\frac{Y^{1/\varepsilon_L}}{K^{\varepsilon_K/\varepsilon_L} \cdot L}\right), \quad (6.11)$$

from which we have:

$$A = \frac{Y^{1/\varepsilon_L}}{K^{\varepsilon_K/\varepsilon_L} \cdot L}. \quad (6.12)$$

Thus, if Equation (6.12) is used as an index for total factor productivity Equation (6.10) gives the TPF rate of growth.[1]

6.4 The "Productivity Slowdown Puzzle"

Table 6.1 displays the evolution of the growth rates of labor productivity (measured by $\overset{o}{y}=[\overset{o}{Y/L}]$) and the growth rates of total factor productivity ($\overset{o}{A}$) for the seven major economies of the world (the so-called "G-7 group") over the past few decades. (Note that when we compute $\overset{o}{A}$ on the basis of the Cobb–Douglas aggregate production function $Y_t = K_t^{\alpha}[A_t L_t]^{1-\alpha}$, we have $\overset{o}{A}=\overset{o}{y}$. Why?) A striking phenomenon emerges from the observation of Table 6.1, namely: there is a worldwide slowdown in productivity growth since the 1970s. This is a puzzling development because it means, looking at the data from the point of view of the S&S model, that *technical progress* slowed down during the same period (for, according to the S&S model, labor productivity $[y = Y/L]$ grows at the same rate as the level of technology) whereas common observation of reality (with all its advances in electronics, communications, information processes, and so on, made during this period) *would* suggest the opposite, namely an *acceleration* in labor efficiency gains. Among the possible explanations for this "puzzle" we have the following:

(1) The "Worldwide Productivity Slowdown" was first detected in 1973–1974 and it exacerbated again in 1979–1980, thus it went *pari passu* with the

---

[1]Equation (6.12) is only one of the many TFP indices possible. For instance, in his original paper on growth accounting Solow (1957) uses as production function $Y_t = A_t F(K_t, L_t)$ instead of $Y_t = F(K_t, A_t L_t)$. Hence the growth accounting equation, the residual, and the TFP index become: $\overset{o}{Y}=\overset{o}{A} +\varepsilon_K \overset{o}{K} +\varepsilon_L \overset{o}{L}$, $\overset{o}{A}=\overset{o}{Y} -(\varepsilon_K\cdot \overset{o}{K} +\varepsilon_L\cdot \overset{o}{L})$ and $A = Y/(K^{\varepsilon_K} \cdot L^{\varepsilon_L})$, respectively.

two major "oil crises" of our time. Linking the two phenomena is a temptation, and many authors have in fact done so (see, for example, Baily, 1981). The basic argument is that the sudden increase in oil prices made much of the existing capital stock "prematurely obsolete," that is, that because the technology of the time was oil-use (or should we say "oil-abuse"?) intensive, it had either to be abandoned in favor of non-oil based technologies (a kind *reswitching* to less efficient techniques: for example, the return to coal as an important source of energy), or used at a *low pace* (for example, we had very efficient trucks, capable of moving fast, but the speed limits introduced during the oil crisis made them seem like 1930's trucks), or altogether replaced by newer, less oil-consuming technologies (for example, the huge, American-style, cars of the time began to be replaced with small,

Table 6.1: The Slowdown in Productivity Growth Across the World

Country	Growth Rate of y		Growth Rate of TFP	
	1948-1972	1972-1988	1948-1972	1972-1988
Canada	2.9	2.6	(=)	(=)
France	4.3	2.1	(=)	(=)
Germany	5.7	2.2	(=)	(=)
Italy	4.9	2.8	(=)	(=)
Japan	8.2	3.3	(=)	(=)
UK	2.4	2.1	(=)	(=)
USA	2.2	1.7	(=)	(=)

Source: N. Gregory Mankiw (1992); and the author's calculations

more energy efficient cars), all of which implied large investments in new equipment while the one in place was not fully depreciated. Hence, the capital stock raised largely *only in an accounting sense*, for much of it was left idle (that is, there appeared a gap between *measured* capital stock and *true* capacity utilization). Quite logically, growth accounting exercises on this period produce a declining productivity growth as result. However, the empirical estimations show that, although real, the negative impact of the oil crises on productivity is orders of magnitude smaller than the registered productivity slowdown, hence quite insufficient to explain it.

(2) The rise in government regulation of industry, which forced many firms to incur large investments to reduce pollution, increase safety in the work-place, and so on (investments which do not raise *physical output*); *plus* the increase in resources devoted to fight crime and corruption (an investment which also makes little contribution to *physical output*), and

so on, might have contributed to the "measured" productivity slowdown.[2] Once again, however, the empirical estimations indicate that these factors can explain only a little portion of the reported productivity slowdown (see Denison, 1985).

Other explanations have been proposed in recent years; some of them do not fit well within the Solow–Swan model (but see Problem 6.4 for a rather unexplored *conjecture* which does fall within the Solow–Swan model), hence we postpone their review for later chapters (see Chapter 7, Section 7.6). However, neither any of the single explanations so far proposed, nor all of them together, can account empirically for the registered 1970's fall in productivity growth. Thus, the "productivity puzzle" remains largely unresolved. (See "*JEL* Symposium," 1988, for a survey of views.)

6.5   Conclusions from Part II: The Need for "Endogenous" Technical Progress

Consider the following questions: *Who* "produces" technical progress and why? *How* is it *transmitted*? What *payment* does it get and where does this payment *come from*? In the neoclassical model these questions are mainly avoided by assuming that technical progress is "exogenously given" ("It floats down from the outside," to use Solow's own words). On the other hand, the "Solow residual" tells us that a large portion of output growth is due to technical progress. Putting these two things together, it is often argued that in the Solow–Swan model much of the output growth (specifically, the portion of it that is captured by the "Solow residual") goes *unexplained*. However, this is not exactly true. Assuming that A is "exogenous" (or that "it floats down from the outside") is not to say that "it falls from the sky" (the, so to speak, *helicopter theory of A*) or that no real-world origin for it can be devised within the neoclassical model. Far from this; what the assumption means is that technical progress is "produced" outside the economic realm of the private, profit-maximizing firms. Thus it could, for instance, be provided by the state: the government commissions some R&D (research and development) firms to "produce" technical progress, pays them with tax revenues collected from the general public and, finally, makes their "output" (technical progress) available to all firms *gratis*. This scenario fits well the idea of "exogenous technical

---

[2] We emphasize the words "physical output" because although a lower pollution, a higher safety in the work-place, a lower crime, and so on, are all valuable goods, they are not measured in GNP (as "physical output" is), hence they are not accounted for in *growth accounting exercises.*

progress" that is present in the Solow–Swan model and whose only purpose is to convey the tale that all firms have access to *A free of charge.*

Hence, the trouble with the assumption of "exogenous technical progress" is not that it leaves the existence of A without a *plausible* explanation; for, as we have seen, the intervention of the state is sufficient to account for that;[3] indeed, it is undeniable that much technical progress is produced in that way, particularly in the so-called "basic research." The *real* trouble is that, by attributing the entire production of A to state-financed R&D firms, we are unfaithful to reality, for we know that much technical progress is generated by private, profit-maximizing firms which are *not* state-financed: they produce technical progress in exactly the same conditions other firms produce their widgets, namely incurring a cost to produce a good which *they* sell to other private, profit-maximizing firms *at a price.* To this effect, technical progress is like any other commodity. This means that in reality it is not completely "exogenous."

If this is so, and it obviously is, why is it not acknowledged in the Solow–Swan model? Simply because if it were (that is, if the model recognized that much technical progress is produced in this manner), it could no longer be assumed that all firms have access to A *gratis*, in which case the Solow–Swan model would not stand up. Why? Because in this model the payments made to the other inputs (K and L) already exhaust the total output, thus leaving nothing to compensate A. This is easy to show. In the Solow–Swan model, capital and labor are paid their marginal products; hence, assuming for simplicity that the production function is Cobb–Douglas of the type $Y_t = K_t^\alpha (A_t L_t)^{1-\alpha}$, we have $MPK = \alpha(Y_t/K_t)$ and $MPL = (1-\alpha)(Y_t/L_t)$, therefore it is $MPK \cdot K_t + MPL \cdot L_t = Y_t$ (that is, the total output is exhausted). Thus, if besides paying for K and L the firms also had to pay for *at least* some of the A-input, their revenues would fall short of their costs and they would go under. Hence, the Solow–Swan model stands up only insofar as *it does not recognize the role that private, profit-maximizing firms play in the generation of technical progress.*

One might wonder whether this is an essential issue or only a minor one; after all, theory in this area of economics generally takes place at high levels of abstraction and we do accept other simplifying tales (for example, the existence of an aggregate production function). Unfortunately, it *is* an essential issue, both for theoretical reasons (which we will explain in a later chapter, Chapter 8) and for the following practical one: the model itself tells us that technical progress is the engine of growth (see Chapter 2, Sec-

---

[3] Solow (1994, p. 48) makes this point clear: "A criticism of the neoclassical model: a theory of growth that leaves the main factor of economic growth unexplained. There is some truth in that observation, but also some residual misconception. To say that the rate of technological progress is exogenous is not to say that it is always mysterious."

tion 2.5), hence technical progress is so important that we should devote great efforts to designing good policies to promote it, yet this requires us to have the correct answers to the questions posed above (that is, who "produces" technical progress and why, what payment it receives and where this payment comes from, and so on). For if we answer these questions, we will be able to design wiser policy measures to spur economic growth. Hence, there is a need to make a portion of technical progress *endogenous* (that is, determined within the model as the output of *private, profit-maximizing firms*), as indeed it *is* in reality.

Economics has in fact made advances in this direction recently. In the next two chapters we will review some of the relevant literature in this area, but a warning about it is in order at this point: since a unified theory of endogenous economic growth is still lacking, the models to be presented do not have the "roundness" of the Solow–Swan model. However, they do take up the right questions.

Suggested Reading

Barro, Robert J. and Xavier Sala-i-Martín (1995). From Ch.10, Sections 10.4.3 to 10.4.6.

Problems

Problem 6.1. Consider the following aggregate production function that is Cobb–Douglas in capital (K_t) and effective labor $(A_t L_t)$:

$$Y_t = F(K_t, L_t, A_t) = K_t^\alpha (A_t L_t)^{1-\alpha}.$$

(a) Show that the elasticities of output with respect to the capital and labor inputs are α and $1 - \alpha$ respectively.
(b) Derive the growth accounting equation corresponding to this production function.
(c) Derive the "Solow residual."
(d) Derive the corresponding index for TFP.

Problem 6.2. Consider the following aggregate production function that is Cobb–Douglas in capital (K_t) and labor (L_t):

$$Y_t = F(K_t, L_t, A_t) = A_t K_t^\alpha L_t^{1-\alpha}.$$

(a) Solve the same questions as in Problem 6.1. In light of the results, does it make a *qualitative* difference for growth accounting exercises whether we assume the production function to be $Y_t = K_t^\alpha (A_t L_t)^{1-\alpha}$ or $Y_t = A_t K_t^\alpha L_t^{1-\alpha}$? Why (or why not)?

Problem 6.3. To abound on the question asked in Problem 6.2, use the table below to compute the growth rates of TFP in the U.S. economy with two different specifications of the aggregate production function: first, $Y_t = K_t^\alpha (A_t L_t)^{1-\alpha}$, and secondly, $Y_t = A_t K_t^\alpha L_t^{1-\alpha}$. (Hint: To check the calculations, note that in both cases the contributions of K, L and A to economic growth must add up to $\overset{o}{Y}$.) **Note:** $\overset{o}{Y}$ is the growth rate of real GNP, $\overset{o}{K}$ is the growth rate of the nonresidential capital stock, and $\overset{o}{L}$ is the growth rate of total employment times average weekly hours. The parameter α in the production function is assumed to be 0.3.

Table 6.2: Growth Accounting Information for the US Economy

USA	$\overset{o}{Y}$	$\overset{o}{K}$	$\overset{o}{L}$	$\overset{o}{A}$ for $Y = K^\alpha (AL)^{1-\alpha}$	$\overset{o}{A}$ for $Y = AK^\alpha L^{1-\alpha}$
1950-1960	3.3	4.0	0.7	(?)	(?)
1960-1970	3.8	4.0	1.4	(?)	(?)
1970-1980	2.8	2.6	1.8	(?)	(?)
1980-1985	2.5	3.6	1.2	(?)	(?)

Source: N. Gregory Mankiw (1992); and the author's calculations

Problem 6.4. In Section 6.4 we gave a brief account of some possible reasons for the worldwide productivity slowdown of the 1970s and 80s (reasons which, no doubt, make good sense). Now consider the following *conjecture*:

> In a way, we should not be surprised that per capita income (or, what amounts to the same thing, productivity) growth fell so much during the 1970s and 80s. After all, much of the high growth of the 1950s and 60s was spurious, for it resulted from the fact that following WWII the capitalist world began to move towards a higher steady state path. Hence, the higher-than-usual (that is, above the historical trend) growth rates lasted only for as long as lasted the transition to the new, higher steady state. Therefore we should have been expecting the "slowdown" to happen.

Do you think that this conjecture makes sense? Does it have any theoretical basis? (Well, if you think so, you may have a thesis before you: All [!] you have to prove is that there is good empirical support for the basic premise, namely that following WWII the capitalist world *did* begin to move towards a higher steady-state path.)

Part III
The Theory of Economic Growth with "Endogenous" Technical Progress

"I think that the real value of endogenous growth theory will emerge
from its attempt to model the endogenous component of
technological progress as an integral part of the
theory of economic growth."
(Robert M. Solow)

Chapter 7

Learning-by-Doing, Knowledge Spillovers and Economic Growth

7.1   Introduction

The theory of endogenous economic growth owes much of its present form to Paul Romer's insightful and continuous work in the field. In a series of articles springing out of his 1983 doctoral dissertation, he provides many of the ideas on which the most promising research agenda in this area is currently based. However, before we proceed to a formal presentation of those ideas (or some of them, for others lay beyond the scope of this book) it will be useful to clarify Romer's understanding of "technical progress," which is central to his theory.

Recall that the Solow–Swan model identifies technological progress with *"anything* that raises labor efficiency." Romer is more specific: he identifies it with increases in the stock of *knowledge*, that is, with *new knowledge on how to produce more efficiently*. This includes *scientific discoveries* (be they major "breakthroughs" or small advances) as well as the *know-how* to use them in production. For discoveries alone do not, by themselves, increase labor efficiency. This is clear in the following example: new machines incorporating the latest technological breakthrough replace operating equipment of an older technological vintage: Is this technical progress? The answer might be "no." For it may well be the case that the labor force do not know how to use the new machines, so output falls; now, if this is true of machines incorporating the latest breakthrough, it must be truer of the breakthrough itself. Thus, for our purpose, *new knowledge* or "technical progress" means new discoveries *plus* the know-how to use them in production.

New discoveries come from R&D activity and job-practice (in ways to be explained below), and the "know-how" results from job-practice (in ways also to be explained below) and formal training, or education. Arrow (1962) was the first to propose an ingenious model of knowledge generation by job-practice. Paul Romer's first contributions to the theory of *endogenous* economic growth (Romer, 1986, 1987) are based on it. Specifically, he combines Arrow's analysis with the assumption of instantaneous and costless dissemination ("spillover") of knowledge. The result is the pathbreaking model presented in this chapter.[1]

7.2 The Learning-by-Doing and Knowledge Spillover Hypotheses

7.2.1 The Hypothesis of "Learning-by-Doing"

Romer's starting point is Arrow's (1962) hypothesis that the accumulation of knowledge (that is, the discovery of new methods to produce more efficiently and the development of the necessary skills to use them in production) is largely a byproduct of mechanization. Why? Because as Arrow (1962) points out, each new machine is capable of modifying the production environment in such a way that *learning* (and often, *invention*) receives continuous stimulae. An example can make this point clear. Imagine that a firm has 20 workers and two machines and that a new machine is brought in, thus raising the firm's level of mechanization (a higher capital–labor ratio). Several things will then happen. First, as the firm's workers operate the new equipment they progressively become accustomed to it, know it better and learn how to obtain the most out of its use. In other words, they learn the latest techniques by actually using them. Second, in the process of adapting to the larger (and usually newer) equipment they often devise *new* forms of *organization* of production and (or) find new ideas to improve on the *equipment itself* (by making, for instance, a change in the structure of some of its components).

---

[1] We use a version of Arrow's analysis that differs from Arrow's own presentation in two ways, one insubstantial (that is, only a matter of form), the other less so. As a result of this, our presentation of the "learning-by-doing, knowledge spillover" model of economic growth also differs a little from Romer's original presentation. For pedagogical reasons, however, we postpone making these differences explicit until the end of the chapter (Section 7.7).

This process is known as "learning-by-doing" but, as presented here, a more appropriate name could be "learning-*and-inventing* by investing-and-doing." It has two sides: on the one hand, people learn a new technique by actually using it in production (this is the "learning side" of the process); on the other hand, from the use of the new technique they derive ideas to improve upon the new technique itself (the "inventive side" of the process). Hence, higher levels of mechanization (which we choose to represent by a higher capital–labor ratio) and increases in the stock of knowledge are two faces of the process of capital accumulation.

This hypothesis can be formalized as follows. Let A_{it} be the stock of knowledge of firm i ($i = 1, 2, ..., N$) at time t. Our "story" says that whenever a firm raises its level of mechanization, its stock of knowledge increases through the process of "learning-by-doing." The precise amount by which this happens is an empirical matter, but for the sake of the theory we postulate that A_{it} rises at θ percent per each 1 percent rise in K_{it}/L_{it}, that is, the learning-by-doing *elasticity* of A_{it} with respect to K_{it}/L_{it} is θ:

$$\theta = \frac{d \log A_{it}}{d \log(K_{it}/L_{it})}, \quad (\theta > 0), \tag{7.1}$$

that is to say:

$$d \log A_{it} = \theta \cdot d \log \left(\frac{K_{it}}{L_{it}} \right). \tag{7.2}$$

This is the "firm's learning-by-doing curve." It can be written in *levels* form as follows:

$$\int d \log A_{it} = \theta \int d \log \left(\frac{K_{it}}{L_{it}} \right)$$

$$\log A_{it} + \log \mu = \theta \log \left(\frac{K_{it}}{L_{it}} \right) + \log \eta,$$

where $\log \mu$ and $\log \eta$ are the usual integration constants, which we write as logarithms merely for convenience. Given that $\log \eta - \log \mu = \log(\eta/\mu) = \log \xi$, where $\xi = (\eta/\mu)$, we have:

$$\log A_{it} = \log \xi + \theta \log \left(\frac{K_{it}}{L_{it}} \right)$$

$$A_{it} = \xi \left(\frac{K_{it}}{L_{it}} \right)^{\theta}, \quad (\theta > 0). \tag{7.3}$$

7.2.2 The Empirics of "Learning-by-Doing"

The idea of "learning-by-doing" has a wide empirical support, at least at the firm and industry levels. Evidence from the airplane construction (provided by Wright, 1936, and Asher, 1956) and the shipbuilding industry (Searle, 1946, and Rapping, 1965) is often quoted, but evidence is also found in other industries.

So for instance (and more relevant to the "learning-and-inventing by investing and doing" case as presented in this chapter), Schmookler (1966) provides detailed evidence from various unrelated industries that in each case the number of patents is closely correlated with investment in physical capital. Specifically, patents follow investment with a lag of one period. This suggests that new knowledge (which obviously must precede new patents, that is, behind each new patent there is always a *new idea*) springs from capital accumulation. Therefore, the "learning-by-doing" story provides an explanation for this empirical relationship.[2]

7.2.3 The "Knowledge Spillover" Hypothesis

Knowledge in general is a very slippery thing. But *technical knowledge* in particular, is impossible to hide. A firm that possesses technical knowledge which other firms do not have, exposes it to the public by using it in production, hence it becomes known to others and is likely to be used by them. Of course, this is neither instantaneous (for it takes time to learn), nor is it without a cost (the legal system of patents will see to it

---

[2]This wealth of *academic* evidence in support of the "learning-by-doing hypothesis" must not surprise. For consider what "the firm's learning-by-doing curve" actually says. Equation (7.3) tells us that, because of "learning-by-doing," there should be a direct relationship between the level of mechanization and the level of technical knowledge. Now, a higher technical knowledge means a higher *productivity of labor* (that is how we define technical progress, namely as an increase in knowledge that raises the productivity of labor). Hence, it is as well to write the firm's "learning-by-doing curve" as follows:

$$y_{it} = \frac{Y_{it}}{L_{it}} = q \left(\frac{K_{it}}{L_{it}} \right)^{\theta} \quad \text{or, what is the same,} \quad \ell_{it} = \frac{L_{it}}{Y_{it}} = m \left(\frac{K_{it}}{L_{it}} \right)^{-\theta}$$

That is to say, the hypothesis of "learning-by-doing" predicts that *the amount of labor needed to produce one unit of output* should decline with mechanization. Is this not what the "casual observer" of production can see in virtually every economic activity? Furthermore, we may write "the firm's learning-by-doing curve" yet in another form: If the amount of labor needed to produce one unit of output should fall with mechanization, in the short run (that is, with a given real wage) the *cost per unit of output* should also decrease with it. Now, also in this setting the empirical evidence in support of Arrow's hypothesis is abundant. For instance, Mansfield (1990) refers to the well-known case that "between 1908 and 1923, the price of Henry Ford's famous model T automobile fell from over \$3,000 to under \$1,000, owing in considerable measure to cost reductions that were due to learning ..."

that whoever uses new knowledge created by someone else will pay a price
to him). But Romer (1986) abstracts from this, so he makes the extreme
assumption that technological knowledge spills over *instantaneously* and all
firms can use it *gratis*.

Now, it is one thing to say that new knowledge spills over, either at
once or slowly; it is another to assume that all firms are free to use it. For
as long as the patent-system exists, no *profit-maximizing* firm in possession
of new knowledge will allow others to use it unless they pay for it. Only
if the firm is unconscious of possessing the new knowledge could other
firms use it gratis. Hence, assuming that every firm has free access to all
knowledge is tantamount to assuming that profit-maximizing firms produce
new knowledge *unconsciously*. On scrutiny, therefore, this is what Romer
(1986) assumes.[3]

7.2.4 The Implications of "Learning-by-Doing" with Free Access to New Knowledge

Coupled with Arrow's "learning-by-doing," Romer's hypothesis of "instantaneous and *costless access* to knowledge" has a number of important implications. For instance:

(1) Whatever knowledge a firm gains through its own "learning-by-
doing," it becomes immediately available to all other firms (and *gratis*).
Thus, firm i will see its own learning-by-doing leaking out to all other
firms, but at the same time it will benefit from the knowledge that the
other firms generate through their "learning-by-doing." Hence, "everyone
knows everything that there is." Thus, at any time t the level of knowledge
is the same for all firms, hence equal to the *economy-wide* knowledge, A_t.
Thus we have:

$$A_{it} = \xi \left(\frac{K_{it}}{L_{it}} \right)^\theta = A_t \quad \text{for all } i \ (i = 1, 2, ..., N). \tag{7.4}$$

(2) From this expression it follows that for any two firms, i and j,
$(i \neq j)$ it is:

$$\frac{K_{it}}{L_{it}} = \left(\frac{A_t}{\xi} \right)^{1/\theta} = \zeta_t \Rightarrow K_{it} = \zeta_t L_{it}, \forall i (i = 1, 2, ..., N), \tag{7.5}$$

---

[3]Romer makes this assumption in his 1986 paper and in some derivatives of it (Romer,
1987), but not in subsequent work. As of 1986, he had a reason to assume "costless
access to knowledge," namely, a technical difficulty (to which we shall refer in due time)
in modeling the patent system. Later, Romer (1990) himself found a way to resolve this
difficulty and removed his assumption. However, at this point it is convenient, if only
for pedagogical purposes, to use his initial assumption and postpone to a later chapter
the analysis of the patent system.

thus we have:

$$\sum_{i=1}^{N} K_{it} = \zeta_t \sum_{i=1}^{N} L_{it} \Leftrightarrow K_t = \zeta_t L_t, \qquad (7.6)$$

or what is the same:

$$\frac{K_t}{L_t} = \zeta_t = \frac{K_{it}}{L_{it}}, \forall i (i = 1, 2, ..., N), \qquad (7.7)$$

that is to say, the capital–labor ratio is the same for all firms and equal to the aggregate capital–labor ratio. This implies that A_t (that is, the level of knowledge or, what comes to be the same thing, the level of technology), which is given by Equation (7.4), becomes:

$$A_t = \xi \left(\frac{K_t}{L_t} \right)^{\theta}. \qquad (7.8)$$

Hence, Arrow's hypothesis of learning-by-doing *plus* Romer's assumption of instantaneous, complete and free of charge dissemination of knowledge lead to the conclusion that an index for the level of technology is given by Equation (7.8). Note that with this index the value of A_t in a given period is no longer exogenously determined: it depends on the period's capital–labor ratio, which is decided by the firms. Hence, it is determined by *actions of the economic agents* (that is to say, is *endogenous*). The firms, however, are unaware of this fact (Romer, 1986).

(3) Since the firms are unconscious of their production of knowledge, they always take A_t as *given*. In other words, they regard the level of knowledge as an *input* which, whatever might be the reason, exists and they can use at zero cost.

7.3   The Arrow–Romer Model

7.3.1   Description of the Model

There is a large number of firms named i $(i = 1, 2, ..., N)$ in the economy, all identical, and with labor-augmenting production function $Y_{it} = F(K_{it}, A_t L_{it})$, which for simplicity we assume to be of the Cobb–Douglas type, that is:

$$Y_{it} = K_{it}^{\alpha}(A_t L_{it})^{1-\alpha}; \quad (0 < \alpha < 1). \qquad (7.9)$$

The number of firms, N, is sufficiently large to ensure that none of them has market-power, therefore they are price-takers. We also assume that new knowledge (that is, technical progress) is "learning-by-doing" generated and, by Romer's (1986) assumption, that all firms can use it *gratis*.

Therefore, at each time the individual firms see the level of technology (A_t) "as given," hence they regard their production function as "strictly neoclassical," that is, with CRTS and positive and diminishing MPK and MPL. The profits of the individual firm i ($i = 1, 2, ..., N$) are given by:

$$\Pi_{it} = Y_{it} - \rho_t K_{it} - \omega_t L_{it} = K_{it}^{\alpha}(A_t L_{it})^{1-\alpha} - \rho_t K_{it} - \omega_t L_{it} \qquad (7.10)$$

and the firm's problem is to choose K_{it} and L_{it} so as to maximize Π_{it}, given the *perceived* value of A_t, that is:

$$\max_{\{K_{it}, L_{it}\}} \cdot \left\{ \Pi_{it} | A_t = K_{it}^{\alpha}(A_t L_{it})^{1-\alpha} - \rho_t K_{it} - \omega_t L_{it} \right\}. \qquad (7.11)$$

The first order conditions for the solution of this program are the following:

$$\alpha A_t^{1-\alpha}\left(\frac{K_t}{L_t}\right)^{\alpha-1} = \rho_t \qquad (7.12)$$

$$(1-\alpha)A_t^{1-\alpha}\left(\frac{K_t}{L_t}\right)^{\alpha} = \omega_t. \qquad (7.13)$$

We shall use these conditions later. For now, we can obtain the aggregate production function by simple summation of the individual production functions as follows: From Equation (7.9) we have:

$$\sum_{i=1}^{N} Y_{it} = A_t^{1-\alpha}\sum_{i=1}^{N}\left(\frac{K_{it}}{L_{it}}\right)^{\alpha} L_{it} = A_t^{1-\alpha}\left(\frac{K_t}{L_t}\right)^{\alpha}\sum_{i=1}^{N} L_{it}, \qquad (7.14)$$

that is to say:

$$Y_t = A_t^{1-\alpha}\left(\frac{K_t}{L_t}\right)^{\alpha} L_t = A_t^{1-\alpha}K_t^{\alpha}L_t^{1-\alpha}, \qquad (7.15)$$

therefore:

$$Y_t = K_t^{\alpha}(A_t L_t)^{1-\alpha}. \qquad (7.16)$$

7.3.2 Solution of the Model for the Steady State

As shown by Equation (7.16), the aggregate production function is Cobb–Douglas in capital and effective labor. Hence, if A_t were an exogenous variable growing at a constant rate, the model would be the same as the Solow–Swan model and would have a steady state capable of satisfying the "stylized facts of growth." (This we saw in Section 2.4.) But A_t is now an *endogenous* variable, for it depends on the level of mechanization (the capital–labor ratio) that the firms choose at each time. Thus, this model differs in nature from the Solow–Swan model. But they do share the same mathematical form, so that if A_t, regardless of its endogenous nature, still grew at a constant rate, this model, like Solow and Swan's, would have a steady state capable of satisfying the "stylized facts of growth." At what rate does A_t grow? From Equation (7.8) we obtain:

$$\overset{\circ}{A_t} = \theta \left(\frac{\overset{\circ}{K_t}}{L_t} \right) = \theta \, \overset{\circ}{k_t} \, . \tag{7.17}$$

Thus, if k_t grows at a constant rate so will the level of technology. Hence, we have to find $\overset{\circ}{k_t}$. From $k_t = K_t / L_t$ we have:

$$\dot{k}_t = \frac{dk_t}{dt} = \frac{(dK_t/dt)L_t - (dL_t/dt)K_t}{L_t^2} = sy_t - (\delta + n)k_t. \tag{7.18}$$

From the aggregate production function we obtain per capita output as follows (using Equation [7.8] to substitute for A_t):

$$y_t = A_t \frac{Y_t}{L_t} = \left(\frac{K_t}{L_t} \right)^\alpha A_t^{1-\alpha} = ak_t^{\alpha+\theta(1-\alpha)}, \tag{7.19}$$

where $\xi^{1-\alpha} = a$ (only a constant). Thus we have:

$$\dot{k}_t = \frac{dk_t}{dt} = sak_t^{\alpha+\theta(1-\alpha)} - (\delta + n)k_t, \tag{7.20}$$

therefore it is:

$$\overset{\circ}{k_t} = \frac{\dot{k}_t}{k_t} = sak_t^{[\alpha+\theta(1-\alpha)]-1} - (\delta + n). \tag{7.21}$$

We can see from this expression that $\overset{\circ}{k_t}$ (the growth rate of the capital–labor ratio) will be constant *only if* $\alpha + \theta(1 - \alpha) = 1$; that is to say (for it is the same thing), *only if* $\theta = 1$. Hence, the model has a "suitable" steady state (in the sense that it satisfies the "stylized facts of growth") only if the *elasticity of learning-by-doing* (that is, the parameter θ) is *exactly* equal to one. But then, the aggregate production function (thus the model itself) becomes as simple as this:

$$Y_t = aK_t, \tag{7.22}$$

that is to say: at the aggregate level, output is proportional to the capital stock. This equation is often called the "*AK* model," a name that can easily create confusion, for the symbol A is used in the economic growth literature to represent the level of knowledge whereas the "a" that appears in Equation (7.22) is only a constant of proportionality. Thus, we shall refer to this equation as the "linear-in-K model." Indeed, it is a peculiar model: to begin with, where is L? Is Equation (7.22) suggesting in any way that output can be produced without using any labor? The answer, of course, is *no*; what the model simply says is that the level of output happens to be in proportion to the capital stock. But behind this *arithmetic* relation there is, of course, an "economic story." However, for the sake of continuity we will postpone it for now. At this moment, it is convenient to complete the characterization of the model's steady state.

From Equation (7.21) we have, with $\theta = 1$, $\overset{o}{k}_t = sa - (\delta + n)$, which, for $sa > (\delta + n)$, is both positive and constant. But is $sa > (\delta + n)$? It is, as we shall see in a moment, so that we are safe on this condition. From Equation (7.19) we obtain, with $\theta = 1$, $\overset{o}{y}_t = \overset{o}{k}_t = sa - (\delta + n) > 0$, hence the model satisfies the "stylized fact **(1)**." Since $\overset{o}{k}_t = \overset{o}{y}_t$, it follows that K_t/Y_t is constant (this also follows immediately from Equation [7.22]), hence the model satisfies the "stylized fact **(2)**." From Equation (7.13) we have (replacing A_t with its value given by Equation [7.8] and using $\theta = 1$):

$$\rho_t = \alpha \xi^{1-\alpha} \left(\frac{K_t}{L_t} \right)^{\theta(1-\alpha)} \left(\frac{K_t}{L_t} \right)^{\alpha-1} = \alpha a, \qquad (7.23)$$

which is constant, hence the model satisfies the "stylized fact **(3)**." Finally, since $\overset{o}{y}_t = sa - (\delta + n)$ and countries differ substantially in the parameters s, a, δ and n, the model seems to also account for the "stylized fact **(4)**" (that is, that there is a great variety of per capita income growth rates across the world). Thus, the "linear-in-K" model has a "suitable" steady state. Besides, it is a *balanced growth* steady state. This can be easily shown. By definition, we have $i = sy$; hence, with a constant rate of savings it is $\overset{o}{i} = \overset{o}{y}$. On the other hand, and also by definition, we have $c = y - i = y - sy = (1-s)y$, thus $\overset{o}{c} = \overset{o}{y}$. This means that in the steady state per capita variables all grow at the same rate, the following:

$$\overset{o}{y} = \overset{o}{k} = \overset{o}{i} = \overset{o}{c} = sa - (\delta + n), \qquad (7.24)$$

therefore (this is obvious on the face) *level* variables also grow all at the same rate, namely the per capita rate *plus* the population growth rate, that is:

$$\overset{o}{Y} = \overset{o}{K} = \overset{o}{I} = \overset{o}{C} = sa - \delta \qquad (7.25)$$

Hence, the steady state growth path is *balanced*. (This, as noted in Chapter 2, does not matter much. What really matters is that the steady state satisfies the "stylized facts of growth.")

7.3.3   Predictions of the Model and Empirical Discussion

The "linear-in-K" model makes some interesting predictions, as indicated below. (Since we will use them later in this chapter, we number them as P.1, P.2, and so on.)

(P.1) (From Equation [7.24]) In the long run, per capita income grows at the rate $sa - (\delta + n)$, and total income grows at the rate $sa - \delta$. How well do these predictions fare against the actual data of reality? Before we answer this question, recall that the predictions at hand are subordinated to the condition that $sa > \delta + n$, and we said that this condition was safe. Now is the moment to prove it. As noted in Chapter 5, for the US economy the stock of physical capital is about two-and-one-half times the annual flow of output, that is, $K_t = 2.5Y_t$. Therefore it is $Y_t = (1/2.5)K_t = 0.4K_t$. Comparing this datum with Equation (7.22) we immediately see that $a = 0.4$ (estimation for the 1950–1985 period). Also in Chapter 5 we said that physical capital depreciates at an average annual rate of about 4 percent, that is, $\delta = 0.04$ (same economy, same period of estimation). Further, we noted in Chapter 6 that the US population grows at an average annual rate of about 1.5 percent, that is, $n = 0.015$ (same period of estimation). Finally, Blanchard (1997, Ch. 23) reports that in the US economy, from 1950 to date, savings average the annual rate of 18.7 percent, that is, $s = 0.187$. In sum, for the US economy we have the following data (annual averages, 1950 onwards): $s = 0.187, a = 0.4, n = 0.015$ and $\delta = 0.04$. Clearly, for the US economy $sa > \delta + n$, and it is very unlikely that similarly developed countries behave differently. Now we turn to the model's predictions concerning the rates of growth. Using the US data, the model predicts that over the period considered (from 1950 to approximately 1990), per capita output should have grown at the rate given by Equation (7.24), that is to say, the following:

$$\overset{o}{y} = sa - (\delta + n) = 0.0198 = 1.98\%.$$

The model also predicts that total output should have grown at the rate given by Equation (7.25), that is:

$$\overset{o}{Y} = sa - \delta = 0.325 = 3.25\%.$$

How good are these results? They are very accurate indeed.

(P.2) (From Equation [7.24]) $\overset{o}{y}$ is positively affected by s; that is to say, *caeteris paribus* an increase (decrease) in the rate of savings will raise (lower) the growth rate of per capita income. As we know, this also happens in the

Solow–Swan model. Note, however, that there is a difference between the two cases: in the Solow–Swan model this happens *only during the transition* to the corresponding new steady state: once the latter is achieved, the growth rate of per capita income reverts to its previous value (equal to the exogenous growth rate of technical progress); but in the present model the effect is *permanent*, that is, an increase (decrease) in s raises (lowers) $\overset{o}{y}$ permanently. Hence, the model predicts that countries with higher rate of savings will, other things being equal, tend to grow faster in per capita terms. The available empirical evidence shows that this prediction conforms to reality.

(P.3) (From Equation [7.24]) $\overset{o}{y}$ is negatively affected by n and δ. As before, this is also true in the Solow–Swan model; the difference, once again, is that in the present model the effect is permanent, whereas in the Solow–Swan model it is only transitory. Thus, the model predicts that, other things being equal, countries with higher rates of population growth and (or) depreciation of the capital stock will tend to grow more slowly in per capita terms. The empirical evidence indicates that this prediction is consistent with the data.

(P.4) Economic integration will raise the rate of growth of the integrated economic space *permanently*. This is an important prediction (and a very subtle one). Moreover, it brings clearly into light how the present model differs from the Solow–Swan model. This we will see as we go forward with it.

Consider what might well happen when various countries integrate into the same economic space. By eliminating trade barriers and freeing the movement of commodities and people, economic integration will force the firms of each and every integrated economy to compete with one another. This will, at least partly, remove economic inefficiencies in the use of the available resources, and this, in turn, will raise output for the existing amounts of inputs. *In terms of the Solow–Swan model*, this initial effect is therefore equivalent to a "once-and-for-all upward shift" of the aggregate production function due to an increase in A_t. (Actually, A_t remains the same, of course; but it is used more wisely, which amounts to the same thing as A_t having increased.[4]) Since the production function shifts up, so does the savings function: this is trivial, for if output is now higher, the same saving rate will deliver a higher amount of savings. In terms of the

---

[4] An example might help to clearly understand the point: Our "existing knowledge" tells us (if we took economic theory seriously) that trade barriers are unwise. Hence, if countries used *this* knowledge wisely, there would be no trade barriers. But in fact there *are* trade barriers and, because of it, inefficiencies. One thing integration does is to eliminate trade barriers (so, at last!, the *existing* knowledge is "used wisely"), thus it removes inefficiencies.

Solow–Swan model, the integration will push the new economic space out of its steady state, and it will begin to move towards a new, higher steady state path. Why higher? Because since savings are higher than what they would normally be, the capital stock will grow more than it would have otherwise, hence output will follow sway. While the transition to the new steady state lasts, the rate of growth will be higher than the pre-integration rate, and will return to its previous level once the transition is over. What will happen afterwards? In terms of the Solow–Swan model, the integrated economy will settle on the new steady state path, along which it will grow again at the pre-integration rate. But the integrated economy will be better off than before: for although it will grow at the pre-integration rate, it will be *on a higher steady state path*, thus enjoying higher levels of output, consumption, and so on, than it would have otherwise (that is, had not occurred the integration).

Therefore, *in terms of the Solow–Swan model* this is what is expected to happen when integration takes place: **(a)** There will be a "short-run (in fact, an *immediate*) effect" consisting of a rise in output out of the same resources due to an immediate efficiency gain. It is like having a "once-and-for-all" upward shift in the aggregate production function. **(b)** There will be a "medium-run effect" consisting of higher growth rates for a *limited* number of years (specifically, for as long as it takes the economy to reach its new steady state). Hence, we may reasonably conceive in terms of the Solow–Swan model that integration is good, for the reasons so far given.

However, *in terms of the "linear-in-K" model* integration is more than merely good: it appears to be magnificent. Why? Because according to this model the "medium-run effect" to which we referred above will have an unending life, that is, the increase in the rate of growth will be *permanent*, and not merely transitory as the S&S model predicts. How is this result achieved? The mathematics of the case are very simple: The "short-run effect" of the integration, which consists of a rise in output with the same amounts of inputs, is the same. Now, in terms of the "linear-in-K" model this means an increase in a, the proportionality constant of the aggregate production function (Equation [7.22]). Specifically, a increases by the following amount (from Equation [722]):

$$da = \frac{1}{K_t}dY_t - Y_t dK_t = \frac{1}{K_t}dY_t$$

(because, since K_t is the same, $dK_t = 0$), therefore the new proportionality constant is the following:

$$a^* = \frac{Y_t + dY_t}{K_t} > \frac{Y_t}{K_t} = a.$$

Hence, the economy's rate of growth, given by Equation (8.24), will *permanently* increase. Figure 7.1 depicts the two situations: when integration occurs, the rate of growth is predicted to increase for a transitory period in the Solow–Swan model, so in this case per capita income is expected to follow the path $\{\mathcal{A} \to \mathcal{B} \to \mathcal{C} \to \mathcal{D}...\}$; but the "linear-in-$K$" model predicts that integration will increase the growth rate *permanently*, hence per capita income is expected to follow the path $\{\mathcal{A} \to \mathcal{B} \to \mathcal{C}' \to \mathcal{D}'...\}$. The difference in per capita income gains predicted by the two models is obvious (and a similar difference applies, of course, to per capita consumption, investment, and all the remaining variables, including the level of knowledge).

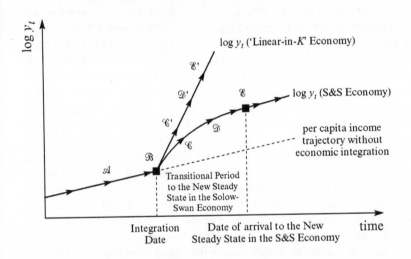

Figure 7.1: Per Capita Income Gain From Economic Integration

In sum, when integration occurs the rate of growth rises in both, the Solow–Swan-type economy and the "linear-in-K" economy. However, in the S&S economy the increase in growth is temporary (that is, it cannot be maintained indefinitely) whereas in the "linear-in-K" economy the rise in growth is permanent (that is, it is maintained forever). What is the reason for this? The answer is very simple: the productivity of capital is not the same in both cases. This can be readily seen. In the S&S economy (we know this from Chapter 2) $MPK = \alpha(K_t/Y_t)$; however, in the "linear-in-K" economy (we know this from Equation [7.22]) $MPK = a = (K_t/Y_t)$. Since $\alpha < 1$, it is clear that the MPK is higher for the "linear-in-K" economy. Let the MPK in the S&S economy be represented by $MPK_{S\&S}$, and the MPK in the "linear-in-K" economy be represented by MPK_{aK}

(we do this for later use), thus we have:

$$MPK_{aK} > MPK_{S\&S}. \qquad (7.26)$$

Hence, although economic integration brings about the same *initial* extra increase in Y and therefore the same *initial* extra increase in K in both types of economies (the so-called "short-run effect"), the *initial* increase in growth will be higher for the "linear-in-K" economy (because its MPK is higher). Moreover, besides having $MPK_{aK} > MPK_{S\&S}$, $MPK_{S\&S}$ is *decreasing* (we know this from Chapter 2) whereas MPK_{aK} is *constant* (this we know from $MPK_{aK} = a = constant$). Therefore, it is obvious in these conditions that the initial gain in growth resulting from integration will slowly disappear in a S&S economy; but not in a "linear-in-K" economy.

Thus the whole story boils down to explaining the following: (1) Why the MPK_{aK} is higher than the $MPK_{S\&S}$; and (2) why the MPK_{aK} is constant (when, by the very logical law of diminishing productivity of inputs, we almost "naturally" should expect it to decline). Concerning the first question, the MPK is higher for the "linear-in-K" economy because in this type of economy an additional unit of capital raises output in two ways: first, because *caeteris paribus* simply there is more of one input (which is capital, of course); and second, because the extra unit of K raises the capital–labor ratio, thus creating "learning-by-doing" which raises the level of knowledge and this, in turn, raises output. In other words, attached to each additional unit of capital there is an *externality* (under the form of new knowledge from which everyone benefits) in the "linear-in-K" economy, but this externality is absent in the S&S economy. Now for the second question: this "learning-by-doing" externality clearly *counteracts* the tendency for MPK to diminish. It appears, therefore, that the magnitude of the externality is such that it *exactly* overturns the tendency for the MPK to fall: *exactly* of that magnitude, not a bit more, nor less (we shall come back to this later).

An interesting application of this prediction of the "linear-in-K" model (concerning the growth benefits of economic integration) has been made by Baldwin (1989) for the case of the *1992 Unification Act* of the economic space of the European Union. Using the "linear-in-K" model, he estimates that the economic integration could have raised the growth rate of the Union by 0.5 percentage points *permanently*. (Actually, Baldwin estimates the increase to be in the range of 0.2 to 0.9 but, for our present purpose, there is no wrong-doing in taking the mean value of the interval.) If accurate (Baldwin himself recognizes that, "given the exploratory nature of the new growth theory" [on which the numbers are based], his estimates might be inaccurate), this would mean a considerable welfare gain for the Europeans derived from the integration. How good this prediction was, is uncertain. Some easy econometric tests can be designed to know it, but they cannot be implemented until more time has elapsed since the unification: perhaps ten, maybe fifteen years from now.

(P.5) (From Equation [7.13]) ω rises with the level of mechanization (that is, with the capital–labor ratio). This can be shown by simplifying Equation (7.13) as follows (and of course we let $\theta = 1$):

$$\omega_t = (1-\alpha)\xi^{1-\alpha}\left(\frac{K_t}{L_t}\right)^{\theta(1-\alpha)}\left(\frac{K_t}{L_t}\right)^{\alpha} = a(1-\alpha)\left(\frac{K_t}{L_t}\right). \qquad (7.27)$$

Hence, the model predicts that other things equal countries with higher K_t/L_t tend to have higher real wages. This suggests a reason why labor tends to migrate from poor countries (that is, countries with low K_t/L_t) to rich ones.

7.4 Policy Analysis

In Chapter 6 we argued that the need for models with endogenous technical progress is imposed by our desire to come up with sound policies for sustained economic growth. The present model goes a long way in that direction, for it offers interesting suggestions for policy measures, as indicated below. Note, however, that "the world out there" is composed of many more pieces than the present model (or indeed any model) can possibly handle, hence it may be advisable to take these policies with a grain of salt. (But then, this is always the case, for the role of science is to serve as a basis for rational decision-making, not to generate "Biblical instructions.")

7.4.1 Knowledge Spillovers, Market Inefficiency and Subsidies to Capital Accumulation

Firms take A_t as given (that is, they ignore that their actions have an influence on A_t) and behave competitively, thus using capital and labor up to the level where their prices are equal to their marginal products, as these are *perceived* by the firms. Now, this behavior leads to an economic outcome that is *not* Pareto-optimal. To see why, imagine that one firm buys an additional unit of capital, thereby raising its capital–labor ratio. As a result of this, the firm's level of knowledge rises through the process of "learning-by-doing," thus increasing the firm's efficiency of labor and, hence, its level of output. The firm that makes the investment thus benefits from it. However, this is not the end of the story: since the firm's additional knowledge spills over to the whole economy, the other firms too benefit from its investment. This is so because the new knowledge, which they acquire at zero cost, also raises their labor efficiency and, hence, their level of output. Thus, by ignoring this *externality*, the firm that makes the investment *undervalues* its contribution to output; that is to say, it underestimates the marginal product of capital. This can also be seen mathematically. The individual firm values the marginal product of capital as (from Equation [7.9]):

$$MPK|_A = \frac{\partial Y_{it}}{\partial K_{it}}|_A = \alpha A_t^{1-\alpha} \left(\frac{K_{it}}{L_{it}}\right)^{\alpha-1}, \tag{7.28}$$

that is to say (using Equations [7.7] and [7.8] and taking $\theta = 1$), the following:

$$MPK|_A = \alpha a. \tag{7.29}$$

But (as we have already shown) the true marginal product of capital (that is to say, MPK_{aK}) is (from Equation [7.22]):

$$MPK_{aK} = \frac{\partial Y_t}{\partial K_t} = a, \tag{7.30}$$

therefore (since $0 < \alpha < 1$) we have $MPK|_A < MPK_{aK}$.

The immediate consequence of this situation is that investment in physical capital falls short of the social optimum. This is so because, by acting competitively, the individual firm uses physical capital up to the level where $MPK|_A = \rho$, thus giving rise to an economic outcome in which $MPK_{aK} > \rho$. Since MPK_{aK} is the true contribution of one additional unit of capital to total output, and hence equal to the marginal benefit society gets from using an additional unit of physical capital, and ρ is the price, hence the cost to society, of each unit of capital, we have a situation in which society would benefit from using additional units of capital. In other words, more investment in physical capital is socially desirable. However, firms will *not* invest more than they do. This is so because by using physical capital up to the level where $MPK|_A = \rho$ they believe to be maximizing profits already. The competitive outcome is, therefore, *suboptimal*.

As a matter of policy, the government could do something to improve this outcome. For instance, it could *subsidize* investment in physical capital by offering a tax rebate to firms that invest in physical capital. This is equivalent to lowering the price of capital to the firm to a level $\rho - subsidy$. In this way the individual firm, still acting under its myopia, will use physical capital (that is, it will invest) beyond the previous level.

7.4.2 Externalities from Capital Accumulation and Balance of Trade Policy

Recall from Prediction (P.2) that a higher savings rate leads to a permanently higher rate of growth of per capita income. The transmission mechanism, from the model's logic, is as follows: a higher s implies higher levels of investment. Hence, for given values of n and δ a higher s means a higher K_t/L_t, from which there is a higher accumulation of knowledge and, thereby, a higher efficiency of labor. Thus the main point is: a higher s leads to a higher $\overset{o}{y}$ only because the former implies a higher accumulation of capital. Hence, a country could achieve a permanently higher $\overset{o}{y}$ by either increasing domestic savings (which is costly in terms of foregone current consumption) or absorbing savings from other countries (that is, by attracting foreign investment). Therefore the model suggests that, so long as it is based on capital goods imports, running a balance of trade deficit is a sound growth-oriented policy. Of course, this conclusion goes against the received wisdom on trade policy. Yet some empirical evidence in its favor is found in the fact that

> by the time that each was surpassed as a world leader in productivity, the Netherlands had accumulated net foreign assets of over 3 times GDP, the U.K. assets totaling roughly 1.5 times GD (Romer, 1987, p. 198).

This suggests that the US recent trend of "rapidly accumulating foreign debt" (rather than doing the opposite, as the traditional teachings would advise) may be well oriented.[5]

7.4.3 Wage Policy and Economic Growth

Recall from Prediction (P.2) that $\overset{o}{y}$ is negatively affected by n. The transmission mechanism behind this prediction is not obvious within the model,

---

[5]Romer (1987, pp. 188–199) does appear to be convinced of the goodness of this policy, as it is clear from the following quotation:

> Holding constant the level of consumption (and this caveat is essential) the advantages of being a net foreign debtor are enormous; we should be running as deep a trade deficit as possible for as long as we can get away with it ... Had the United States [done as previously did the Netherlands and the UK], diverting domestic investment abroad, it too may have been surpassed by a new borrowing country. So perhaps, because of recent economic policies, the United States is back, standing tall, rapidly accumulating foreign debt.

but a fitting story can be devised as follows: an increase in the rate of population growth raises the growth rate of the labor supply, thus lowering the growth in real wages, thereby raising the relative price of capital, ρ/ω, above the level that it otherwise would have. Firms respond to this distortion in relative factor prices by using more of the relatively cheaper input (in this case, labor) and less of the relatively more expensive one (in this case, capital). Hence,

> an increase in the rate of growth of the labor force, with the implied decrease in the rate of growth of wages, could cause a decrease in innovation, and hence a decrease in knowledge spillovers from innovation (Romer, 1987, p. 166).

This implies that the reverse, that is, an increase in the growth rate of real wages, tends to raise labor efficiency, as follows: the higher real wage growth lowers the relative price of capital relative to the level that it would otherwise have, and firms respond by using relatively more capital and less labor, thus raising their capital–labor ratios. This leads to a higher accumulation of knowledge (through greater "learning by-doing" and spillover of knowledge) and, thereby, to a higher efficiency of labor.

Hence, the model suggests that a policy of high growth in real wages tends to spur economic growth. Thus, "there may be a rationale for the policies followed in Europe to reduce total hours worked and keep wage growth rates high" (Romer, 1987, p. 198).

Note, however, that the higher real wage growth not only increases productivity growth but, in the short-to-medium-run (and this qualification is essential), *also* the rate of unemployment (for it provokes short-to-medium-run labor displacement). Hence, the model suggests that there is a (again, short-to-medium-run) trade-off between productivity growth and unemployment, the same idea used by some European economists to explain the observed "ability" of the European economy to generate long-lasting unemployment. (See, for example, Mairesse, 1982.) The present model adds theoretical ground to this view.

This may be really bad news: real wages growth is kept high to induce innovation and spur productivity growth on the hope that the latter will create employment, yet the very policy is short-to-medium-run labor-displacing, hence it raises the rate of unemployment. The conclusion, from the perspective of the present model *alone*, seems to be the following: whether a policy of high growth in real wages is advisable depends on how much value society places upon these two opposing outcomes: a higher productivity growth and a higher short-to-medium-run rate of unemployment.

7.4.4 Economic Integration

Recall from Prediction (P.4) that economic integration raises the growth rate of the integrated economy *permanently*. Therefore, the current trend of economic integration of countries into larger economic spaces taking place around the world (think of the European Union; the North-American Single Market, which includes Mexico, the USA and Canada; and the recently declared goal of the USA Administration to make the whole American continent a free-trade zone by the year 2005) seems a sound growth-oriented global policy.

7.5 The "Convergence Hypothesis"

Equation (7.24) tells us that $\overset{\circ}{y}$ does *not* depend on y. In other words, the rate at which per capita income will grow in the future is *not* influenced by the current level of per capita income. Hence the model does *not* predict cross-country convergence of per capita income of any kind.[6] This must be correctly understood: The model does *not* suggest that countries that are currently poor will be poor forever (or reciprocally, that countries that are currently rich will necessarily remain so in the future). What the model says is that, so to speak, *economic inertia* will not reduce the gap between rich and poor countries.

However, poor countries need *not* rely on *inertia*. They may instead raise s, lower n, and implement many other sound policies as those described above. (Economic integration with other countries seems particularly useful in the context of this model.) By the same token, rich countries, by following unsound policies (such as engaging themselves in "trade wars," and so on) may fall behind in the future. This shows how important it is for countries to have wise governments.

---

[6] Not even of each economy to its *own* steady state. The reason is that a "linear-in-K" economy *always is* in steady state, hence it does not display any dynamics towards the long-run equilibrium: the short-run equilibrium and the long-run equilibrium are the same in this type of economy. How do we know that the "linear-in-K" economy always is in steady state? A simple means to obtain this conclusion is the following: we know that in steady state $\overset{\circ}{Y}=\overset{\circ}{K}$, thus, in steady state Y_t/K_t is constant. But for the "linear-in-K" economy $Y_t = aK_t$ at all t, therefore it always is $Y_t/K_t = a$ (constant), that is, a "linear-in-K" economy is *permanently* in steady state (which does *not* imply that the steady state must be always the same, of course).

7.6   The Model and the Worldwide "Productivity Slowdown Puzzle"

As previously noted, one of the main tenets of the present model is that "an increase in the growth rate of labor will be accompanied by a fall in the rate of growth of labor productivity" (Romer, 1987). This provides one reason (one, for there will likely be others) for the "worldwide slow-down in productivity growth." To be sure, the growth rate of US labor supply speeded up starting in the mid 1960s due to the following factors: (1) Incorporation to the labor force of the post-WWII "baby boom"; (2) incorporation to the labor force of the female population; and (3) a sharp increase in immigration, all of which kept the growth rate of the real wage low (or, perhaps better said, "under control"), thus slowing down the pace of US innovation and, thereby, of labor productivity.

Now, this explanation of the productivity *puzzle* does not square well with the European experience, for the following reason. The same three factors cited above also apply to the European economy. However, as already noted, Europe followed a policy of reducing per capita hours worked and keeping real wages growing at a faster rate than the US, and this, according to the model, should have compensated (at least partially) for the negative effect that the above-mentioned factors had on productivity. Thus, we would expect the slowdown in productivity growth to have been smaller in Europe than in the USA, which is *not* (see Chapter 6, Table 6.1) what in fact happened.

Hence, there are only two ways of reconciling this explanation with the facts, namely: either the three factors cited above had a much stronger effect in Europe than in the USA (in which case the question of *why* immediately arises), or (more probably) other factors besides those considered here also plaid a role in the slowdown of productivity growth. Either way, the *puzzle* remains alive. However, the *contribution* of this model to a full explanation of the issue is highly valuable, for it is unlikely that the world-wide slowdown in productivity growth responded to one single cause.[7]

---

[7] As Romer (1987) rightly indicates, given the amount of effort economists have devoted to disentangle the productivity puzzle, "it would be surprising if this effort [that is, the explanation provided by this model] were a complete success. One suspects that any area that has received this much attention will be subject to a conservation law, the conservation of puzzles" (p. 163).

7.7 The Original Version of the A&R Model (Arrow, 1962; Romer, 1986)

In the "Introduction" to this chapter (see footnote 1) we noted that our presentation of the Arrow–Romer model differs in two ways, one of mere form, the other more substantive, from the original versions of Arrow (1962) and Romer (1986, 1987). These differences come from the way in which the idea of "learning-by-doing" is understood (the more substantive difference) and modeled (the merely formal difference). Beginning with the former, we described Arrow's (1962) idea of learning-by-doing as "learning-*and-inventing*," not as "learning" *alone*, that is, we have added an "inventing side" to the original (Arrow's) "learning side" of the investment process. We did this on purpose because, as Solow (1997) remarks, if mechanization only offers a "learning side" as byproduct, it becomes rather far-fetched to use Arrow's idea as an appropriate foundation for *sustained* economic growth. This is so because without the "inventing side" we cannot realistically hope that mechanization (that is, more capital) per se will increase A *unceasingly*. Through a "learning side" alone, we will "learn" how to use a *given* "invention" better, but there must be a moment in which everything that there was to be extracted (learned) from that invention is already known. Thus, unless *another invention* comes along from somewhere, labor efficiency will not rise any further, that is, the capacity of the "learning side" alone to increase A is most surely *bounded*, hence it cannot deliver unceasing growth. Adding an "inventing side" to Arrow's original idea seems therefore necessary. A different matter is whether this trick is legitimate, that is, whether, as Solow (1997) questions, the flow of capital investment actually creates anything worth calling "inventions" (or new technologies *proper*). For now, we assume it does (but we will come back to this issue in Chapter 8, Section 8.5.2).

As to the purely formal difference with the Arrow–Romer original versions, we made "learning-by-doing" a byproduct of mechanization, which we chose to represent by a rising *capital–labor ratio*. Arrow (1962) and Romer (1986) represent the rising mechanization by a rising capital stock (that is, by *continuous capital investment*). Thus, their "learning curve" is not Equation (7.1) but the following:

$$\theta = \frac{d \log A_{it}}{d \log K_{it}}, \quad (\theta > 0), \tag{7.31}$$

that is to say (the equivalent of Equation [7.2]):

$$d \log A_{it} = \theta \cdot d \log K_{it} \tag{7.32}$$

which, written in *levels*, takes the following form (the equivalent of Equation [7.3]):

$$A_{it} = \xi K_{it}^{\theta}. \tag{7.33}$$

Going through the same steps of our presentation, we obtain the following expression for the economy-wide level of knowledge (the equivalent of Equation [7.8]):

$$A_t = \xi K_t^{\theta} \tag{7.34}$$

and the following expression for the aggregate production function (the same as Equation [7.16]):

$$Y_t = K_t^{\alpha} (A_t L_t)^{1-\alpha} \tag{7.35}$$

or equivalently (using Equation [7.34] to substitute for A_t):

$$Y_t = a K_t^{\alpha + \theta(1-\alpha)} L_t^{1-\alpha}. \tag{7.36}$$

Does this alternative specification of the A&R model make any difference? In substance, none whatsoever. Using the same argument of Section 7.3.2, we again conclude from the aggregate production function Equation (7.35) that the model has a "suitable" steady state if (and only if) A_t grows at a constant rate. Now, from Equation (7.34) we have the following:

$$\overset{\circ}{A}_t = \theta \overset{\circ}{K}_t, \tag{7.37}$$

that is to say, A_t will grow at a constant rate (and hence the model will have a "suitable" steady state) only if K_t grows at a constant rate. Under what conditions will K_t grow at a constant rate? By definition we have the following:

$$\overset{\circ}{K}_t = \frac{dK_t/dt}{K_t} = \frac{sY_t - \delta K_t}{K_t} = s\frac{Y_t}{K_t} - \delta, \tag{7.38}$$

hence K_t (and therefore A_t) will grow at a constant rate only if Y_t/K_t is constant. Now, from the aggregate production function Equation (7.36) we have the following expression for Y_t/K_t:

$$\frac{Y_t}{K_t} = a K_t^{(\alpha-1)+\theta(1-\alpha)} L_t^{1-\alpha}. \tag{7.39}$$

Thus, Y_t/K_t will be constant if and only if $\theta = 1$ *and* L_t is constant. In that case, however, the aggregate production function reduces to the following expression:

$$Y_t = \left(aL^{1-\alpha}\right) K_t. \tag{7.40}$$

that is, the A&R model becomes "linear-in-K." The only difference with the previous presentation of the model is that the proportionality constant (see Equation [7.22]) is $aL^{1-\alpha}$ instead of a, but a constant anyway. Consequently, the per capita growth rate (see Equation [7.24]) is in this case the following:

$$\overset{\circ}{y}= saL^{1-\alpha} - \delta, \tag{7.41}$$

which is constant. There are (minor?) differences with the growth rate obtained in the previous presentation, however. First, n does not appear in Equation (7.41), thus this version of the model predicts that the rate of population growth has no bearing on the per capita rate of *economic* growth. (Is this a reasonable prediction?) Second, what does appear in Equation (7.41) (as opposed to Equation [7.24]) is the population size, and this spells trouble. For it is telling us that, *other things equal, countries with more population will tend to grow faster in per capita terms,* but this "scale effect" of population on growth does not have a clear empirical support.[8] To circumvent this complication some authors give an interesting (and ingenious) interpretation for why L (the population size) appears in Equation (7.41), namely:

> It is possible that the scale variable *for spillovers, L,* does not relate closely to aggregates measured at the country level. The relevant scale can, for example, be larger than the size of the domestic economy if producers benefit from knowledge accumulated in other countries. (Barro and Sala-i-Martín, 1995, p. 151; emphasis added.)

This is a plausible explanation, no doubt. But it is the kind of "escape route" which makes the model untestable (or, at least, very difficult to *falsify*) with aggregate economic data. The reason is that it becomes difficult (to say the least) to ascertain the economic space relevant for spillover effects (for example, the specific country we are dealing with, whichever it might be? This *plus* its inmediate neighbors? Only the northern portion of the country at hand? Or the whole world in a piece...?). Many economists feel uncomfortable with this kind of models. On the other hand, if we are to assume a constant population, then it is the same to model "learning-by-doing" in terms of investment (that is, increases in the capital stock) or in

---

[8] Scale effects on the growth rate of per capita income, according to which "large countries" tend to grow faster than small ones (where "large" is measured either by population size, as it is here, or by other variables, such as output size, human capital size, and so on) are generated not only by this version of the "learning-by-doing, knowledge spillover" model but also by other models of economic growth (see Chapter 8). The empirical evidence, however, is never clearly supportive of the "scale effect." (See Backus, Kehoe and Kehoe, 1992. We suggest that the reading of this book be first completed.)

terms of the more mundane idea of mechanization (that is, a rising capital–labor ratio). Hence, we might as well choose the previous presentation of the A&R model and avoid these little complications.

To finish this brief presentation of the original version of the model, we call attention to a fact that might create some confusion as to what the "learning-by-doing, knowledge spillover" model is about. By looking at Equation (7.36) we immediately realize that production *always* exhibits *increasing returns to scale* in capital and labor because $\alpha + \theta(1-\alpha) + (1-\alpha) > 1$ whatever the value of θ. This fact created some confusion when the A&R model first appeared in that it seemed as if endogenous growth was tied to the existence of IRTS. In fact, that is not the case, as the previous presentation of the model shows (note that the aggregate production function Equation [7.16], with A_t given by Equation [7.8], exhibits *constant*, not *increasing* returns to scale in capital and labor).

The existence of IRTS in capital and labor is, first, unesential to this model; and second, not a sufficient condition to generate unceasing economic growth (for instance, the present version of the A&R model exhibits IRTS, but if θ happens to be smaller than one unceasing growth is impossible [Why? See Problem 7.4]). Romer (1989, p. 93–94) makes a warning about this potential source of confusion. Commenting on the case $\theta < 1$ he clearly remarks how "this [case] shows that IRTS [in capital and labor] are not by themselves enough to sustain persistent growth."

What *is* essential to this model, though, is that there be *constant returns* to accumulatable factors of production (that is, constant marginal productivity of physical capital, or human capital, or the aggregate measure of both [see Appendix Section 7.A.2 below in connection with the use of K, H, or the aggregate measure of both in this model]). Technically, the point is a simple one: what generates unceasing growth in the A&R model is *not* IRTS (which might or might not exist in this model, depending on which version of it we use) but the fact that the externality from capital (be it physical, human, or the aggregate measure of both) accumulation eliminates the tendency for the MPK to diminish as K grows.

This is not to say that aggregate IRTS are not present in the real world. They may well be. To be sure, many economists hold the view that IRTS are a *pervasive* feature of reality. All we are saying here is that the "learning-by-doing, knowledge spillover" model does *not* rely on aggregate IRTS to generate unceasing growth.

Appendix 7.A. Comments on Some Special Features of the Arrow-Romer Model

Now that we have completed the basics of the Arrow–Romer version of the "learning-by-doing, knowledge spillover" approach to economic growth, it will be convenient to take up some very peculiar features of the model that we have so far set aside. They will bring some light on the nature of this very influential model. (These comments apply equally to the original version of the model [Arrow, 1962, and Romer, 1986] and the version presented in this chapter. For the sake of continuity we work with the latter.) The discussion is based on Solow (1994, 1997).

7.A.1. The Elasticity of "Learning-by-Doing" and the Steady State of the Model

We have seen that the Arrow–Romer model possesses a *suitable* steady state (that is, one that satisfies the "stylized facts" growth) only if the *elasticity* of "learning-by-doing" is *exactly* equal to one or, what amounts to the same thing, only if the "learning-by-doing, knowledge spillover" *externality* attached to each additional unit of capital has the precise magnitude to *exactly* overturn the tendency for the MPK to decline, in which case the Arrow–Romer model becomes simply "linear-in-K." Therefore, the "linear-in-K" model is a *very special* case of the Arrow–Romer version of the "learning-by-doing, knowledge spillover" approach to economic growth. Hence, to fully capture the status of this model in the theory of economic growth, we must further analyze the fact that it is a *very special* case. An in depth analysis, however, involves the use of (rather complex) mathematics, which is one thing we do not want to do in this book; hence, the analysis will have to be mostly intuitive.

Imagine that the elasticity of learning-by-doing (that is, the parameter θ in Equation [7.1]) deviates, however small the deviation might be, from the *precise* value of one. For instance, imagine that $\theta < 1$. Using Equation (7.8) to substitute for A_t in Equation (7.16), we can write the aggregate production function thus:

$$Y_t = aK_t^{\alpha+\theta(1-\alpha)}L_t^{1-[\alpha+\theta(1-\alpha)]} \qquad (7.42)$$

which, in per capita terms, takes the following form (Equation [7.19], reproduced here for convenience):

$$y_t = ak_t^{\alpha+\theta(1-\alpha)}. \qquad (7.43)$$

Since $\alpha + \theta(1 - \alpha) < 1$ when $\theta < 1$, we immediately see that in this case the capital stock will exhibit *diminishing* marginal productivity. Hence, each additional unit of capital will produce an ever-decreasing amount of additional output which, coupled with the constant saving rate, will generate an ever-decreasing addition to the capital stock. In per capita terms (that is, we now fix our attention in Equation [7.43]) this implies that k_t, the capital stock per capita, will eventually stop growing and, therefore, so will per capita income, y_t. In other words, with $\theta < 1$ (and hence, diminishing marginal productivity of capital) there must come a time beyond which the per capita variables will purely *reproduce* their values, that is, the economy will reach a steady state along whose path the per capita rate of growth will be *zero*. Therefore, with $\theta < 1$ the Arrow–Romer model produces the same outcome as the Solow–Swan model *without technical progress* (see Section 2.5 of Chapter 2). This is logical because if k_t will eventually stop growing, so will the level knowledge A_t (we know this from Equation [7.17]), and with a constant A_t the Arrow–Romer model is mathematically the same as the Solow–Swan model *without technical progress*.[9] In sum, if $\theta < 1$ the Arrow–Romer model does not yield the unceasing per capita growth that we observe in the real world.

Now imagine that $\theta > 1$. In this case, $\alpha + \theta(1 - \alpha) > 1$, hence the capital factor will exhibit *increasing* marginal productivity. Each additional unit of capital will produce an ever-increasing amount of additional output which, coupled with a constant saving rate, will generate an ever-increasing addition to the capital stock, and so on (the argument goes in reverse to the previous case). Thus, the economy will keep growing at an ever-*rising* per capita rate, therefore never reaching a steady state. Moreover, the model is *explosive* in this case. By this we mean that, with $\theta > 1$, the Arrow–Romer model produces a rate of growth that rises *so rapidly that output must reach infinite value in a finite period of time*. How long will this period of time be? The precise answer to this question would take us too far aside mathematically. Suffice it to say that Solow (1994) has made some (in fact, conservative) calculations: he shows that with θ only mildly above one, the Arrow–Romer model will produce such an ever-rising growth rate that "a country like Germany or France will achieve infinite output in about 200 hundred years, or even a shorter period from *now*" (Solow, 1994, p. 50).

---

[9]Note the irony of this: we are unsatisfied with the finest version of the Solow–Swan model because it assumes *exogenous* technical progress, hence we have initiated the search for a model of economic growth in which technological progress is generated *endogenously*. We have found one such model, namely the Arrow–Romer version of the "learning-by-doing, knowledge spillover" production of technical progress. Curiously enough, however, if the *elasticity* of "learning-by-doing" happens to be smaller than one, this model (in which, to repeat the idea, technical progress is *endogenous*) ends up being possibly worse than the Solow–Swan model with *exogenous* technical progress.

(Surely, that is growing much too fast!)

7.A.2. How Factual Can the "Linear-in-K" Model Be?

The discussion above makes it clear that only if θ is *exactly* equal to one is the Arrow–Romer model useful, for it is only in this *special case* that the model satisfies the "stylized facts of growth." Thus, of the Arrow–Romer model only the "linear-in-K" version works. Now, how factual can this *special case* be? If θ is exactly equal to one (that is to say, for it is the same thing in this case, if production exhibits *exactly* constant returns to capital) everything works alright; any deviation from this, and the model predicts either an "economic Big Bang" $(\theta > 1)$ *or* an "economic collapse" $(\theta < 1)$. Might nature be so "capricious?" As Professor Solow would say (see Solow, 1997), the very law of gravitation is less severe than that: Newton's theory, which involves the *square* power of the distance between two celestial bodies, works alright; but his theory does not predict that the planets will either drift away or collapse for a minor deviation from that precise *square power*. However, the "linear-in-K" model does not allow any leeway. To tell the truth, there are grounds for being suspicious.

Some authors have suggested that although "the *absence of diminishing returns* [to capital] may seem unrealistic, the idea becomes more plausible if we think of K in a broad sense to include human capital" (Barro and Sala-i-Martín, 1995, p. 39; emphasis added). This, however, does not solve the problem posed by Solow. It is true that in the "linear-in-K" model we can think of K in the "broad sense," to include in it not only *physical* capital (as we have done so far) but *human* capital also.[10] This is perfectly possible because the same "learning-by-doing" story that is at the root of the model can be told in either case. After all, what *really* puts the mechanism of "learning-by-doing" into motion is *the breaking-down of routine* in the workplace, and this will happen with either a new (and usually different) machine *or* a new (and usually innovative) manager

---

[10] The reader may have noticed at once that this "extension" of the "linear-in-K" model invalidates the *calibration* test presented in Section 7.3.3 (**P.1**). Will the "linear-in-K" model still predict the growth rates with the same degree of accuracy? It might. If K is the broad measure of capital, the relation $K_t = 2.5Y_t$ has to fall short of reality, that is, the "capital" stock has to be more than 2.5 times the annual flow of income. How much more? We do not know. Since until very recently economists were used to think of K as physical capital only, the empirical computations for the broad concept of capital are infant and unreliable. But, in any case, $a = Y_t/K_t$ must be well below 0.4. On the other hand, the rate of savings must be well above the value of 18.7 percent of income. Hence, the two changes in the data work in opposite directions. Do they compensate each other so that the model still predicts the growth rates with accuracy? We do not know.

or engineer, and so on, *or* both at the same time. Thus, the "learning-by-doing" story would not change by telling it in terms of H instead of K (as in Lucas, 1988) or by merging both into an *aggregate*. This will, surely enough, *increase the magnitude* of the externality attached to each additional unit of "capital," thus helping to counteract the tendency for the "MPK" to decline. However, Solow's complaint is not directed to a possible (note: only possible) "absence of diminishing returns to capital" but to the necessity (note: *necessity*) of *exactly constant* returns to capital. So the question remains even with the broad concept of K: Why not *still* diminishing returns to "capital?" Why not (and now with a greater reason) increasing returns to "capital?" Unfortunately, econometrics is of little help in this case because it faces the problem (quite common in economics nowadays) of *observational equivalence*: the same data are consistent with more than one theory, that is, it would be

> all but impossible to make a convincing empirical case. Observations consistent with constant returns to capital would inevitably also be consistent with a fair range of increasing and decreasing returns to capital. (Solow, 1997, p. 16)[11]

So, what are we to make of all this? The "linear-in-K" version of the New (that is, *endogenous*) Theory of Economic Growth is useful. Thanks to it, we have been able to speculate on policy measures, re-think a number of issues (such as the benefits of economic integration, the influence of savings on growth, the productivity slowdown of the 1970s and 80s, and so on), and the conclusions seem to accord with *common sense* (which, in our modest opinion, is of the greatest importance). So, perhaps, Solow dramatizes a little. But his point must be well taken. After all, it is only telling us that *even if everything else were fine* with the "linear-in-K" model, we would still do well not to rest at peace with it (that is, that while using this model we should keep searching for a less demanding one). All in all, Solow's (1997, pp. 13–14) observation is wise:

> [With] the ["linear-in-K"] version of the New [i.e. endogenous] Economic Growth Theory ... nature must do exactly the right thing or else the theory evaporates in one way or another. ... The world could just happen to be exactly like that. But you would have to be a real plunger to rest the theory of economic growth on one powerful long-shot coincidence.

---

[11] For instance: The capital–output ratio is constant both in the steady state of the Solow–Swan model and in the "linear-in-K" model, hence the aggregate data on Y and K may be generated by (and therefore be consistent with) either the Solow–Swan model or the "linear-in-K" model. Thus, we will not be able to discriminate between the two models on the basis of aggregate data on Y and K.

Appendix 7.B: The Existence of a Steady State and the Acceptability of Models of Economic Growth

From our previous discussions (in this chapter and in the entire book) the reader might be forming the impression that a reason to reject a model of economic growth is the lack of a steady state or, at least, of a "suitable" steady state. In either case, this would be a wrong impression. On purely methodological grounds, the possession of a steady state is neither a necessary nor a sufficient condition for a model of economic growth to be acceptable. All that is required of an economic growth model is that it accommodates the "stylized facts" of Chapter 1 (and other "facts" that might eventually come to our knowledge). The possibilities are thus the following:

(a) A model that possesses no steady state but satisfies the "stylized facts of growth." On purely methodological grounds, one such model will be acceptable. (No examples of this kind of model will appear in this book, but they might appear somewhere else.)

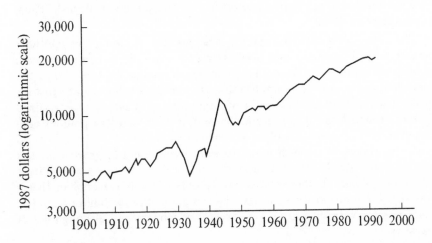

Figure 7.2: US Per Capita Income. *Source*: US Bureau of Census (*Historical Statistics of the United States: Colonial Times to 1970*) and US Department of Commerce

(b) A model that possesses no steady state and does not satisfy the "stylized facts of growth." On methodological grounds, one such model will not be acceptable. But the reason for its rejection will not be the absence of a steady state but the model's inability to satisfy the "stylized facts of growth." The Arrow–Romer model with *elasticity* of "learning-by-doing" greater than one (that is, $\theta > 1$), falls into this category. We have rejected this case of the A&R model, but *not* because of its lack of a steady state, that is, *not* because it generates an ever-rising growth rate, but because *that* rate is *explosive*. One might be willing to accept that the rate of growth is not constant but increasing (Romer, 1994, p. 11, quotes evidence from Kremer, 1993, purporting that such is in fact the case, although a simple look at Figure 7.2 gives us another impression; but this, of course, is no more than "eye inspection"); but one can hardly accept a model of economic growth according to which *scarcity* will disappear within a few generations.

(c) A model that possesses a steady state but does not accommodate the "stylized facts of growth." On methodological grounds, one such model will be rejected. The Solow–Swan model *without technical progress* discussed in Section 2.5 and the A&R model with $\theta < 1$ belong into this category. They possess a unique steady state (the variables grow at constant rates) but cannot accommodate the "stylized facts of growth" (the constant rate at which the per capita variables grow is zero, that is, those models do not yield the *unceasing per capita growth* that we see in the real world). Thus, we also rejected them.

The above rules notwithstanding, it is true that economic growth theorists like to build models which possess a steady state. To be sure, they seem to have a fixation with them. There are three reasons for this: First, the possession of a steady state implies that the variables will grow at constant rates. This, as long as those rates are appropriate to satisfy the "stylized facts of growth," can do no harm. Second, it *does* seem (as pointed out) that economic growth takes place at constant rates. Third, and surely of no least importance, it is much easier to work with economic growth models that possess a steady state: models with no steady state are quite difficult to handle. When all these things are considered, it is reasonable, therefore, that economic growth theorists have a preference for building models which possess a steady state: It is a matter of convenience, although not of necessity.

Suggested Reading

Romer, Paul M. (1987).
Barro, R. J. and Xavier Sala-i-Martín (1994). Ch. 6, Section 6.2.
Solow, Robert M. (1994) and (1997). Ch. 1.

Problems

Problem 7.1. Consider an economy with N firms $i(i = 1, 2, ..., N)$. (N is large enough to ensure that no firm in particular has significant market power, that is, firms are price-takers, hence they behave competitively). Each individual firm has a production function of the following form (Cobb–Douglas in physical capital and effective labor):

$$Y_{it} = F(K_{it}, A_t L_{it}) = K_{it}^{\alpha}(A_t L_{it})^{1-\alpha} \quad (i = 1, 2, ..., N),$$

where A_t represents the efficiency of one unit of labor, hence it may be interpreted as an index for the level of technology. Consider further that A_t evolves through time according to the following rule (the "learning-by-doing" process of knowledge creation and, thereby, labor-efficiency augmentation):

$$A_t = \xi \left(\frac{K_t}{L_t} \right) \quad (i = 1, 2, ..., N).$$

Obviously, whenever one firm $i(i = 1, 2, ..., N)$ increases its capital–labor ratio, it affects the economy-wide efficiency of labor, A_t (the "knowledge spillover effect" is at work). However, the individual firm ignores this effect, so that for its decision-making it takes A_t as given.

1. Determine: (a) the unit retributions to capital and labor inputs, (b) the aggregate volume of production, (c) the growth rate of per capita income.
2. Is this economy's system of retribution to factor inputs feasible?
3. In terms of promoting efficiency, is there a role for government intervention in this economy? *Why?* (or why *not?*) and *which role?* (if any).

Problem 7.2. In the version of the Arrow–Romer model presented in this Chapter the true marginal product of labor is zero (i.e. $MPL = 0$). *Why* is this so (that is, explain the *economic story* behind this peculiarity of the model; thus avoid the mathematical obviety that $MPL = \partial Y / \partial L = 0$). *Hint*: The "economic story" is explained in this chapter (also in Romer, 1987, p.166, last paragraph).

Problem 7.3. The "linear-in-K" version of the "learning-by-doing, knowledge spillover" approach to economic growth presented in this chapter (the Arrow–Romer model), predicts that a decrease in the length of the working day (or, for that matter, of the working week: for instance, from the current 40 hours per week to 35 hours per week) keeping the corresponding (that is, the per day, or per week) real wage the same (that is, reduce hours worked but *not* the wage paid) will produce a permanent increase in the growth rate of per capita income and, therefore, a gain in social welfare.

1. Explain why.

2. Do you think that this prediction of the Arrow–Romer model gives theoretical ground to those who, in light of the high unemployment rate currently affecting the European Union, and with the aim of reducing it, propose to reduce the length of the working week without reducing the week's wage? *Why?* (or why *not?*)

Problem 7.4. In the Arrow–Romer original version of the "learning-by-doing, knowledge spillover" model of economic growth presented in Section 7.7, show that if the *elasticity* of "learning-by-doing" (the parameter θ) is smaller than one the model has a steady state but it does not satisfy the "stylized facts" of economic growth because the steady state per capita rate of growth is zero. What is the economic intuition behind this result?

Chapter 8

Schumpeterian Models of Economic Growth

8.1 Introduction

The Arrow–Romer model presented in Chapter 7 is appealing because it makes technical progress endogenous, that is, as resulting from "things people do." Yet the model is not entirely satisfactory, for it assumes that technical progress results from "things people do *unconsciously*": Firms invest in physical capital guided by the maximization of their profits and, *without explicitly seeking it*, this behavior gives rise, through the process of learning-by-doing and knowledge spillover, to increases in the level of knowledge. Thus, technical progress occurs as an *unintended byproduct* of the economic activity of the firms. In real life, however, technological progress is intentionally sought: there are firms (to which we may refer as "research and development, or R&D, firms") whose activity is precisely the invention of new ways to increase economic efficiency, that is, "to produce" technical progress. Now this activity requires that some resources be devoted to it, and it is obvious that no firm would ever do that unless it had a profit attached. In other words, technical progress entails a conscious investment for which the firms that incur it must be compensated. Clearly, this is not the scenario described in the Arrow–Romer model. There, firms do not purposely invest in the production of technical progress: this simply occurs as a side effect of the economic activity of the firms and is regarded by them as "heaven's gift" for which no retribution is necessary.

Now, this amounts to saying that everyone can use A (and, by extension, the increase in it or "technical progress") free of charge. Such a tale is unavoidable because if the firms had to pay for A either totally or partially, the Arrow–Romer model would not stand up. Why? Because the payments made to the other inputs (capital and labor) already exhaust the total output, thus leaving nothing to compensate A. This is easy to show: in the Arrow–Romer model, capital and labor are paid their marginal products as these are *perceived* by the firms. The profit rate and the real wage are thus given by Equations (7.12) and (7.13), respectively, which, using Equation (7.8) to substitute for A_t and taking $\theta = 1$ become Equations (7.23) and (7.27), respectively, hence we have $\rho_t K_t + \omega_t L_t = \alpha a K_t + (1-\alpha) a K_t = a K_t = Y_t$, that is, the total output is exhausted. Hence, if in addition to paying for K and L, the firms had to pay for A, they would not survive: the model stands up only because it assumes that A is *gratis* to the firms. In this regard, the Arrow–Romer model makes no progress with respect to the Solow–Swan model, where A is also assumed to be costless to the firms for exactly the same reason: if firms had to pay for it, the model would not stand up (see Chapter 6, Section 6.5). Hence, this is the situation: To accommodate the assumption that all firms have free access to A (which is false), the Solow–Swan model makes technical progress "exogenous" *in its entirety* (which is also false), thus ignoring the role that private, profit-maximizing firms play in the generation of technical progress. To do the same (that is, to accommodate the assumption that all firms have free access to A) the Arrow–Romer model "endogenizes" A in a curious way, namely: private, profit-maximizing firms produce A *unconsciously* (whence they do it *gratis*, making their A output a free input for everyone). This is a clever trick, but it falsifies the role that private, profit-maximizing firms play in the generation of A, hence not much progress is made.

In sum, to be faithful to reality we need models of economic growth in which technical progress (and, by extension, its accumulated level A) is both endogenous as output *and* user-retributed as input. In the Solow–Swan model, it has neither of these properties; in the Arrow–Romer model, it only has the first. Therefore, this needs to be corrected. It turns out, however, that the treatment of technical progress (and, by extension, of its accumulated level, A) as an "endogenous output *and* user-retributed input" runs into a technical difficulty, namely, *it is incompatible with the assumption of perfect competition throughout the economy.* The present chapter will show, first, that this conclusion, although disturbing, is inescapable;[1] and second, that it can be surpassed, for it is possible to build models of eco-

---

[1] Why should it be "disturbing" to us that the treatment of A as an "endogenous output *and* user-retributed input" be incompatible with the assumption of perfect competition throughout the economy? Simply because, as economists, we *like* to use the assumption of perfect competition in our models, for we know very well how to work with it (that is, it is a comfortable analytical setting for us).

nomic growth which account for the "endogenous, user-retributed" nature of technical progress based on the assumption of *imperfect* competition.

8.2 The Nature of Technical Progress: A "Non-rival, Partially Excludable Good"

Economists classify economic goods according to their degrees of *rivalry* and *excludability* (Cornes and Sandler, 1986). A good is said to be "excludable" when it is possible to confine its use (benefits) to selected persons. Thus for instance, an apple is an excludable good: if you are not willing to pay for it, you will not have it (here the price system provides a means to make the good excludable). A light house, however, is a "non-excludable" good, for it is impossible to exclude any ship from its benefits. The interesting thing about "*non*-excludable" goods is that their provision by private firms is impossible without government intervention. The reason is that, once produced, a non-excludable good will be available to everyone whether or not they pay for it. Thus, private firms will be unable to raise any revenue from their provision of one such good unless the government, using the tax system, collects money from the public and uses it to pay them.

However, in the real world we find that many R&D firms, the activity of which is the production of *knowledge*, are not financed by government-raised taxes but by direct sale of their output (the new knowledge they produce, that is, "technical progress"). Thus, "technical progress" (and by extension, the accumulated level of it, the *stock of knowledge A*) must be a good *at least* "partially excludable," for otherwise we would not see private firms providing it without government financing. So it is: the inventor of a new design to produce widgets cannot prevent another inventor from *learning* it, thus effectively accumulating the new *knowledge* in his mind, and using it to produce other designs; but he can certainly prevent anyone from using his design ... to produce widgets. For this, all he has to do is to patent the design and enforce his exclusive rights over it by means of the legal system.[2]

---

[2] "Knowledge enters into production in two distinct ways. A new design enables the production of a new good. A new design also increases the stock of knowledge. The inventor of a design has property rights over its use in the production of [the new good] but not over its use in research. If an inventor has a patented design for widgets, no one can make or sell widgets without the agreement of the inventor. On the other hand, other inventors are free to spend time studying the patent application for the widget and learn knowledge that helps in the design of a wodget. This means that the benefits from the first productive role of a design are completely excludable, whereas the benefits from the second are completely non-excludable. In an overall sense, [designs, that is, 'knowledge'] are partially excludable" (Romer, 1990, p. S84-S85).

A good is said to be "rival" if its use by one person precludes its use by another. Thus for instance, an apple is a rival good: if you eat it, the apple is gone, nobody else can eat it too. A light house, however, is a "non-rival" good because its use by one ship in no way precludes its use by another (the light-signal from a light house can be used simultaneously by many ships). The interesting thing about "*non*-rival" goods is that a firm that uses them as inputs will be unable to carry out its production under perfect competition if it (the firm) *must pay for them*. This is easy to show. Imagine that a firm uses a *non*-rival input z along with a set of *rival* inputs $\{x_1, x_2, ..., x_N\}$ according to the following production function:

$$Y = F(x_1, x_2, \cdots, x_N, z). \tag{8.1}$$

Since the amount of z does *not* diminish with its use (because of the non-rival characteristic), the firm could double its output by simply replicating (doubling) the rival inputs $x_1, x_2, ..., x_N$. There is no need to replicate the *non*-rival input also, for the same z can be used an unlimited number of times *simultaneously* (for instance, in two different factories). This means that, although $x_1, x_2, ..., x_N$ *and* z are used as inputs, production exhibits CRTS in $x_1, x_2, ..., x_N$, i.e. in the *rival* inputs *alone*. Thus, the production function (8.1) is homogeneous of degree one in $x_1, x_2, ..., x_N$, hence the following equality holds (by Euler's theorem):

$$\frac{\partial F}{\partial x_1} x_1 + \frac{\partial F}{\partial x_2} x_2 + \cdots + \frac{\partial F}{\partial x_N} x_N = Y. \tag{8.2}$$

This means that by paying the *rival* inputs according to their marginal products (as perfect competition requires), the firm already exhausts its revenue. If in addition it must reward the *non*-rival input with its marginal product (as perfect competition would again require), payments would exceed revenue because:

$$\frac{\partial F}{\partial x_1} x_1 + \cdots + \frac{\partial F}{\partial x_N} x_N + \frac{\partial F}{\partial z} z > \frac{\partial F}{\partial x_1} x_1 + \cdots + \frac{\partial F}{\partial x_N} x_N = Y, \tag{8.3}$$

therefore the firm would incur a loss and it would have to close down.

The same result can be reached with the following (though of course equivalent) argument: since the production function (8.1) is homogeneous of degree one in $x_1, x_2, ..., x_N$ (that is, since production exhibits CRTS in the *rival* inputs alone), it must be homogeneous of degree greater than one in $x_1, x_2, ..., x_N$ *and* z, that is, production must exhibit IRTS when all inputs, rival and non-rival, are considered together. Now a firm that faces IRTS has its average costs above the marginal cost at all levels of output.[3] Hence, if it must price its output by the marginal cost (as perfect competition would force it to do), it would face a loss at all levels of production, and it would have to close down.

Now of course the *stock of knowledge* A (and, by extension, the increase in it, or "technical progress") is a *non*-rival good because a theorem, and so on (in general, any blueprint "for mixing together raw materials" [Romer, 1990]) can be used by an unlimited number of persons simultaneously (for its use by one person does *not* diminish the "amount" of it available to others). Thus, A is exactly like the hypothetical z-input of our previous argument. Besides, it intervenes in every production process of the real world. Thus, to the extent that in reality there are firms which use as inputs certain blueprints (designs, and so on) for which *they* must pay, we are forced to give up the assumption of perfect competition in our models.[4]

In the Solow–Swan model this difficulty is avoided by making the stock of knowledge A *exogenous* to the private activity of the firms. In Solow's words, "it floats in from the outside." For instance, it could be provided by the state: the government raises revenue from taxes, uses it to finance the production of knowledge and, finally, makes this knowledge freely available to everyone. The trouble with this scenario is that it avoids giving up the assumption of perfect competition only at the expense of giving up reality itself: it is *not* true that all technical progress is funded by the state (though a portion of it, particularly in the so-called "basic research," surely is). In other words, the Solow–Swan model recognizes that A is a non-rival good, but also assumes that it is "non-excludable" whereas it is at least *partially* excludable in reality. In sum, the Solow–Swan model retains the assumption of perfect competition only at the expense of denying the role that private, profit-maximizing firms play in the generation of technical progress (Romer, 1990).

In the Arrow–Romer version of the "learning by doing, knowledge spillover" model, technical progress is a non-rival good and it does not "float in from outside" the private activity of the firms. In fact, it is produced by private, profit-maximizing firms. The trouble is that they do not carry out this production on purpose: it is merely an unintended "side effect"

---

[3] This is a standard result in microeconomics and it can be shown as follows: let AC be the average cost; obviously, it is a function of the level of production, that is, $AC = f(Y)$. If TC represents the total cost, $TC = AC \cdot Y$. Marginal cost is thus $MC = dTC/dY = f'(Y) \cdot Y + AC$. If AC is decreasing with Y, *as it is under IRTS*, $f'(Y) < 0$ always, therefore $MC < AC$ at all levels of Y.

[4] True, many pieces of knowledge (that is, at least a portion of A) are available to firms at zero cost. This is the case, for instance, of government-provided statistics of the "business clime," and so on. But that is not the case with, for instance, a patented computer software: only those firms that pay for it are allowed to use it.

of their investments in the production of other goods and they completely disregard its existence. They thus provide *technical progress* (that is, "new knowledge") in exchange for nothing. Hence, perfect competition is possible because, although the "new knowledge" (and, by extension, its accumulated level A) is a non-rival good, its users do *not* have to pay for it. This, however, amounts to assuming that A is also *non*-excludable, for otherwise, if it were at least partially excludable, its producers would demand a compensation for it, no matter how unintended its production.

Hence, there seems to be no escape from the following conclusion: if we want to acknowledge the "non-rival, partially excludable" character of A, thus accounting for the role that private, profit-maximizing firms play in the generation of technical progress, we must abandon the assumption of perfect competition and explicitly introduce market power in our models. Here, too, the pioneering work of Paul Romer (1990), building on some basic ideas by Schumpeter (1942) and others (see, for example, the survey articles by Marris and Mueller, 1980, Section III, pp. 59–69, and Romer, 1994, pp. 17–19), is essential.[5]

8.3   Romer's Schumpeterian Model

The model economy uses four basic inputs: capital, human capital (that is, "skilled" labor), raw (that is, "unskilled") labor, and the level of technology (that is, the "stock of knowledge") and it is organized in three

---

[5] It may be of some value to explain how the name of Schumpeter has come to enter into this area of economics. In his book *Capitalism, Socialism, and Democracy*, Schumpeter (1942) recognizes explicitly that market power exists in real economies and suggests that we are fortunate that it be so because, to the extent that R&D activities are a major force of economic growth, some degree of market power is more efficient than none. He rests this view on the argument that what gives incentives to R&D is the prospect of securing its potential benefits. In perfect competition firms are at liberty to adopt inventions made by others without having to pay for them, hence no firm can secure the benefits of its investments in R&D. Therefore, perfect competition provides no incentives for innovation. In monopolistic markets, however, inventions cannot be freely adopted by everyone, hence the monopolistic firm has the prospect of securing the benefits of innovation and this provides the incentive to invest in R&D activities.

That this thesis (almost as briefly expounded by Schumpeter as it is in these lines) bears upon the issues raised by Romer (1990), is undeniable; that there are other economic growth-related (and equally vague) intuitions proposed by Schumpeter, such as his notion of "creative destruction" (see Subsection 8.5.1 later in this chapter), is also undeniable; that for those contributions Schumpeter deserves to be considered a "classic" in this area, however, might be an exaggeration. In this regard, Solow (1994, p. 52) is probably accurate: "Schumpeter is a sort of patron saint in this field [and he] should be treated like a patron saint: paraded around one day each year and more or less ignored the rest of the time." In any case, models of economic growth which explicitly introduce the idea of market power are usually labeled "Schumpeterian."

sectors: (1) The research sector uses human capital and the stock of knowledge to produce new knowledge. Specifically, it produces "designs" for new intermediate capital-goods; (2) the final-good sector uses human capital, raw labor and the available intermediate capital-goods to produce a final-good output, which can either be consumed or saved; (3) the intermediate capital-goods sector produces intermediate capital-goods using as inputs the output not consumed (that is, saved) of the final-good sector together with the designs produced by the research sector. In this way, the intermediate capital-goods are simple forgone consumption of the final-good. Of course, in real life the research sector also uses unskilled labor as an input; however, this sector is likely to be more human-capital intensive than labor intensive; therefore, ignoring that it uses unskilled labor while acknowledging the use of human capital is merely one form of saying that this sector is assumed to be human-capital intensive. Similarly, in real life the intermediate capital-goods sector also uses human capital and raw labor as inputs; however, this fact is accounted for by the assumption that the intermediate capital-goods are simple forgone consumption of the final-good (because in the production of the latter human capital and unskilled labor intervene as inputs). The working of the model is described below and for this purpose Figure 8.1, which shows the input–output flows of the postulated model economy, may prove helpful.

8.3.1 Description of the Model

The Final-Good Sector

Output of the final-good Y is produced with human capital (skilled labor) H, unskilled labor L, and a variety of intermediate capital-goods $\{x_j\}$ ($j = 0, 1, 2, ...$). To keep the model tractable, we assume that H and L are fixed and inelastically supplied (hence total population, $H + L$, is also fixed). Firms in the production of the final-good Y act competitively, that is, there are a large number of them, named i ($i = 1, 2, ..., N$), they are price-takers in the inputs and output markets, and each produces at time t an amount Y_{it} of the final-good according to the following technology:

$$Y_{it} = F(H_{Yi,t}, L_{it}, x_{0i,t}, x_{1i,t}, x_{2i,t}, \cdots), \qquad (8.4)$$

where $H_{Yi,t}, L_{it}, x_{0i,t}, x_{1i,t}, x_{2i,t}, ...$ are the amounts of the different inputs used by the i-th firm ($i = 1, 2, ..., N$). For simplicity, we assume that the technology in Equation (8.4) is of the following form:

$$Y_{it} = H_{Yi,t}^{\alpha} L_{it}^{\beta} \left(x_{0i,t}^{1-\alpha-\beta} + x_{1i,t}^{1-\alpha-\beta} + x_{2,t}^{1-\alpha-\beta} + \cdots \right), \qquad (8.5)$$

which is an almost-but-not-exactly Cobb–Douglas specification; the difference is that in the exact Cobb–Douglas form

> all capital goods are perfect substitutes. One additional dollar
> of capital in the form of a truck has the same effect on the
> marginal productivity of mainframe computers as an additional
> dollar's worth of computers, [whereas Equation (8.5)] expresses
> output as an additively separable function of all the different
> types of capital goods so that one additional dollar of trucks
> has no effect on the marginal productivity of computers (Romer,
> 1990, p. S81).

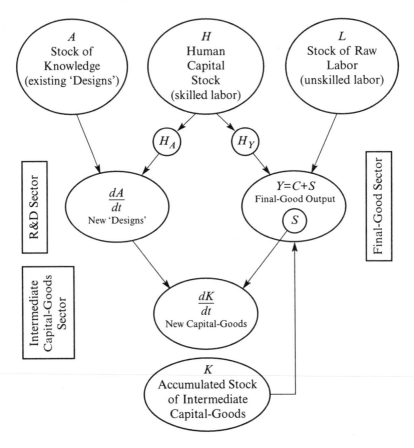

Figure 8.1: The Input–Output Flows Structure in Paul Romer's Schumpeterian Model of Economic Growth (Romer, 1990)

Since the firms producing the final-good Y are competitive, and the production function (Equation [8.5]) exhibits CRTS (that is, it is homogeneous of degree one), we can aggregate across the N firms in the production of the final-good as follows:

$$NY_{it} = (NH_{Yi,t})^{\alpha}(NL_{it})^{\beta} \left([Nx_{0i,t}]^{1-\alpha-\beta} + [Nx_{1i,t}]^{1-\alpha-\beta} + \cdots\right), \quad (8.6)$$

that is to say:

$$Y_t = H_{Yt}^{\alpha} L_t^{\beta} \left(x_{0t}^{1-\alpha-\beta} + x_{1t}^{1-\alpha-\beta} + x_{2t}^{1-\alpha-\beta} + \cdots\right), \quad (8.7)$$

hence "output in the final-good sector can be described in terms of the actions of a single, aggregate, price-taking firm" (Romer, 1990, p. S81).

Now, each intermediate capital-good corresponds to a particular "design," and each design is a piece (that is, *one unit*) of "knowledge." Thus, at any time t the *level* of knowledge, A_t, can be measured by the existing number of designs, therefore by the number of intermediate capital-goods discovered and, hence, available to that date. In other words, in this model technological *progress* takes the form of *an increase in the number of* designs, therefore in the number of intermediate capital-goods discovered and, hence, available. It follows that at any *given* time t there is always a *finite* number of designs, therefore of intermediate capital goods available, A_t (that is, at any *given* time the sum $[x_{0t}^{1-\alpha-\beta} + x_{1t}^{1-\alpha-\beta} + x_{2t}^{1-\alpha-\beta} + \cdots]$ in Equation [8.7] is *finite*). Thus we have:

$$Y_t = H_{Yt}^{\alpha} L_t^{\beta} \left(\sum_{j=0}^{A_t} x_{jt}^{1-\alpha-\beta}\right). \quad (8.8)$$

Let the final-good be taken as *numeraire* (that is, we will express every other price in terms of units of the final-good), hence we make $P_Y = 1$ in each period. Further, let ω_{Ht} be the price of the human capital input (the *real*, that is, expressed in units of the final-good Y, wage of skilled labor) at time t; ω_{Lt}, the price of unskilled labor; and P_{jt} $(j = 0, 1, 2, \cdots, A_t)$, the price of the j-th intermediate capital-good. The typical firm in the competitive final-good sector takes these prices as given and demands of each input $(H, L, x_j; j = 1, 2, \cdots, A_t)$ up to the level where profits are maximized. Thus, at each time t we can derive from Equation (8.8) the *aggregate* demand for the j-th intermediate capital-good input in particular, as follows:

$$\max_{\{x_{jt}\}} \cdot \left\{\Pi_t = Y_t - \omega_{Ht}H_{Yt} - \omega_{Lt}L_t - \sum_{j=0}^{A_t} P_{jt}x_{jt}\right\}, \quad (8.9)$$

that is to say:

$$\max_{\{x_{jt}\}} \cdot \left\{ \Pi_t = H_{Yt}^\alpha L_t^\beta \sum_{j=0}^{A_t} x_{jt}^{1-\alpha-\beta} - \omega_{Ht} H_{Yt} - \omega_{Lt} L_t - \sum_{j=0}^{A_t} P_{jt} x_{jt} \right\}. \quad (8.10)$$

The first order condition for the solution of this program is given by:

$$\frac{\partial \Pi_t}{\partial x_{jt}} = (1 - \alpha - \beta) H_{Yt}^\alpha L_t^\beta x_{jt}^{-\alpha-\beta} - P_{jt} = 0; \; (j = 0, 1, \cdots, A_t), \quad (8.11)$$

which implies:

$$(1 - \alpha - \beta) H_{Yt}^\alpha L_t^\beta x_{jt}^{-\alpha-\beta} = P_{jt}; \; (j = 0, 1, \cdots, A_t), \quad (8.12)$$

and this is the aggregate demand for the j-th intermediate capital-good, expressed in inverse form.

The Intermediate Capital-Goods Sector

Contrary to the final-good sector, the intermediate capital-goods sector cannot be described as competitive. This is so because each producer in this sector holds a *patent* on the design of the capital-good they produce, either because they have invested in research and development (R&D) to invent the j-th design, or because they have bought from its inventor the exclusive rights (that is, the patent) to use the design in the production of the corresponding capital-good. In either case, theirs is the only firm legally entitled to use the design *for the production of the corresponding capital-good*. Therefore, each producer in the intermediate capital-goods sector is a *monopolist* in the production of their good. For simplicity, we assume that the patent rights last forever and that, although in real life there are firms that do their own R&D, there exists a separate R&D sector in which all the designs are invented and the rights (patents) to use them in the production of the corresponding capital-goods sold to the firms which produce those goods in the intermediate sector.

Within this setting, imagine that once the monopolist producers of the intermediate capital-goods sector have incurred the fixed cost of buying the production rights (patents) on the corresponding design, they can produce one unit of their good with η units of the final-good Y. Let r be the interest rate (for simplicity, we assume it to be fixed). Thus, the unit *variable cost* of producing the j-th intermediate capital-good is $r P_Y \eta = r\eta$ because $P_Y = 1$ by choice of numeraire.

In each period, the monopolist producers in the intermediate capital-goods sector take the aggregate demand for their good (Equation [8.12]) as given and choose *either* the price to be charged *or* the quantity to be produced of the good, for they cannot choose both: if they choose the price, the quantity to be produced is automatically determined by the demand-side of their business; if they choose the quantity to be produced, the aggregate demand for the good automatically determines the price to be charged; the fact that they are monopolists gives them control over *either* the price charged *or* the quantity produced, but not over both. In any case, either if they fix the price or the quantity, they will be guided by the maximization of profits. Therefore, their behavior can be described by the following program:

$$\max . \{\Pi_{jt} = P_{jt}x_{jt} - r\eta x_{jt}\}, \qquad (8.13)$$

that is to say (using Equation [8.12]):

$$\max_{\{x_{jt}\}} . \left\{\Pi_{jt} = (1 - \alpha - \beta)H_{Yt}^{\alpha}L_t^{\beta}x_{jt}^{1-\alpha-\beta} - r\eta x_{jt}\right\}. \qquad (8.14)$$

The first order condition for the solution of this program is given by:

$$\frac{\partial \Pi_{jt}}{\partial x_{jt}} = (1 - \alpha - \beta)^2 H_{Yt}^{\alpha}L_t^{\beta}x_{jt}^{-(\alpha+\beta)} - r\eta = 0 \qquad (8.15)$$

for each j $(j = 1, 2, ..., A_t)$, and from this equation we obtain the precise quantity produced (and demanded, therefore *used*) of the j-th intermediate capital-good at time t, that is:

$$x_{jt} = \left[\frac{(1 - \alpha - \beta)^2 H_{Yt}^{\alpha}L_t^{\beta}}{\eta r}\right]^{1/(\alpha+\beta)} ; \ (j = 0, 1, \cdots, A_t). \qquad (8.16)$$

Once the quantity produced of the j-th capital-good has been chosen by its monopolist producer, the aggregate demand for the good determines its price P_{jt}. Thus, substituting x_{jt} into Equation (8.12) we obtain:

$$P_{jt} = \frac{\eta r}{1 - \alpha - \beta} = \bar{P} \qquad (8.17)$$

for all j at all t (that is, the price is the same for all intermediate capital-goods and, moreover, it is constant over time). Given that each intermediate capital-good enters the production function of the final-good Y symmetrically, we can deduce that there is a common level of use of all intermediate capital-goods (that is, that they are all used in the same amounts: $x_{0t} = x_{1t} = \cdots = x_{A_tt}$):

$$x_{jt} = \bar{x}_t \text{ for all } j \ (j = 0, 1, \cdots, A_t). \qquad (8.18)$$

This is easy to show. Take any two intermediate capital goods; for instance, $j=0$ and $j=1$. According to Equation (8.16) we have:

$$\frac{x_{0t}}{x_{1t}} = \frac{\left[(1-\alpha-\beta)^2 H_{Yt}^\alpha L_t^\beta / \eta r\right]^{1/(\alpha+\beta)}}{\left[(1-\alpha-\beta)^2 H_{Yt}^\alpha L_t^\beta / \eta r\right]^{1/(\alpha+\beta)}} = 1, \qquad (8.19)$$

therefore $x_{0t} = x_{1t}$, and so on. Thus it is:

$$x_{jt} = \bar{x}_t = \left[\frac{(1-\alpha-\beta)^2 H_{Yt}^\alpha L_t^\beta}{\eta r}\right]^{1/(\alpha+\beta)} ; \; (j = 0, 1, \cdots, A_t), \qquad (8.20)$$

and using this expression we can write the aggregate production function of the final-good (Equation [8.8]) as follows:

$$Y_t = H_{Yt}^\alpha L_t^\beta A_t \bar{x}_t^{1-\alpha-\beta}. \qquad (8.21)$$

From Equation (8.18) we know that an amount $\bar{x}_t$ is produced (and used) of each intermediate capital-good at time t. Since there are A_t intermediate capital-goods available at time t, the total amount of intermediate capital goods used at that time is $A_t \bar{x}_t$. Since it takes η units of Y to produce one unit of any intermediate capital-good, it takes $\eta A_t \bar{x}_t$ units of Y to produce the amount $A_t \bar{x}_t$ of capital-goods actually used in time t. Hence, $\eta A_t \bar{x}_t$ is the amount of capital (expressed in units of the final-good Y) actually used in production in year t, that is:

$$K_t = \eta A_t \bar{x}_t, \qquad (8.22)$$

therefore:

$$\bar{x}_t = \frac{K_t}{\eta A_t}, \qquad (8.23)$$

and substituting this result into Equation (8.21) we obtain:

$$\begin{aligned}
Y_t &= H_{Yt}^\alpha L_t^\beta A_t \left(\frac{K_t}{\eta A_t}\right)^{1-\alpha-\beta} \\
&= H_{Yt}^\alpha L_t^\beta A_t^{\alpha+\beta} K_t^{1-\alpha-\beta} \cdot \eta^{\alpha+\beta-1} \qquad (8.24) \\
&= (A_t H_{Yt})^\alpha (A_t L_t)^\beta K_t^{1-\alpha-\beta} \cdot \eta^{\alpha+\beta-1}.
\end{aligned}$$

The Research Sector

New designs are obtained by investing two inputs in research and development activities, namely, human capital H_A and the existing stock of knowledge A. Now, the "existing stock of knowledge" coincides with the current *level* of A, that is, with all the designs already invented. This is so because although each design cannot be used in the production of the corresponding intermediate capital-good except by the monopolist producer that owns the patent rights for that purpose (that is, designs are *excludable* goods in "that" direction), as soon as they are used once to manufacture the corresponding intermediate capital-goods in the intermediate sector, they become "common knowledge," hence their use by scientists (that is, by the human capital engaged in research, H_A) to invent new designs is unavoidable (that is, designs are *non-excludable* goods in "this" direction). Therefore, the stock of knowledge, A, evolves according to the following rule (the "production function of knowledge"):

$$\frac{dA_t}{dt} = f(H_{At}, A_t), \tag{8.25}$$

which, by his own choice, Romer (1990) particularizes as follows:

$$\frac{dA_t}{dt} = \delta H_{At} A_t, \tag{8.26}$$

and this implies:

$$\overset{\circ}{A} = \frac{dA_t/dt}{A_t} = \delta H_{At}. \tag{8.27}$$

The research and development (R&D) sector can be described as competitive for the following reason: The typical firm in this sector uses two inputs, H and A, to produce new designs. Input A is *gratis*, but H is not: there are many individuals who possess (and therefore offer) H (skills) and many firms which demand this input (not only those in the R&D sector, but also those in the final-good sector).[6] The market for H is, therefore, competitive, and it gives rise to a uniform price of H, ω_H, which firms in the R&D sector take as *given*. On the other hand, when one of these firms produces a new design, it faces a large number of potential buyers for it, namely all the firms in the intermediate capital-goods sector interested in having the patent rights over the design. These firms will, therefore, bid up the price of the patent rights over the design to a level P_{At} which the R&D

---

[6] In real life, also the firms in the intermediate capital-goods sector will demand H, of course; but since we assume in this model that capital-goods are simple forgone consumption (that is, *not consumed* output of the final-good sector), there is no need to account for this fact here.

firm must take as *given* (what that price is, we will shortly see). Hence, the typical R&D firm takes its "output" (a *new design*) and input H prices as given, thus acting competitively. Therefore, output in the R&D sector can be described in terms of the actions of a single, aggregate, price-taking firm much as it could be done with output in the final-good sector. New designs will thus be produced so as to maximize profits, therefore the behavior of the R&D sector can be described by the following program:

$$\max_{\{H_A\}} . \{\Pi_{A_t} = P_{At}\delta H_{At}A_t - \omega_{Ht}H_{At}\} . \tag{8.28}$$

The first order condition for the solution of this program is given by:

$$\frac{\partial \Pi_{A_t}}{\partial H_{At}} = P_{At}\delta A_t - \omega_{Ht} = 0, \tag{8.29}$$

which implies:

$$\omega_{Ht} = P_{At}\delta A_t. \tag{8.30}$$

Now, how much is a new patent worth to the intermediate capital-goods producers, that is, what is P_{At}? We can find out by reasoning thus: When a new design is invented, whoever buys the rights (that is, the patent) to use it in the production of the corresponding capital-good, will enjoy the monopoly profits of that production forever: they will produce the profit-maximizing monopoly quantity x_{jt} and sell it (or *rent* it out, and for reasons that will soon be clear this description is more appropriate in this model) to the producers of the final-good Y at the (*rental*) price P_{jt}. Thus, each year t from the current period $t=0$ in which they buy the patent rights to $t=\infty$, they will extract a monopoly (or "extra normal") profit $\Pi_{jt} = P_{jt}x_{jt}-r\eta x_{jt}$. Hence, the *annual flow* of monopoly profit to be derived from the possession of the patent rights over a new design is given by $\Pi_{jt} = P_{jt}x_{jt}-r\eta x_{jt}$. It follows that the potential buyers of the patent rights over a new design will bid up its price to the level at which the *present discounted value* of the future stream of monopoly profits accruing from owing the patent rights equals its price, that is:

$$P_{At} = \sum_{t=0}^{\infty} \frac{P_{jt}x_{jt} - r\eta x_{jt}}{(1+r)^t} = \sum_{t=0}^{\infty} \frac{(P_{jt} - r\eta)x_{jt}}{(1+r)^t}. \tag{8.31}$$

It was shown above that $P_{jt} = \bar{P}$ for all j at all t (see Equation [8.17]), and also that $x_{jt} = \bar{x}_t$ for all j (see Equation [8.18]). Thus we have:

$$P_{At} = \sum_{t=0}^{\infty} \frac{(\bar{P} - r\eta)\bar{x}_t}{(1+r)^t}. \tag{8.32}$$

Solution of the Model for the Steady State Equilibrium

Equation (8.24) shows that, concerning the production of the final-good Y, technical progress is labor and human capital augmenting ($A_t L_t$ and $A_t H_{Yt}$, respectively), but it is detached from K, that is, production in the final-good sector is characterized by Harrod-neutrality. Hence, at the aggregate level this model must behave "just like the neoclassical (that is, Solow–Swan) model with labor and human capital augmenting technological change" (Romer, 1990, p. S89). Our experience with that model suggests that this one too must be consistent with a *steady state equilibrium* along whose path all variables: Y, K, C, and A, grow at the *same* constant exponential rate, that is, a *balanced growth path*. (Since we are assuming total population $L + H$ to be constant, the absolute and per capita levels of the variables are analytically the same thing, hence we need not distinguish them here.) Also by reference to the augmented Solow–Swan model, we can deduce that this one too must exhibit transitional dynamics towards the steady state equilibrium. However, this dynamic process appears to be so complicated that it remains unexplored. Therefore, we will only solve the model for the steady state equilibrium, ignoring whatever dynamics the model displays towards it.

Given that along the steady state balanced growth path all variables grow at the same rate, $\overset{\circ}{K} = \overset{\circ}{A}$. Therefore, along the steady state balanced growth path the ratio K_t / A_t remains constant, and this, together with Equation (8.23), implies that $\bar{x}_t$ must also be constant along the steady state path (because $\overset{\circ}{\bar{x}}_t = \overset{\circ}{K}_t - \overset{\circ}{A}_t = 0$), that is:

$$\bar{x}_t = \bar{x} \text{ for all } t \text{ along the steady state balanced growth path} \quad (8.33)$$

That is to say, in the steady-state equilibrium not only x_{jt} is the same for all j (see Equation [8.20]) but it is also constant over time. Using this condition, Equation (8.29) becomes:

$$P_{At} = \sum_{t=0}^{\infty} \frac{(\bar{P} - r\eta)\bar{x}}{(1+r)^t} = (\bar{P} - r\eta)\bar{x} \sum_{t=0}^{\infty} \frac{1}{(1+r)^t} = (\bar{P} - r\eta)\bar{x}\frac{1}{r}. \quad (8.34)$$

Thus, replacing $\bar{P}$ with its value given by Equation (8.17), and re-arranging terms, we obtain:

$$P_{At} = \left(\frac{r\eta}{1 - \alpha - \beta} - r\eta\right)\bar{x}\frac{1}{r} = \frac{(\alpha + \beta)\bar{P}\bar{x}}{r}, \quad (8.35)$$

that is to say, along the steady-state balanced growth path (on which we are concentrating our attention) P_{At} is a constant $\bar{P}_A$ (that is, the price of a patent is constant both for all designs and over time). Using Equation (8.23), P_{At} can now be written as follows:

$$P_{At} = \frac{\alpha + \beta}{r} \cdot (1 - \alpha - \beta) H_{Yt}^{\alpha} L_t^{\beta} \bar{x}^{1-\alpha-\beta} = P_A = constant. \qquad (8.36)$$

The full characterization of the steady state equilibrium requires that we determine the growth rate for the different variables. Since Y, K, C and A all grow at the same rate, it will be sufficient to determine the growth rate of anyone of them, for instance $\overset{\circ}{A}$, the growth rate of the level of technology. Equation (8.27) provides this rate, but to make use of the equation we need to know the (steady state) value of H_{At} first. This, however, is easily obtained as follows: Recall that the real wage paid to human capital must be the same in the R&D and final-good sectors where it is used as an input. The reason has already been explained (see the description of the R&D sector above) but an alternative, equivalent explanation is the following: if ω_H were not the same in both sectors, H would move from one sector to the other until its relative shortage (or abundance) made ω_H equal everywhere. In our discussion of the R&D sector we found (Equation [8.30]) $\omega_{Ht} = P_{At} \delta A_t$. Since the final-good sector is competitive, the real wage of human capital in that sector will be equal to the MPH_Y, that is (from the second row of Equation [8.24]):

$$\omega_{Ht} = MPH_Y = \frac{\partial Y_t}{\partial H_{Yt}} = \alpha H_{Yt}^{\alpha-1} L_t^{\beta} A_t \bar{x}^{1-\alpha-\beta}, \qquad (8.37)$$

and since ω_H must be equal in the R&D and final-good sectors, we have:

$$P_{At} \delta A_t = \alpha H_{Yt}^{\alpha-1} L_t^{\beta} A_t \bar{x}^{1-\alpha-\beta}. \qquad (8.38)$$

Replacing P_{At} with its value from Equation (8.36), and simplifying, we obtain:

$$H_{Yt} = \frac{1}{\delta} \cdot \frac{\alpha}{(\alpha + \beta)(1 - \alpha - \beta)} \cdot r, \qquad (8.39)$$

which is constant for a given r. Since we have assumed that H is fixed and inelastically supplied, the above equilibrium condition implies that H_{At} must also be constant, that is:

$$H_{At} = H - H_{Yt} = H - \frac{1}{\delta} \cdot \frac{\alpha}{(\alpha + \beta)(1 - \alpha - \beta)} \cdot r = constant. \qquad (8.40)$$

Using this result in Equation (8.27), we obtain:

$$\overset{\circ}{A} = \delta H_A = \delta H - \frac{\alpha}{(\alpha + \beta)(1 - \alpha - \beta)} \cdot r = g, \qquad (8.41)$$

which is constant for the given r. Therefore, along the steady state balanced growth path, Y, K, and C will all grow at the rate g of the level of technology given by Equation (8.41).

To see that this conclusion holds, recall that along the steady state path H_{Yt}, L_t and $\bar{x}_t$ are all constant; hence, from Equation (8.23) we obtain $\overset{o}{K}=\overset{o}{A}= g$, and from Equation (8.24), $\overset{o}{Y}=\overset{o}{A}= g$. Finally, by definition we have:

$$C_t = Y_t - I_t = Y_t - \frac{dK_t}{dt}, \qquad (8.42)$$

therefore:

$$\frac{C_t}{Y_t} = 1 - \frac{dK_t/dt}{Y_t} = 1 - \frac{dK_t/dt}{K_t} \cdot \frac{K_t}{Y_t} = 1 - \overset{o}{K} \cdot \frac{K_t}{Y_t}. \qquad (8.43)$$

Given that along the steady state path the capital–output ratio remains constant (because H_{Yt}, L_t and $\bar{x}_t$ are constant), that is, since (from Equations [8.24] and [8.25]):

$$\frac{K_t}{Y_t} = \frac{\eta A_t \bar{x}_t}{H_{Yt}^\alpha L_t^\beta A_t \bar{x}_t^{1-\alpha-\beta}} = \frac{\eta \bar{x}_t^{\alpha+\beta}}{H_{Yt}^\alpha L_t^\beta} = \gamma, \qquad (8.44)$$

we obtain $C_t = \gamma Y_t$ and $\overset{o}{C}=\overset{o}{Y}= g$. Therefore, in steady state all variables grow at the same rate as the level of technology, that is:

$$\overset{o}{Y}=\overset{o}{K}=\overset{o}{C}=\overset{o}{A}= g = \delta H - \frac{\alpha}{(\alpha + \beta)(1 - \alpha - \beta)} \cdot r, \qquad (8.45)$$

which is constant for the given r. Letting:

$$\frac{\alpha}{(\alpha + \beta)(1 - \alpha - \beta)} = \Lambda, \qquad (8.46)$$

the rate of growth can be written as follows:

$$g = \delta H_A = \delta H - \Lambda r. \qquad (8.47)$$

8.3.2   Predictions of the Model

(P.1) A large population is irrelevant. What is relevant is the amount of human capital relative to the amount of raw labor (that is, the distribution of the population between skilled and unskilled labor, H/L) and the amount of human capital devoted to research relative to the total amount of human capital (that is, the distribution of skilled labor between research and other activities, H_A/H_Y). These conclusions follow from Equation

(8.47), which gives the rate of growth. If the total population were important in determining the rate of growth, we would have g as a function of $H + L$ (total population), which is not the case. Thus, the total population is irrelevant. On the other hand, although Equation (8.47) gives g as a function of H, it ought to be recalled that we are keeping L constant by assumption, therefore the equation says that "*for a given L, g is higher the higher H*." Thus the model predicts that, *other things equal*, countries with a higher H/L ratio will tend to grow faster. Further, Equation (8.47) gives g as an increasing function of H_A; however, we are keeping H constant by assumption, hence we read this form of the equation as follows: "*for a given L and a given H, g is higher the higher H_A.*" Thus, the model predicts that, *other things equal*, countries with a higher H_A/H ratio will grow faster." To the extent that, as Romer (1990) points out, "the fraction of human capital devoted to research is apparently highest in the most developed countries of the world," the prediction above helps to explain why today's poor economies find it so difficult to "catch up" with the rich ones.

(**P.2**) Equation (8.47) shows that economic growth will not occur unless $\delta H > \Lambda r$, that is, $H > \frac{1}{\delta} \Lambda r$ (see Figure 8.2). Of course, this particular threshold level of H must not to be taken literally, for it might be concomi-

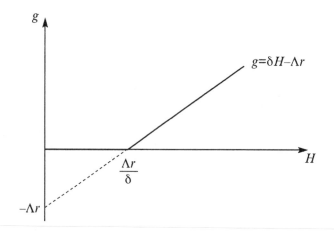

Figure 8.2: Rate of Growth and Human Capital Requirements

tant with the specific functional forms used here. However, the model's prediction is clear: some minimum level of human capital is necessary for growth to begin taking place. The economic explanation that is behind this prediction appears to be the following: economic growth can only occur if new designs are invented (that is, if A grows), and this requires that some human capital be employed in research; on the other hand, the production of the final-good Y (which is needed for survival, for after all the final-good Y encapsulates the consumer goods) requires the use of some human capital. Hence, either the amount of H is above the level required to produce the socially-decided amount of Y, or no human capital will be available to be employed in research, in which case neither A nor, therefore, the economy could grow.[7]

(P.3) Changes in η (the "technical" unit cost of production of intermediate capital-goods, in terms of units of the final-good Y) have an ambiguous effect on the economy's rate of growth. This conclusion is blurred in the model because in Equation (8.47) the parameter η does not appear, hence one might be tempted to conclude that changes in η do not affect the rate of growth. However, this is not so. From the maximization program of the typical monopolist producer of intermediate capital-goods (Equation [8.13]) it is clear that a reduction in η lowers the monopolist's unit variable cost of production (ηr) and raises its level of output $\bar{x}$, as indicated by Equation (8.20). Now, Equation (8.37) shows that an increase in $\bar{x}$ raises the return to human capital in the final-good sector. Thus, if the return to human capital in the research sector were not affected by the increase in $\bar{x}$, there would be no doubt that the reduction in η would provoke a movement of human capital away from the production of designs and towards the production of the final-good Y, thereby reducing the amount of human capital employed in the research sector and, hence, the economy's rate of growth.

However, the increase in $\bar{x}$ *does affect* the return to human capital in the research sector. This is clear from Equations (8.30) and (8.36): the increase in $\bar{x}$ raises P_A (Equation [8.36]) and this, in turn, increases the return to human capital in the research sector (Equation [8.30]). In sum, a reduction in η raises *both*, the return to human capital in the final-good sector *and* the return to human capital in the research sector. Thus, depending on which return rises more, human capital will move either to or away from the research sector, therefore either raising or lowering the economy's rate of growth. Since η does not appear in Equation (8.47) we must conclude that, *for the functional forms used in the model*, both returns rise the same, hence their effects on the allocation of H cancel each other out: since the human capital factor derives no gain by moving from one sector to the other, its allocation remains unaltered, therefore the economy's rate of growth does not change. However, Romer (1990) points out that this is not a robust

---

[7] "This explanation is reminiscent of the explanation for the absence of growth in prehistoric time that is offered by some historians and anthropologists: civilization, and hence growth, could not begin until human capital could be spared from the production of goods for immediate consumption" (Romer, 1990, p. S96).

result because "if slightly different functional forms were used, [this kind of exact cancellation would not hold, and] the net effect of a decrease in η could be either to increase or to reduce the amount of human capital used in the research sector." Hence, "the correct inference from this model is that the effect of [a change] in η on the rate of growth is ambiguous, something that a priori theorizing cannot solve" (Romer, 1990, p. S94).

(**P.4**) An increase (decrease) in the interest rate lowers (raises) the economy's rate of growth. Mathematically, this conclusion follows immediately from Equation (8.47); however, the transmission mechanism that is behind it is rather subtle. A decrease in the interest rate has the same effect on the unit variable cost $r\eta$ of the typical monopolist producer of intermediate capital-goods as a decrease in η (namely, it lowers $r\eta$), therefore also the same effect on $\bar{x}$ (namely, it raises $\bar{x}$). Hence, a reduction in the interest rate, like a reduction in η, raises both, the return to human capital employed in the final-good sector and the return to human capital employed in research. However, the effect on the latter must be stronger. This is easy to show. Equation (8.39) is the equilibrium condition in the market for human capital. It states that, in equilibrium, the return to human capital in the research sector (the left-hand side of the equation, that is, Equation [8.30]) must equal the return to human capital in the final-good sector (the right-hand side of the equation, that is, Equation [8.37]). Using Equation (8.36), Equation (8.39) becomes:

$$\delta A_t \frac{\alpha + \beta}{r} \cdot (1-\alpha-\beta)H_{Yt}^{\alpha}L_t^{\beta}\bar{x}^{1-\alpha-\beta} = \alpha H_{Yt}^{\alpha-1}L_t^{\beta}A_t\bar{x}^{1-\alpha-\beta}. \qquad (8.48)$$

Now, if this equality remains unaltered by a decrease in η because the resulting increase in $\bar{x}$ raises equally the left-hand side and the right-hand side of the equation (and we know this from our discussion in [**P.2**]), the same cannot happen when $\bar{x}$ rises *and* r falls: in this case, the left-hand side of the equation (that is, the return to human capital in the research sector) must rise more. Therefore, a reduction in the interest rate drives the human capital market out of equilibrium, that is:

$$\delta A_t \frac{\alpha + \beta}{r} \cdot (1-\alpha-\beta)H_{Yt}^{\alpha}L_t^{\beta}\bar{x}^{1-\alpha-\beta} > \alpha H_{Yt}^{\alpha-1}L_t^{\beta}A_t\bar{x}^{1-\alpha-\beta}. \qquad (8.49)$$

The higher return paid in the research sector will attract towards this sector some of the human capital employed in the production of the final-good Y, and as this happen the marginal productivity of H in this latter sector (thus also this sector's return to human capital, for they are the same thing) will increase, thereby restoring equilibrium in the market for human capital. The end result is a lower H_Y and a higher H_A, therefore also a higher rate of growth for the economy.[8]

[8]Under normal circumstances, namely decreasing marginal productivity of H (for a given A) in both sectors, the movement of the human capital factor from the final-good sector to the research sector would not only increase the marginal productivity of H in the production of the final-good, but it would also decrease the marginal productivity of H in the production of designs. In this case the equilibrium in the market for human capital would be restored by means of an increase in the return to H in the final-good sector and some contraction in the return to H in the research sector; hence, neither the required re-allocation of H would be as drastic nor, therefore, as affected the rate of growth. However, by the form in which the production of knowledge has been modeled (Equation [8.26]) the marginal productivity of H is not decreasing (for a given A), hence the restoration of the equilibrium in the market for human capital relays entirely on an increase in the return to human capital in the final-good sector. The final outcome, however, is the same: For the analysis of the effect on g of a change in r, the difference between assuming that the marginal productivity of H in the research sector is constant for a given A (as it is done here) or assuming that it is decreasing, is only of degree, not of direction. It could be changed to be decreasing without any harm for the conclusions, though this would complicate the model considerably. Thus, the assumption made in Equation (8.26) that the production of knowledge is *linear in H_A* for a given A (which is what makes the marginal productivity of H to be constant in the research sector for a given A) is harmless.

However, it may be mentioned in passing that the other assumption made in Equation (8.26), namely that the production of knowledge is also *linear in A for a given H_A* (which makes the marginal productivity of A to be constant in the research sector for a given H_A) is not nearly as harmless. For imagine that we make the production of designs a concave function of A for a given H_A; for example, we may replace Equation (8.26) with the following:

$$\frac{dA_t}{dt} = f(H_{At}, A_t) = \delta H_{At} A_t^{\frac{1}{2}}$$

This production function of knowledge implies a decreasing marginal productivity of A in the production of designs (for a given H_A). But it also implies something else, namely that the marginal productivity of *human capital* in the production of designs is *non*-linear in A, that is:

$$MPH_A = \frac{\partial f}{\partial H_A} = \delta A_t^{\frac{1}{2}}$$

This means that the marginal productivity of human capital employed in the research sector does not grow at the same rate as the level of knowledge but only at $1/2$ of it, that is, $\overset{\circ}{MPH}_A = \frac{1}{2} \overset{\circ}{A}$. On the other hand, Equation (8.21), the structure of which will not change by making the production of knowledge a concave function of A, shows (see Equation [8.37]) that the marginal productivity of human capital employed in the final-good sector does grow at the same rate as the level of knowledge, that is: $\overset{\circ}{MPH}_Y = \overset{\circ}{A}$. Now, MPH_A is the return to human capital in the research sector and MPH_Y is the return to human capital in the final-good sector. Thus, as A becomes larger the return to human capital will grow more slowly in the research sector than in the final-good sector, the human capital factor will continuously fly out of the production of designs and into the production of the final-good, the economy's rate of growth will slow down and it will eventually come to a halt. Thus, if the production function of knowledge is made concave in A for a given H_A (that is, if the marginal productivity of A in the research sector is decreasing for a given H_A) the model does not yield unceasing growth, and this is a problem because it violates the very first of the "stylized facts of growth" laid down in Chapter 1. In sum, "linearity in A is what makes unbounded growth possible, and

(P.5) The amount of research done under the economic environment described in the model falls short of the social optimum, that is, too little human capital is devoted to research and hence the economy's rate of growth is unnecessarily low. A simple way to arrive at this conclusion is the following: a new design brings an additional benefit to society of $\partial Y_t / \partial A_t$ *each year* from the moment in which it is obtained to infinity. Hence, the *total* additional benefit to society brought about by a new design is the present discounted value of the stream of its current and future annual additional benefits, that is to say, the Marginal Social Benefit of a new design (MSB_A) is given by:

$$MSB_A = \sum_{t=0}^{\infty} \frac{MSB_{At}}{(1+r)^t}. \tag{8.50}$$

From Equation (8.21) we can obtain MSB_{At} as follows:

$$MSB_{At} = \frac{\partial Y_t}{\partial A_t} = H_{Yt}^{\alpha} L_t^{\beta} \bar{x}_t^{1-\alpha-\beta}. \tag{8.51}$$

Substituting this result into Equation (8.50) we have:

$$MSB_A = \sum_{t=0}^{\infty} \frac{H_{Yt}^{\alpha} L_t^{\beta} \bar{x}_t^{1-\alpha-\beta}}{(1+r)^t}, \tag{8.52}$$

which (taking into account that H_{Yt} and $\bar{x}_t$ are both constant in the steady state equilibrium, and L_t is fixed by assumption) can be written thus:

$$MSB_A = H_{Yt}^{\alpha} L_t^{\beta} \bar{x}_t^{1-\alpha-\beta} \sum_{t=0}^{\infty} \frac{1}{(1+r)^t} = \frac{1}{r} H_{Yt}^{\alpha} L_t^{\beta} \bar{x}_t^{1-\alpha-\beta}. \tag{8.53}$$

On the other hand, the R&D firm that invents the design receives a compensation P_A which is only (from Equation [8.36]) a portion $(\alpha+\beta)(1-\alpha-\beta)$

in this sense unbounded growth is more like an assumption than a result of the model" (Romer, 1990). Therefore, the question is whether or not the marginal productivity of A is decreasing (for a given H_A), that is, whether or not opportunities in research are actually petering out. Romer's opinion is the following:

> [This] is an empirical question that this kind of theory cannot resolve. The specification [in Equation (8.26)], in which unbounded growth at a constant rate is feasible, was chosen because there is no evidence from recent history to support the belief that opportunities for research are diminishing (Romer, 1990, p. S84).

The problem will still appear, however, if they happen to be *increasing*. For if MPH_A is increasing, there will be a "Big Bang" (the problem being similar to the one explained in Appendix 7.A.1, Chapter 7).

of MSB_A, that is:

$$P_A = (\alpha + \beta)(1 - \alpha - \beta)\frac{1}{r}H_{Yt}^{\alpha}L_t^{\beta}\bar{x}^{1-\alpha-\beta} < MSB_A. \qquad (8.54)$$

Clearly, society would gain from having more designs invented, but this requires that a higher amount of human capital be engaged in research. The obvious economic reason behind this result is that each new design generates a positive externality for which the design's inventor is uncompensated. This happens because "[each] additional design raises the productivity of all future individuals who do research, [for it increases the stock of knowledge A], but because this benefit is nonexcludable, it is not reflected at all in the market price for designs" (Romer, 1990, p. S96).

(P.6) Scientists are undercompensated, that is, they receive a wage below the value of their marginal product; the human capital employed in non-research activities, however, receives a payment according to its marginal productivity. This conclusion is "the other side of the coin" of prediction (P.5): scientists earn a wage $\omega_H = P_A \delta A$ (see Equation [8.30]) which is the *market* value of their marginal product (note that, from Equation [8.26], it is $MPH_A = \partial f/\partial H_A = \delta A$, and a design is sold at the price P_A); however, since the market price P_A is below the *true value* of a design, ω_H is below the true value of the marginal product of H_A. The situation is different for the human capital employed in non-research activities. In this case, the wage is $\omega_H = \alpha H_{Yt}^{\alpha-1}L_t^{\beta}A_t\bar{x}^{1-\alpha-\beta}$ and it coincides with the true value of the marginal product of H_Y (see Equation [8.37] and recall that $P_Y = 1$ by choice of numeraire). Thus, the wage earned by human capital tends to be same across the economy (Equation [8.38]), but whereas the non-scientists receive the true value of their marginal product, scientists are paid less than theirs.

(P.7) Economic integration will enhance growth not because of the resulting larger market as measured by the larger population (as it is usually thought), but because of the resulting larger stock of human capital available to the new, integrated economy. This can be seen by analyzing the form in which economic integration affects the steady state equilibrium of two economies, 1 and 2, which are identical except in their stocks of human capital, H_1 and H_2. From Equation (8.47) we know that the amounts of human capital devoted to research in each economy are:

$$H_{A1} = H_1 - \frac{\Lambda r}{\delta} \qquad (8.55)$$

$$H_{A2} = H_2 - \frac{\Lambda r}{\delta} \qquad (8.56)$$

and their rates of growth are:

$$g_1 = \delta H_{A1} = \delta H_1 - \Lambda r \qquad (8.57)$$

$$g_2 = \delta H_{A2} = \delta H_2 - \Lambda r \qquad (8.58)$$

Once the two economies integrate, the stock of human capital available to the new, integrated economy will be:

$$H^* = H_1 + H_2, \qquad (8.59)$$

and the amount of human capital devoted to research:

$$H_A^* = H^* - \frac{\Lambda r}{\delta} = (H_1 + H_2) - \frac{\Lambda r}{\delta}. \qquad (8.60)$$

Hence, the growth rate of the integrated economy will be:

$$g^* = \delta H_A^* = \delta(H_1 + H_2) - \Lambda r, \qquad (8.61)$$

which is greater than either g_1 or g_2. This happens not only because the amount of human capital devoted to research is greater in the integrated economy (which by itself would speed up technological progress and hence increase the rate of growth) but also because the proportion of human capital devoted to research (the H_A/H ratio) increases with the integration of the two economies.[9] Thus, "the model suggests that what is important for growth is integration not into an economy with a large number of people but rather into one with a large amount of human capital" (Romer, 1990, p. S98).

8.3.3　The Model and the "Stylized Facts of Growth"

Equation (8.47) makes clear (with account of the qualification made in footnote 8) that the model satisfies the "stylized fact (1)" of economic growth, namely that there is unceasing growth (or, what is the same thing, that in the long run per capita income grows at a non-decreasing rate). From Equation (8.44) we know that the model also satisfies the "stylized fact (2)," namely that in the long run the capital–output ratio remains constant. As for the "stylized fact (3)," namely that the rate of profit

---

[9]This is easy to show. From Equation (8.47) we have $H_A/H = (H - \frac{\Lambda r}{\delta})/H$, therefore it is:

$$\frac{d(H_A/H)}{dH} = \frac{\Lambda r/\delta}{H^2} > 0,$$

that is, the steady state fraction of human capital devoted to research rises with the total amount of human capital available to the economy.

exhibits no perceptible trend, the following argument shows that it too is satisfied by the present model: By definition, the rate of profit is $\rho_t = \Pi_t/K_t$; also by definition, $\Pi_t = Y_t - W_t$, and it is clear from the model's structure that $W_t = \omega_{Ht}H_t + \omega_{Lt}L_t = \omega_{Ht}(H_{Yt} + H_{At}) + \omega_{Lt}L_t$. From Equation (8.21) we obtain ω_{Lt} as follows:

$$\omega_{Lt} = MPL = \frac{\partial Y_t}{\partial L_t} = \beta H_{Yt}^{\alpha} L_t^{\beta-1} A_t \bar{x}_t^{1-\alpha-\beta} = \beta \frac{Y_t}{L_t}. \tag{8.62}$$

On the other hand, Equation (8.37) yields:

$$\omega_{Ht} = \alpha H_{Yt}^{\alpha-1} L_t^{\beta} A_t \bar{x}_t^{1-\alpha-\beta} = \alpha \frac{Y_t}{H_{Yt}}. \tag{8.63}$$

Using these two equations the wage bill W can be written thus:

$$W_t = \alpha \frac{Y_t}{H_{Yt}} H_{Yt} + \alpha \frac{Y_t}{H_{Yt}} H_{At} + \beta \frac{Y_t}{L_t} L_t = \alpha Y_t + \alpha \frac{H_{At}}{H_{Yt}} Y_t + \beta Y_t. \tag{8.64}$$

In steady-state equilibrium, H_{Yt} and H_{At} are both constant (see Equations [8.39] and [8.40], respectively), thus we have $\alpha(H_{At}/H_{Yt}) = b$, a constant. Hence:

$$W_t = (\alpha + b + \beta)Y_t, \tag{8.65}$$

therefore:

$$\Pi_t = [1 - (\alpha + b + \beta)]Y_t = (1 - \alpha - \beta - b)Y_t. \tag{8.66}$$

Using Equation (8.44) (that is, in the steady-state equilibrium the capital–output ratio remains constant) we obtain:

$$\rho = \frac{(1 - \alpha - \beta - b)Y_t}{K_t} = \frac{1 - \alpha - \beta - b}{\gamma} = constant, \tag{8.67}$$

thus in the long run the rate of profit remains constant. Finally, predictions **(P.1)** and **(P.2)** suggest that we ought to expect a great cross-section dispersion of growth rates around the world. Hence, the present model is consistent with the fourth "stylized fact of economic growth" as laid down in Chapter 1. Moreover, since as far as aggregate output is concerned the present model is essentially the Solow–Swan model with labor-and-human capital-augmenting technology (the only difference being that the present model provides a more realistic analysis of the origin of technical progress), it should be possible to derive from it a similar cross-country analysis of economic convergence to the one presented in Chapters 3 and 4. Thus, in a way, the present model provides a more rigorous theoretical ground for some of the results obtained in the "catching up" controversy (for example, the suggestion made in Chapter 4 that one reason for the lack of convergence observed in reality is the discrepancy in levels of human capital between the rich and poor countries).

8.4   Policy Analysis

Most policy suggestions from this model are quite apparent in Predictions
(**P.1**) to (**P.7**). For instance, if an ample market as measured by counts of
people were all that mattered (because a large market means a high demand
for goods, as it is often argued), then having a large population would
be a good substitute for economic integration and even for international
trade. This model shows, however, that what really matters for growth is
a large amount of human capital. Thus the model suggests that economic
integration (or, in its absence, trade with other nations) is important even
for countries with a large population, like India or China, because it is
access to a large stock of human capital, not to a large population, that
makes the difference in terms of growth.

Similarly, various predictions of the model, but in particular Prediction
(**P.5**), indicate that any policy that motivates the creation of new "designs"
(such as direct subsidies to research, the protection of intellectual property
rights, and so on) is well advised. In this regard, and contrary to both, the
main conclusion of the "learning-by-doing" model presented in Chapter
7 and the common wisdom, the present model indicates that a policy of
direct subsidies to physical capital accumulation is not necessarily good
for economic growth and it might even be counterproductive. (Why? The
analysis of this issue is left to the reader as an exercise; see Problem 8.1.)

8.5   Beyond Romer's Schumpeterian Model: Some Topics for Further Study

8.5.1   Economic Growth based on "Creative Destruction"

The present model views technical progress as an increase in the "number"
of intermediate capital-goods available (or, generally speaking, in the number of inputs used in production). Surely, very few people, if any at all, will
dispute that this is *one* form in which technical progress often presents itself.
Now consider the following example: we enjoy "canned music" today much
as our ancestors did in the past; however, the record player has experienced
great transformation: first, the gramophone, then the tape recorder, and
now the CD. Since the gramophone was driven out by the tape recorder,
and this, in turn, by the CD, we might say that there was *one* record player
in the past and there is *still one* in the present (which, loosely speaking, is
true). Thus, if we were to take the present model literally, we would have
to conclude that for the enjoyment of "canned music" there has been no

technical progress since the invention of the gramophone (!) Of course, we need not take Romer's model literally; it is simpler, and much better, to acknowledge that technical progress does not always come as an increase in the number of available inputs: very often when a new design appears it drives out an older equivalent (as in our example). In other words, the present model ignores the fact that technical progress often takes the form, not of an increase in the "number" of available inputs, but of an increase in the *quality* of existing ones.

This *quality ladder* feature of technical progress has been studied by Grossman and Helpman (1991) and Aghion and Howitt (1992), among others. A basic aspect of these models is Schumpeter's idea of *creative destruction*: when a new (therefore more efficient) design for the production of an existing good is "created," the firm that begins to use it first will bite into the market share of its competitors, for it can offer the good in a better quality at the same price (or, what comes to be the same thing, in the same quality at a lower price). Hence, the competitors either introduce the same design (or, if unable to do that, introduce a still newer one) or else they will be driven from the market. Now, as they introduce the newer "blueprint," they often stop the use of the old one, even when their investments in the current equipment are not fully depreciated (pure "destruction"). Adding to this mechanism the suggestion, also made by Schumpeter, that firms invest in R&D mostly to be in a position to conquer a larger share of the market (or to avoid losing whatever share they already have), we obtain Schumpeter's vision of technical progress as a process of "creative destruction."[10]

---

[10] In passing, and for the record:

> One capitalist can drive another from the field ... by selling more cheaply. In order to sell more cheaply without ruining himself, he must produce more cheaply ... [This is achieved] with the continual improvement of machinery ... If now, by the utilization of new machines ... one capitalist has found the means of producing [more cheaply] than his competitors, ... how will this capitalist operate? ... He attains the object he wishes to attain if he puts the price of his goods only a small percentage lower than that of his competitors. He drives them from the field, he wrests from them at least a part of their sales ... However, the *privileged position* of our capitalist is not of long duration; other competing capitalists introduce the same machines ... The capitalists find themselves, therefore, in the same position relative to one another as *before* the introduction of the new means of production ... the same game begins again ... That is the law which gives [the capitalist] no rest and continually whispers in [his] ears: "Go on! Go on!" While, therefore, competition continually pursues him with [this] law ..., the capitalist continually tries to get the better of competition by incessantly introducing new machines, ... and by not waiting until competition has rendered the new ones obsolete.

Schumpeter's view of the introduction of new techniques? No, not Schumpeter's; Marx's

One result of these models of "creative destruction" is that there tends to be *overinvestment* in the economy because the firm that introduces a better design for the production of an existing good does not internalize the "destruction" that its innovation provokes (remember that it forces the competing firms to abandon their own "methods of production" even when their current equipment is not fully depreciated). If the innovative firm had to internalize this negative externality (by, for example, compensating the rival firms for their losses), the "innovation" might be unprofitable and hence it would not be effected. But since this kind of compensation never takes place, the "innovation" is carried out.[11]

8.5.2   Bounded "Learning-by-Doing" (Solow, 1997)

Whatever happened to knowledge creation through "learning-by-doing?" In Chapter 7 we presented a model in which *all* knowledge resulted from "learning-by-doing" and none from ad hoc R&D activity; in the present chapter, the opposite happens, that is, *all* knowledge comes from ad hoc R&D activity and none from "learning-by-doing." The justification for moving from the model presented in Chapter 7 to Romer's (1990) Schumpeterian model was clear: in the "learning-by-doing, knowledge spillover" model of Chapter 7 new knowledge, all of it, was produced *unconsciously*; this made it available to all firms gratis, and this, in turn, allowed us to carry out the analysis of economic growth within the framework of perfect competition. But the first premise, that all knowledge is produced unconsciously, is clearly false: some firms, which we identified as R&D firms, produce new knowledge *on purpose*. Hence, the R&D firm that makes an "invention" knows full well that it possesses a new piece of knowledge, and (very far from allowing other firms to use it gratis) it will demand, through the legal system of patents, a monopoly price on its use. Thus, the model presented in Chapter 7 fell short of reality because, first, not all knowledge is produced through "learning-by-doing," much less unconsciously; and second, once we recognize that some knowledge is produced through ad hoc R&D activity, the theory of economic growth cannot be carried out within the framework of perfect competition.

("Wage Labor and Capital," in Marx, 1977, pp. 22-24). But, come to think of it, they do not seem to be very different, particularly when we account for the fact that, in Marx, "competition" does not mean "perfect competition" as we use this concept today but only "struggle for a larger share of the market," and whether this war is fought by many firms or by only a few is of lesser importance.

[11] This result was also advanced by Marx. (However, he might have carried it out too far, as he made it the basis of his "Law of the Tendency of the Rate of Profit to Fall," see Valdés, 1988.)

Now, this does not mean that no knowledge whatever is created through the process of "learning-by-doing," as Romer's (1990) Schumpeterian model implicitly assumes. As Solow (1997) points out, regarding the creation of knowledge there appear to be in the real world two processes at work. One is R&D activity, which generates new knowledge capable of giving a turn to existing industries, or even create entirely new ones. The other, which consists of "continuous improvement" in the *existing* products and processes, is the result of experience in the production and use of such products and processes, that is, the result of "learning-by-doing" proper. Hence, although we cannot, realistically, expect "learning-by-doing" to produce *major breakthroughs* (that is, new knowledge capable of transforming existing industries radically or even create entirely new ones) unless by fluke, it nonetheless gives rise to improvements in the design, quality, reliability, and so on, of *existing* goods, as well as improvements in the use of *existing* processes. In Solow's (1997) words:

> [Although "learning-by-doing"] does not usually create anything worth calling new technology, it does, however, generate useful know-how, improvements in plant layout and materials handling, economies in a number of location of fasteners, time-and-effort-saving changes in the allocation of jobs to people, and a hundred other ways to improve quality and reduce waste in the production of more or less *unchanged products* by more or less *unchanged methods*. (Solow, 1997, p. 24–25, emphasis added.)

Hence, it would be a great step forward to build models in which knowledge sprung from *both*, R&D activity *and* "learning-by-doing." Ideally, however, such models should take into account that (as we hinted in Chapter 7, Section 7.7, and the discussion above makes clear) the capacity of "learning-by-doing" to generate new knowledge is almost certainly *bounded*, its limits being the full possibilities of the (*already existing*) inventions.

For instance: Imagine that a new invention comes up from (as it would normally be the case) R&D activity. When the invention is implemented we cannot expect that its possibilities to increase A will be exhausted (or if you wish, taken advantage of) instantly. This is so because the labor force, even the human capital employed, needs time to acquire full command of the new invention (for example, if the invention is an altogether new good, there is a long way to go in terms of improvements in its design, durability, reliability, and so on; if it is an entirely new process, there is also a long way to go in terms of improving the know-how to operate with it, and so on). It is here where "learning-by-doing" takes its turn at increasing A. Presumedly, its capacity to increase A *within the new invention* will be initially high, hence A_t will increase fast at the beginning. However, as the full possibilities of the new invention are approached, the capacity of "learning-by-doing" to increase A will slowly die out. The process is depicted in Figure 8.3. Initially (time $t = 0$), the level of knowledge is A_0. Then, at time $t = 1$, a new invention comes up from R&D activity which has the potential for raising the level of knowledge to $\widehat{A}_1$, say. The invention is implemented and "learning-by-doing" begins to raise A_t from its current level A_0 towards its potential level *within the new invention,* $\widehat{A}_1$. Initially, A_t will rise quickly, then it will begin to slow down and, unless another invention comes up, it will reach (asymptotically) its potential level $\widehat{A}_1$ and remain there. Imagine, however, that a new invention which has the potential to raise A_t to an upper level $\widehat{A}_2$ does come up at time $t = 2$. Then a new life begins for "learning-by-doing," and so on. Hence, A_t effectively follows the path $\{A_1 \rightarrow A_2 \rightarrow A_3...\}$, which could be modeled thus:

$$A_t = \widehat{A}_t - \frac{1}{\xi \left(\frac{K_t}{L_t}\right)^{\theta}}, \qquad (8.68)$$

so that as capital accumulation takes place (that is, as "learning-by-doing" works its length) A_t approaches the upper limit $\widehat{A}_t$, which will keep rising only in so far as the R&D activity pomps in new inventions.

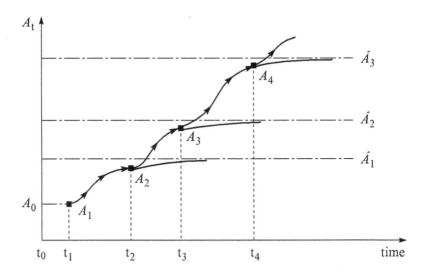

Figure 8.3: Knowledge Creation Through R&D Activity and Bounded Learning-by-Doing

Hence, any model which incorporates this process of knowledge creation must rely on a continual stream of R&D inventions to generate un-bounded economic growth because, once devoided of capacity for inventing *proper*, "learning-by-doing" alone will not deliver an unceasing increase in A_t. Solow (1997) provides one such model. He begins by assuming that inventions are mostly the result of organized R&D activity. However, since (as it is often the case) researchers may end up finding something while look-ing for something else, inventions, though the result of purposeful R&D, are not always "intended," hence there is *some degree of randomness* in their arrival. There is another, even more powerful reason for randomness in the arrival of inventions, and that is the obvious fact that the output of R&D activity (that is, inventions) cannot be *timed* like the production of candies (to give an example) can. For, when a researcher sets out to solve a scientific problem she may find the solution soon, or two years from now, or she may never find it at all. Thus, Solow (1997) assumes that the result of R&D activity is an "erratic stream of inventions." In other words, inventions arrive at random; when one of them occurs, it opens the door for "learning-by-doing" to produce a long (but not indefinite) increase in A_t. Hence, in terms of Equation (8.68), Solow (1997) models $d\widehat{A}_t/dt$ as a (always positive) random walk.[12] (The specifics of the modeling are left to the reader. Note, however, that in this model $\widehat{A}_t$ is *exogenously determined*. Therefore, there is ahead the theoretical challenge to make $\widehat{A}_t$ *endogenously* determined as the output of profit-maximizing R&D activity.)

8.5.3 "Leaders" vs. "Followers" in Research and the Problem of Technological Diffusion

Romer's (1990) Schumpeterian model concludes that, to experience unceas-ing growth, a country must continually increase its stock of knowledge (a conclusion which, as a general statement, is the same as the one obtained from the Solow–Swan model). It follows from this conclusion that whereas

---

[12] Actually, he does not carry out the analysis in terms of A (the level of technical knowledge) but in terms of ℓ (the amount of labor needed to produce one unit of output). However (see Chapter 7, footnote 2), the two concepts are equivalent because ℓ decreases as A increases. Thus, instead of saying that a new invention raises the upper bound of the level of knowledge $(\widehat{A}_t)$ we could say (as Solow does) that it decreases the *lower* bound of the labor requirement per unit of output, $\widehat{\ell}_t$. Thus, he models the process of knowledge creation as follows:

$$\ell_t = \widehat{\ell}_t + \frac{1}{\xi\,(K_t/L_t)^\theta},$$

so that as capital accumulation (that is, "learning-by-doing") takes place, ℓ_t approaches $\widehat{\ell}_t$, the lower bound achievable under the given invention.

the technologically advanced economies will not (in general) be able to increase their stock of knowledge unless *they* keep on *inventing* more efficient "designs," less advanced countries can increase theirs, and therefore experience growth, by "copying" *technologies that already exist but are unknown to them.* This raises the important issue of which policy is best for a developing country, to be a "follower" (imitator) in research or to attempt to be a "leader" at it? Barro and Sala-i-Martín (1995) give a tentative answer to this question. They argue that since imitation is usually cheaper than invention, being a "follower" is the better policy.

The experience of the East Asian tigers (South Korea, Singapore, and so on), and of Japan earlier, is in tune with this result, but a policy of imitation raises questions of its own. For although it might be true that imitation is cheaper than invention, a developing country can follow a policy of imitation only by gaining *access* to better technologies in the first place. This takes us back to the problem of *technological diffusion*: Through what channels is technological knowledge transferred from one nation to another? Why did the East Asian tigers succeed in imitating the technologies of more developed countries while other nations with similar initial endowments (for example, the whole Latin-American basin) did not?

In Chapter 4 (Section 4.4) we touched upon this issue and pointed out that the explanation at hand, although favored by most, does not satisfy everyone because it relies on too many factors; so many, indeed, that it turns vague. Thus, for instance, after noting that "secure property rights, reliable enforcement of contracts, a liberal trade regime, low taxes and public spending, etc." is the way to go, the same editorial of *The Economist* quoted in that section recognizes that "Economists argue about *how much weight to attach to one factor or another* but have come to agree with this [here is the trouble] *broad proposition*: the key to growth is granting producers and consumers the economic freedom to face and respond to incentives" (emphasis added). Hence, as it stands, our knowledge in this area is too fragmented for us to pin down a set of few but *distinctively effective* policies. Therefore, we need fine-tuning work on this issue.

Suggested Reading

Solow, Robert M. (1994). From p.51, 5th paragraph ("I think that the real value of endogenous growth theory, etc.") to the end.
Romer, Paul M. (1994). From p.11, 4th paragraph ("Version #2: The Passing of Perfect Competition") to p.14, 3rd paragraph ("Even though it is obvious in retrospect, etc."); from p.15, 4th paragraph ("In my first paper on growth [Romer, 1986], etc.") to p.16, 2nd paragraph ("For years,

the economic analysis of science and technology, etc."); and from p.17, 3rd
paragraph ("Neo-Schumpeterian Growth," etc.) to the end.
Romer, Paul M. (1990). Particularly, up to p.S79.
Solow, Robert M. (1997). Chapters 2 and 3.

Problems

Problem 8.1. The common wisdom (and some theoretical models, such
as the Arrow–Romer version of "learning-by-doing" presented in Chapter
7) indicate that a policy of direct subsidies to physical capital accumulation (or, if you wish, subsidies to investment in physical capital, or to the
production of capital-goods, for they all amount to the same thing) is good
to spur economic growth. Would you say that the model presented in this
chapter also points in the same direction? Why, or why not? (Hint: A good
procedure to analyze this question might be the following: First, begin by
identifying which parameter of the model could be used to capture the idea
of a subsidy to physical capital accumulation; second, discuss how this parameter would change with the subsidy; third, follow this change through
the relevant equations in the model; fourth, reach a conclusion as to the
convenience of the policy. Finally, *and most important of all*, translate the
analysis into English, that is, tell the *economic story* behind your conclusion.)

Problem 8.2. In several places in this chapter, it was pointed out that to
a large degree Romer's Schumpeterian model behaves like the Solow–Swan
model. Therefore, it is not altogether surprising that some authors question
the need for Romer's model. "If we gain so little in terms of explaining the
facts, why bother at all," they seem to say (though perhaps what is meant is
"bother at all coming up with the assumption of *imperfect* competition...")
Would you embrace this point of view? Explain. (Hint: The **Suggested
Reading** by Romer, 1994, and Solow, 1994, in this chapter will be a good
help.)

Part IV
Concluding Remarks

"[E]*ducational* disadvantages of the tendency ... to exaggerate
differences and represent all knowledge as brand new: It
doesn't breed a scientific spirit but the reverse, viz., a
blind scramble to acquire the new orthodoxies
for fear of being out of fashion."
(Sir Dennis Robertson)

Chapter 9

Theories of Economic Growth: "Old" and "New"

9.1 Introduction

Two different approaches in the theory of economic growth have been presented in this book: one takes technical progress as *exogenous* (that is, produced by means of publicly funded R&D activity), the other takes it as *endogenous* (that is, produced by profit-maximizing, *not* publicly funded firms). The former is often called the "old," and the latter the "new," theories of economic growth. Yet these are only names, signs economists use to understand each other. To be sure, some achievements of the "old" theory (such as the analysis of convergence presented in Chapters 3 and 4 and the "human capital augmented" S&S model) came after the birth of the "new" theory; on the other hand, a few insights on endogenous economic growth are either older than the S&S model (for an account of this, see Nelson, 1997) or nearly as old (for example, Arrow's [1962] hypothesis of the creation of knowledge through "learning-by-doing"). Thus, speaking of old and new in this instance is not very accurate even time-wise.

More important, the adjectives "old" and "new," when used in reference to the theories of economic growth surveyed in this book, should not be taken as synonymous of "outdated" and "modern," respectively. In fact, this chapter gives a few reasons why an evaluation of these theories ought not be made on such terms; for, in many respects, there is no ground to discard the former in favor of the latter. Indeed, since the "old" and the "new" approaches treat different aspects of the creation of knowledge, namely its exogenous and endogenous components, respectively, and given that both components will likely (perhaps inevitably) remain through time, it is reasonable to expect that the two approaches will come to be integrated in a future (and more complete) theory of the production of technology. Thus, it may be appropriate to think of them as "building blocks" in the modeling of the actual process of economic growth and development, rather than as in themselves all-round (and opposing) theories. At any rate, that is the point of view presented in this chapter.

9.2   Endogenous and Exogenous Theories of Economic Growth: An Evaluation

Ever since the new wave of research on growth theory began in the late 1980s, proponents of the two theories have been (on and off) arguing over which of the two approaches is better. One (possibly the first) round of the dispute was fought in the empirical arena. As discussed in Chapter 3, Section 3.5, to meet the empirical finding that $\lambda \approx -0.022$, the parameter α in the aggregate production function $Y_t = K_t^\alpha (A_t L_t)^{1-\alpha}$ has to be approximately equal to 0.7 (consequently, $1 - \alpha \approx 0.3$). In the S&S model factor inputs are paid their marginal products, thus in this model α is the share of K (and $1 - \alpha$ the share of L) in national income.[1] So the model predicted (this was the interpretation at the time) that K must receive about 70 percent of the national income and L about 30 percent of it. However, the national income accounts were indicating the opposite: a 30 percent share for K and a 70 percent for L. Something was wrong: Was it the S&S model? The national accounts? Or was it something else?

The proponents of the new theory took it for certain that it was the S&S model which failed. Specifically, it assumed that K and L were paid their marginal products but in reality K is paid less and L more than that. Why? Because each new bit of K generates an *externality* for which it is not compensated. We explained this story at length in Chapter 7, so there is no need to repeat it here. The important point is that the new theory,

---

[1] This we saw in various occasions in this book but, to refresh our memory, recall that the income share of K is, by definition, $\text{Sh}_K = \Pi_t / Y_t$. If K is paid its marginal product, which is given by Equation (2.10) in Chapter 2, we have:

$$\text{Sh}_K = \frac{\Pi_t}{Y_t} = \frac{MPK_t \cdot K_t}{Y_t} = \frac{(\alpha Y_t / K_t) \cdot K_t}{Y_t} = \alpha,$$

and similarly for Sh_L from Equation (2.11) in Chapter 2.

by means of this externality effect, could explain the observed discrepancy between each factor's marginal product and their actual retributions.

Then as it often happens in intellectual disputes, the old theory had its turn on the issue and the *human capital augmented* S&S model came to its rescue. We explained the intricacies of this extension of the S&S model in Chapter 3, Section 3.5.1, thus again there is no need for repetition here. The point is that the old theory managed to come out of trouble in this issue and, all the more important, keeping its main assumptions untouched, namely, that factor inputs *are* paid their marginal products and that taking technical progress as *exogenous* is as useful an analytical tool as any, at least to tackle the problem at hand. So after all, this round of the dispute ended up with another (economics might be having too much of this by now!) episode of *observational equivalence*: two theories consistent with the same empirical finding. Therefore, the conclusion from this round of the debate, neatly summarized by Romer (1994), is that

> if you are commited to the [old theory], the kind of data [discussed above] cannot be used to make you recant. They do not compel you to give up the convenience of a model in which markets are perfect. They cannot force you to address the complicated issues that arise in the economic analysis of [technical progress] (Romer, 1994, p. 10).

Another round in the debate between the two theories seems to have been constructed over their (as-of-today-known) implications for economic policy. For reasons to be soon explained, however, this discussion is somewhat misleading because it is based on stretching too big a difference between the two theories which may not be as big in *practice* as it looks in theory. To see this, recall from Chapter 7 that both the S&S model and the "linear-in-K" model conclude that economic integration is a sound growth-oriented policy. The same can also be said of many other policies, such as those intended to lower the population growth, or to increase the rate of saving (as, to give only a few examples, policies directed to increase the share of output devoted to investment in physical and human capital, as could be a lower tax on business profits, a direct subsidy to acquiring education, and so on); or even policies designed to promote R&D, such as the creation of a publicly funded research center, and so on. The number of growth-oriented policies that can be devised in light of *both* the S&S model and the "linear-in-K" model is large indeed.

There is, however, a difference between the old and the new theories of economic growth as regards these policies, namely, that the former predicts them to be "good" whereas the latter predicts them to be "magnificent."

More specifically, those policies increase the economy's rate of growth *temporarily* according to the S&S model and *permanently* according to the new, endogenous branch of models. To put this in yet another form, we may say that the old theory predicts those policies to be "trend-lifting" whereas the new one predicts them to be "trend-tilting." Figure 7.1 in Chapter 7 makes this difference clear.[2]

Now, of course, "permanent" is more lasting than "temporary" no matter how long the latter. Hence, this difference between the two theories is no doubt relevant, for it refers to the economy's *rate of growth* and it was shown in Chapter 1 that even small differences in growth rates make for large differences in living standards. Yet it may be wise not to press this difference too far either, for it may actually be minor *in practice*. Why? The *speed of convergence*, which tells us how long it will take an economy (according to the old theory) to settle on a new steady state path following, for instance, an increase in the rate of savings, is essential to this issue. As previously noted, λ (the speed of convergence in the S&S type economy) is about -0.022, thus the old theory predicts that it will take a few decades for an economy to reach the new steady state after a policy change. This means, for example, that if a government policy were to raise the rate of savings, the economy's rate of growth would, *caeteris paribus*, remain at a higher level for a "temporary" period of *a few decades*! Quite a good policy deal, one should be inclined to think.

Of course, to be higher *forever* is better still; but imagine that the exact proportionality between output and the capital stock (whatever measure we use for this), which characterizes much of the literature on endogenous economic growth and is the basis of the policy-induced *permanent* changes in the rate of growth, is false (in Chapter 7, Appendix 7.A.2, and Chapter 8, footnote 8, we gave a number of reasons for not ruling out this possibility).[3] If so, favoring the new theory on the above-mentioned grounds only, would be a decision based on wishful thinking, and as such, a very dangerous one. For it is bound to raise the public's expectations about the power of economic policy by far too much (which will not be beneficial for either the economists or economics). Hence, favoring the new theory over the old on

---

[2]This is Solow's (1997) terminology. He says that he has been unable to come up with better names ("trend-lifting" and "trend-tilting") to describe the difference between the two kinds of models as regards policy, but (in our opinion) those names do describe the situation quite well. There is an alternative terminology to express this difference, and that is to say that, as regards policy, the old theory implies *level effects* whereas the new one implies *growth effects*. But in truth they both imply level *and* growth effects, do they not? So, we prefer to stick to Solow's terminology.

[3]"The power of the new results makes it all the more important to decide whether the powerful assumptions that lead to them are true. Before jumping to the policy conclusions, we must decide whether to accept their foundations" (Solow, 1997, p. 85)

the basis of how long they predict policy effects to last, is somewhat unfair.

So it is clear that the above-mentioned two rounds of the dispute between proponents of the two theories lead us nowhere as regards which theory is better. Better for what? To accommodate the empirical findings at hand? They both do that. Better to decide on growth-oriented policies? For this the new theory, *as it stands* (and this qualifier is essential, hence more about it below), does not really take us much further than the old one (and, besides, we are still at odds with its conclusions). Hence, we do not think that an evaluation of the two approaches to modeling economic growth presented in this book can be posed in terms of which is better. They both have their own pros and cons, their own insights and shortcomings. On the one hand, there is one aspect of the creation of knowledge (itself the main factor of economic growth: no dispute about this) which the old theory will never be able to capture, namely the fact that a portion of technical progress is endogenous (that is, it results from *profit-seeking, privately funded* R&D activity).[4] Thus, to the extent that the new theory tries to model the endogenous portion of technical progress, it will inevitably (and fortunately!) stay with us.

Now the endogenous component of technical progress is not the whole story of the knowledge creation process. For a portion of technical progress *is* exogenous, particularly in the so-called basic research. For instance, in a study of 61 important twentieth-century inventions, Jewkes, Sawers and Stillerman (1959) found that nearly half of them were the product of academic research (that is, hardly describable as a profit-driven, not publicly funded activity). We are still wondering, for another thing, how many important innovations have (and will have!) their origin in research laboratories linked to the, often private, but still government-subsidized, military industrial complex and space exploration programs. These types of research institutions will remain with us, and so, too, the exogenous portion of technical progress. It must be emphasized, also, that (as pointed out in Chapter 7, Section 7.7, and Chapter 8, Section 8.5.2) much technical progress comes from "learning-by-doing," that is, improvements made by people on the shop floor on the basis of new inventions which themselves result from *both*, endogenous and exogenous R&D activity. It so seems, therefore, that a good understanding of the actual process of economic growth calls for the presence of both components of technical progress in our models.

Thus in a way, the new theory is *not* providing so much a model of economic growth as it is providing a model of how the endogenous portion

----

[4] It is of course trivial why the old theory will never accommodate the *fact* that technical progress *is* partially endogenous: If it did, it would no longer be the "old," exogenous theory of economic growth.

of technical progress is "produced." Cheerfully, it has made good progress, so perhaps, as Solow (1997, p. 41) says, "may be the time is ripe for an analytical killing." We ought to wish so; for only then there will be a *solid* step forward in the

> ongoing policy dabates about tax subsidies for private research, antitrust exemptions for research joint ventures, the activities of multinational firms, the effects of government procurement, the feedback between trade policy and innovation, the scope of protection for intellectual property rights, the links between private firms and universities, the mechanisms for selecting the research areas that receive public support, and the costs and benefits of an explicit government-led technology policy. We will be able to address the most important policy questions about growth: In a developing country like the Philippines, what are the best institutional arrangements for gaining access to the knowledge that already exists in the rest of the world? In a country like the United States, what are the best institutional arrangements for encouraging the production and use of new knowledge? (Romer, 1994, p. 20–21)

In sum, a thorough model of the actual process of economic growth should account for both, the exogenous and the endogenous components of technical progress. Furthermore, it may have to deal as well with a few other issues which, though relevant to the case, have been almost forgotten hitherto. For one thing, there is an irreducible degree of *uncertainty* in the process of knowledge creation. We touched upon this issue in Chapter 8, Section 8.5.2. There, this uncertainty was considered amenable to probabilistic treatment. The trouble is that it might *not*. To be sure, "if *Knightian uncertainty* shows up anywhere, it could be here" (Solow, 1994, p. 52; see also Nelson, 1997). If so, we lack the appropriate analytical tools. This may be a serious problem; for it means, not only that a portion of technical progress is exogenous as we use this term, but exogenous *to the economy itself*, that is, the production of technical knowledge might not be a mere matter of "put in more resources and you'll get more output." (And then, what kind of production function for knowledge do we assume in our models?)

Second, and perhaps related to this, is the fact that, to this date, mainstream economics has kept the modeling of economic growth within the canons of *general equilibrium* analysis (the literature surveyed in this book, both the old and new theories alike, testifies to this assertion). Moreover, retaining this framework of analysis appears to be a basic goal in the research strategy of mainstream economics. Some economists, however, begin to question whether this framework, productive as it has been, is flexible enough to let us progress much further in the analysis of economic growth and development. So, for instance, Nelson (1997, p. 33) shows deep concern that the commitment to "conform to a general equilibrium model may restrict what we know about how economies grow rather than expand our knowledge," and he invites the profession "to think a bit about what is gained and what is lost by operating under this constraint." We leave the scrutiny of Professor Nelson's view to the reader (but also take occasion to point out that his arguments deserve careful consideration).

9.3 Conclusion

The analysis of economic growth is an all-deserving area of research, for nothing can be more important to an economist *as such*, than to help society find the way to increasing her living standards, "to uplifting those most in need." Yet, as it happens, nothing that is really good ever comes easy and finding the means to achieving the highest possible rate of *sustainable* economic growth is no exception. On the contrary, it is a complicated issue to uncover. In this chapter, we have tried to remind the reader that although much progress has been made in recent years, there is a long way to go before we can let the bells go off. The problems to be addressed are rather clear, but even how to go about them represents a difficulty. Perhaps *modesty* (to value our findings for what they are worth, and not more; to accept that other scholars besides economists can also contribute to a better knowledge of these issues, so that we are prepared to consider what they have to say to us, and so on) will increase our own chances of success.

Suggested Reading

Nelson, R. (1997).
Romer, Paul M. (1994).
Solow, R. (1997). Chapter 4 ("Policies for Economic Growth"), pp. 69–92.
(*Suggestion*: Perhaps the optimal reading sequence is Romer–Solow–Nelson).

Mathematical Appendices

Mathematical Appendix A

A.1. The Growth Rate Operator

Let x and z be two variables that evolve through time, $x = x(t)$ and $z = z(t)$. The following equalities hold:

$$\overset{\circ}{xz}=\overset{\circ}{x} + \overset{\circ}{z} \ \text{ and } \ \overset{\circ}{x/z}=\overset{\circ}{x} - \overset{\circ}{z}$$

Proof. By definition, we have:

$$\overset{\circ}{xz}= \frac{d(xz)/dt}{xz} = \frac{(dx/dt)z + (dz/dt)x}{xz} = \frac{dx/dt}{x} + \frac{dz/dt}{z} = \frac{\dot{x}}{x} + \frac{\dot{z}}{z} = \overset{\circ}{x} + \overset{\circ}{z}.$$

Similarly:

$$\overset{\circ}{x/z} = \frac{d(x/z)/dt}{x/z} = \frac{[(dx/dt)z - (dz/dt)x]/z^2}{x/z} = \frac{(dx/dt)z - (dz/dt)x}{z^2(x/z)}$$

$$= \frac{(dx/dt)z}{zx} - \frac{(dz/dt)x}{zx} = \frac{dx/dt}{x} - \frac{dz/dt}{z} = \frac{\dot{x}}{x} - \frac{\dot{z}}{z} = \overset{\circ}{x} - \overset{\circ}{z}.$$

Now let a be a constant and $y = y(t)$. Then, if $x = y^a$ the following equality holds:

$$\overset{\circ}{x}= a\, \overset{\circ}{y}$$

Proof. Taking logarithms in $x = y^a$ we have:

$$\log x = a \log y,$$

therefore it is:

$$\frac{d\log x}{dt} = a\frac{d\log y}{dt},$$

that is to say:

$$\overset{\circ}{x} = a\,\overset{\circ}{y}$$

We will use these basic "growth rate operators" very frequently in this book.

Mathematical Appendix B

B.1. Proof of Equation (3.1)

Time subindices are suppressed for convenience. We thus have:

$$
\begin{aligned}
\overset{\circ}{\tilde{y}} &= \frac{d\tilde{y}/dt}{\tilde{y}} = \frac{f'(\tilde{k}) \cdot (d\tilde{k}/dt)}{f(\tilde{k})} = \frac{\tilde{k} \cdot f'(\tilde{k}) \cdot (d\tilde{k}/dt)}{f(\tilde{k}) \cdot \tilde{k}} = \frac{\tilde{k} \cdot f'(\tilde{k})}{f(\tilde{k})} \cdot \overset{\circ}{\tilde{k}} \\
&= \frac{MPK \cdot K/(AL)}{Y/(AL)} \cdot \overset{\circ}{\tilde{k}} = \frac{K \cdot MPK}{Y} \cdot \overset{\circ}{\tilde{k}} = \frac{\Pi}{Y} \overset{\circ}{\tilde{k}} = \mathrm{Sh}_K \cdot \overset{\circ}{\tilde{k}}
\end{aligned}
$$

B.2. Proof of Equation (3.7)

Before we solve this problem it will be convenient to explain what a "Taylor expansion" is. Imagine that a function $z_t = f(x_t)$ exists but we don't know its values except for $x_t = x_0$. In other words, all we know about this function is that for $x_t = x_0$ it takes the value $f(x_0) = z_0$. Is there any procedure by which we could, based on this little information, obtain more knowledge about this function? The answer is *yes*. We can obtain the (approximate) value of the function for an $x_t = x_1$ which is a bit larger (or a bit smaller) than x_0, that is, we can obtain the approximate values of $f(x_1)$ when x_1 is "a bit to the right" ("a bit to the left") of x_1. (Figure B.1 below may help to clarify this idea. We assume in this figure that x_1 is a bit larger than x_0.) To see this, imagine that we know the shape of the function (we do *not* really know it, which is precisely the trouble; but *imagine* that we do), and that it is as depicted in Figure B.1. Clearly we have:

$$z_1 = f(x_1) = f(x_0) + CD.$$

On the other hand, by definition:

$$f'(x_0) = \tan \widehat{B} = \frac{\sin \widehat{B}}{\cos \widehat{B}} = \frac{CE}{BC} = \frac{CE}{x_1 - x_0}.$$

Now, as we can see, CE is larger than CD; but clearly, the closer x_1 is to x_0 the more approximate are CE and CD; thus, for values of x_1 very close to x_0, we may replace CE with CD. (Sure, no matter how close x_1 will be to x_0, we will make an error by doing this substitution: That is why the results of this exercise are only *approximate* to the truth.) We have:

$$f'(x_0) = \frac{CD}{x_1 - x_0},$$

therefore:

$$CD = f'(x_0)(x_1 - x_0),$$

and substituting this result in the first equation above we obtain:

$$z_1 = f(x_0) + f'(x_0)(x_1 - x_0),$$

that is to say, in general:

$$z_t = f(x_t)|_{x_t = x_0} + f'(x_t)|_{x_t = x_0}(x_t - x_0).$$

This procedure is known as the (first order) Taylor expansion of $z_t = f(x_t)$ around the (known) value of $x_t = x_0$.

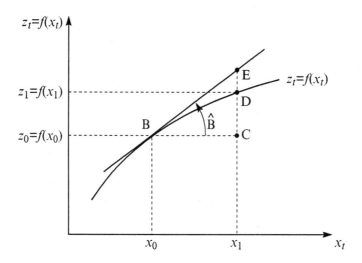

Figure B.1: Taylor's First Order Expansion of $z_t = f(x_t)$
Around the Value $x_t = x_0$

What this procedure means, of course, is that we are "linearizing" $z_t = f(x_t)$ for no reason other than either we do it or no further progress will be made, given our ignorance about the true form of the function. (Needless to say, this procedure may not be innocuous.)

With this in mind we can work out our problem, which is similar. We have a function for the growth rate of per capita income, Equation (3.6), which gives $\overset{o}{y}_t$ as a function of y_t (or, if you wish, of $\log y_t$). We do not know anything about this function *except* that for $y_t = y_t^*$ (or, if you wish, for $\log y_t = \log y_t^*$) the function takes the value $\overset{o}{y}_t = g$, that is, in the steady state the rate of growth of per capita income *is* the growth rate of the level of technology, g. Thus we know one value of the function and so a Taylor expansion around this value can be performed, as follows (time subindices are suppressed for convenience):

$$
\begin{aligned}
\overset{o}{y} &= \left(\overset{o}{y}\right)_{y=y^*} + \left(\frac{d\overset{o}{y}}{d\log y}\right)_{\log y \,=\log y^*} \cdot (\log y - \log y^*) \\
&= g + \left[sA^{(1-\alpha)/\alpha} \cdot \alpha \cdot \frac{\alpha-1}{\alpha} \cdot e^{\log y \cdot (\alpha-1)/\alpha}\right]_{y=y^*} (\log y - \log y^*) \\
&= g + \left[sA^{(1-\alpha)/\alpha} \cdot (\alpha-1) \cdot y^{(\alpha-1)/\alpha}\right]_{y=y^*} (\log y - \log y^*) \\
&= g + (\alpha-1)\left[sA^{(1-\alpha)/\alpha} \cdot y^{(\alpha-1)/\alpha}\right]_{y=y^*} (\log y - \log y^*).
\end{aligned}
$$

B.3. Solving Equation (3.21)

For convenience, we let:

$$\log \tilde{y}_t = z_t \text{ for all } t \text{ and } -\lambda \log \tilde{y}^* = \phi \text{ (a constant)},$$

so that we have:

$$z_{t+1} = (1+\lambda)z_t + \phi$$

or, what is the same (retarding one period):

$$z_t = (1+\lambda)z_{t-1} + \phi.$$

Thus, for $t = 1$ we have:

$$z_1 = (1+\lambda)z_0 + \phi.$$

For $t = 2$:

$$z_2 = (1+\lambda)z_1 + \phi = (1+\lambda)[(1+\lambda)z_0 + \phi] + \phi = (1+\lambda)^2 z_0 + (1+\lambda)\phi + \phi.$$

For $t = 3$:

$$z_3 = (1+\lambda)z_2 + \phi = (1+\lambda)^3 z_0 + (1+\lambda)^2 \phi + (1+\lambda)\phi + \phi,$$

and so on. Hence, for $t = T$ we obtain:

$$z_T = (1+\lambda)^T z_0 + (1+\lambda)^{T-1}\phi + (1+\lambda)^{T-2}\phi + ... + (1+\lambda)\phi + \phi$$

$$= (1+\lambda)^T z_0 + \phi[(1+\lambda)^{T-1} + (1+\lambda)^{T-2} + ... + (1+\lambda) + 1].$$

The expression in brackets is the sum of terms of a geometric progression in $(1+\lambda)$, therefore we have:

$$z_T = (1+\lambda)^T z_0 + \phi\frac{1-(1+\lambda)^T}{1-(1+\lambda)} = (1+\lambda)^T z_0 - \frac{\phi}{\lambda}[1-(1+\lambda)^T].$$

Since $(1+\lambda)^T = \exp[T\log(1+\lambda)]$ and $\log(1+\lambda) \approx \lambda$ (this approximation is obtained by means of a Taylor expansion of $\log[1+\lambda]$ around the value of $\lambda = 0$), we have: $(1+\lambda)^T = \exp(\lambda T)$, therefore:

$$z_T = e^{\lambda T} z_0 - \frac{\phi}{\lambda}(1 - e^{\lambda T}),$$

that is to say (reverting to the notation above):

$$\log \tilde{y}_T = e^{\lambda T} \log \tilde{y}_0 + (1 - e^{\lambda T}) \log \tilde{y}^*.$$

B.4. Proof that $\log y_T - \log y_0 = \overset{\circ}{y}_{[0,T]}$ (the growth rate of per capita income for the entire $[0,T]$ period).

By definition:

$$\overset{\circ}{y}_{[0,T]} = \frac{y_T - y_0}{y_0} = \frac{y_T}{y_0} - 1,$$

from which it follows that:

$$\frac{y_T}{y_0} = \overset{\circ}{y}_{[0,T]} + 1,$$

therefore:

$$\log \frac{y_T}{y_0} = \log(\overset{\circ}{y}_{[0,T]} + 1) \approx \overset{\circ}{y}_{[0,T]},$$

where the approximation is obtained by means of a Taylor expansion of $\log(\overset{\circ}{y}_{[0,T]} + 1)$ around the value of $\overset{\circ}{y}_{[0,T]} = 0$.

Mathematical Appendix C

C.1. Solving Equation (5.12)

To obtain the first order conditions for the maximization of total utility write $\mathcal{U} = \sum_{t=0}^{\infty} \frac{1}{(1+\varrho)^t} U\left(A_t[f(\tilde{k}_t) - (n+\delta+g-1)\tilde{k}_t - \tilde{k}_{t+1}]\right)$ in expanded form, as follows:

$$
\begin{aligned}
\mathcal{U} \;=\; & \frac{1}{(1+\varrho)^0}U\left(A_0[f(\tilde{k}_0)-(n+\delta+g-1)\tilde{k}_0-\tilde{k}_1]\right) \\
+\; & \frac{1}{(1+\varrho)^1}U\left(A_1[f(\tilde{k}_1)-(n+\delta+g-1)\tilde{k}_1-\tilde{k}_2]\right) \\
+\; & \frac{1}{(1+\varrho)^2}U\left(A_2[f(\tilde{k}_2)-(n+\delta+g-1)\tilde{k}_2-\tilde{k}_3]\right) \\
+\; & \cdots
\end{aligned}
$$

and note that $A_t[f(\tilde{k}_t)-(n+\delta+g-1)\tilde{k}_t-\tilde{k}_{t+1}]=c_t$ for all t. Since the choice variables are $\tilde{k}_1$, $\tilde{k}_2$, $\tilde{k}_3$, and so on, the first order conditions for the maximization of $\mathcal{U}$ are obtained by setting its partial derivatives with respect to $\tilde{k}_1$, $\tilde{k}_2$, and so on, equal to zero. (Be careful: it is very easy to leave terms behind while taking each partial derivative [that is why it is convenient to write $\mathcal{U}$ in expanded form, so that, for instance, we can see how many times $\tilde{k}_1$, for example, appears in the objective function].) This provides a system of simultaneous equations which we can write in compact form as: $\partial\mathcal{U}/\partial\tilde{k}_t = 0; (t = 1, 2, ..., \infty)$, where $\partial\mathcal{U}/\partial\tilde{k}_t = 0$ is obtained by simple analogy with any equation in the system, that is:

$$
\frac{\partial\mathcal{U}}{\partial\tilde{k}_t} = -\frac{U'(c_{t-1})A_{t-1}}{(1+\varrho)^{t-1}} + \frac{U'(c_t)A_t[f'(\tilde{k}_t)-(n+\delta+g-1)]}{(1+\varrho)^t} = 0,
$$

which may be rearranged as follows:

$$
f'(\tilde{k}_t) - (n+\delta+g-1) = (1+\varrho)\frac{A_{t-1}}{A_t}\cdot\frac{U'(c_{t-1})}{U'(c_t)}; \quad (t = 1, 2, ..., \infty).
$$

References

A

AGHION, Philippe and Peter Howitt (1992). "A Model of Growth through Creative Destruction," *Econometrica*, 60, 2 (March), 323–351.

ARROW, Kenneth J. (1962). "The Economic Implications of Learning by Doing," *Review of Economic Studies*, 29 (June), 155–173.

ARROW, Kenneth J. (1963). *Social Choice and Individual Values*, New Haven: Yale University Press.

ASHER, H. (1956). *Cost-Quantity Relationships in the Airframe Industry*, R-291, Santa Monica: The Rand Corporation.

B

BACKUS, David K., P. J. Kehoe and T. J. Kehoe (1992). "In Search of Scale Effects in Trade and Growth," *Journal of Economic Theory*, 58, 377–409.

BAILY, Martin N. (1981). "Productivity and the Services of Capital and Labor," *Brookings Papers on Economic Activity*, 1, pp. 1–50.

BALDWIN, Richard (1989). "The Growth Effects of 1992," *Economic Policy* (October), 247–281.

BARRO, Robert J. (1991). "Economic Growth in a Cross Section of Countries," *Quarterly Journal of Economics*, 106, 2 (May), 407–443.

BARRO, Robert J. (1997). *Determinants of Economic Growth: A Cross-Country Empirical Study*, Cambridge, Mass., The MIT Press.

BARRO, Robert J. and Xavier Sala-i-Martín (1991). "Convergence across States and Regions," *Brookings Papers on Economic Activity*, 1, 107–182.

BARRO, Rober J. and Xavier Sala-i-Martín (1992). "Convergence," *Journal of Political Economy*, 100, 2 (April), 223–251.

BARRO, Rober J. and Xavier Sala-i-Martín (1995). *Economic Growth*, New York, McGraw-Hill.

181

BLANCHARD, Olivier (1997). *Macroeconomics*, New York, Prentice Hall.

BURDA, Michael and Charles Wyplosz (1993). *Macroeconomics: A European Text*, New York: Oxford University Press.

C

CASS, David (1965). "Optimal Growth in an Aggregative Model of Capital Accumulation," *Review of Economic Studies*, 32 (July), 233–240.

CORNES, Richard and Todd Sandler (1986). *The Theory of Externalities, Public Goods, and Club Goods*, Cambridge: Cambridge University Press.

CHRISTENSEN, Laurits R., Dianne Cummings and Dale W. Jorgenson (1980). "Economic Growth 1947–1973: An International Comparison," in John W. Kendrick and Beatrice Baccara (eds), *New Developments in Productivity Measurement and Analysis*, NBER Conference Report, Chicago: University of Chicago Press.

D

DENISON, Edward F. (1991). *Trends in American Economic Growth, 1929–1982*, Washington, D.C.: The Brookings Institution.

DOUGHERTY, Christopher (1991). *A Comparison of Productivity and Economic Growth in the G-7 Countries*, PhD dissertation, Harvard University.

E

ELIAS, Victor J. (1990). *Sources of Growth: A Study of Seven Latin American Economies*, San Francisco, ICS Press.

F

FISHER, Stanley (1993). "Macroeconomic Factors in Growth." Presented at World Bank conference, "How Do National Policies Affect Growth?" Washington D.C., February.

FRIEDMAN, Milton (1992). "Do Old Fallacies Ever Die?," *Journal of Economic Literature*, 30, 4, pp. 2129–2132.

G

GALTON, Francis (1886). "Regression Towards Mediocrity in Hereditary Stature," *Journal of the Anthropological Institute of Great Britain and*

Ireland, 15, 246–263.

GROSSMAN, Gene M., and Elhanan Helpman (1991). *Innovation and Growth in the Global Economy*, Cambridge, Mass.: The MIT Press.

GROSSMAN, Gene M., and Elhanan Helpman (1994). "Endogenous innovation in the theory of growth," *Journal of Economic Perspectives*, 8, 1 (Winter), pp. 23–44.

H

HARROD, Roy F. (1937). "Review of Joan Robinson's 'Essays on the Theory of Employment'," *Economic Journal*, 326–330.

HARROD, Roy F. (1948). *Towards a Dynamic Economics: Some Recent Developments of Economic Theory and their Applications to Policy*, London: Macmillan.

J

JEL "Symposium" (1988). "Symposium on the Slowdown of Productivity Growth," *Journal of Economic Literature*, Fall 1988.

JEWKES, John, David Sawers and Richard Stillerman (1959). *The Sources of Invention*, New YorK: St. Martin's Press.

JONES, Hywel G. (1976). *An Introduction to Modern Theories of Economic Growth*, New York: McGraw-Hill.

K

KALDOR, Nicholas (1961). "Capital Accumulation and Economic Growth." In F. A. Lutz and D. C. Hague (eds), *The Theory of Capital*, New York: St. Martin's Press, pp. 177–222.

KEYNES, John M. (1936). *The General Theory of Employment, Interest and Money*, London: Macmillan.

KEYNES, John M. (1930). "F. P. Ramsey," *Economic Journal* (Mar.) Reprinted in J. M. Keynes, *Essays in Biography*, London: Macmillan.

KREMER, Michael (1993). "Population Growth and Technological Change: One Million B.C. to 1990," *Quarterly Journal of Economics*, 108, 3 (August), 681–716.

KOOPMANS, Tjalling C. (1965). "On the Concept of Optimal Economic Growth," in *The Econometric Approach to Development Planning*, Amsterdam: North Holland.

KUZNETS, Simon (1946). *The National Product since 1869*, New York: National Bureau of Economic Research.

L

LEVINE, Ross and David Renelt (1992). "A Sensitivity Analysis of Cross-Country Growth Regressions," *American Economic Review*, 82, 4, 942–963.
LUCAS, Robert E., (1988). "On the Mechanics of Economic Development," *Journal of Monetary Economics*, 22 (July), 3–42.

M

McALEER, Michael (1994), "Sherlock Holmes and the Search for Truth: A Diagnostic Tale," *Journal of Economic Surveys*, 8, 4, pp. 317-30.
MADDISON, Angus (1982). *Phases of Capitalist Development*, Oxford: Oxford University Press.
MADDISON, Angus (1987). "Growth and Slowdown in Advanced Capitalist Economies: Techniques of Quantitative Assessment," *Journal of Economic Literature*, 25 (June), 649–698.
MADDISON, Angus (1989). *The World Economy in the Twentieth Century*, Paris: OECD.
MADDISON, Angus (1991). *Dynamic Forces in Capitalist Development*, Oxford: Oxford University Press.
MAIRESSE, J (1982). Comments on "Economic Policy in the Face of Declining Productivity Growth," by W. D. Nordhaus, *European Economic Review*, 18 (May), pp. 159–162.
MANKIW, N. Gregory (1992). *Macroeconomics*, New York: Worth Publishers.
MANKIW, N. Gregory, David Romer and David N. Weil (1992), "A Contribution to the Empirics of Economic Growth," *Quarterly Journal of Economics*, 107, 2 (May), 407–437.
MANSFIELD, Edwin (1990). *Managerial Economics: Theory, Applications, and Cases*, New York: W.W. Norton.
MARGLIN, Stephen A. (1963). "The Social Rate of Discount and the Optimal Rate of Investment," *Quarterly Journal of Economics*, 95–111.
MARRIS, Robert and Dennis Mueller (1980), "The Corporation, Competition, and the Invisible Hand," *Journal of Economic Literature*, March (Section III, pp. 50–60.)
MARX, Karl (1898). "Wage Labor and Capital," in *Marx-Engels Collected Works*, 9, pp. 197–228, New York: International Publishers (1977).

N

NELSON, Richard R. (1997). "How New Is New Growth Theory," *Challenge*, 40, 5, September/October, pp. 29–58.

NELSON, Richard R. and Edmund S. Phelps (1966). "Investment in Humans, Technological Diffusion, and Economic Growth," *American Economic Review*, 56, 2 (May), 69–75.

P

PACK, Howard (1994). " Endogenous Growth Theory: Intellectual Appeal and Empirical Shortcomings," *Journal of Economic Perspectives*, 8, 1 (Winter), 55–72.

PASINETTI, Luigi L. (1977). *Lectures on the Theory of Production*, New York: Columbia University Press.

PHELPS, Edmund S. (1961). "The Golden Rule of Accumulation: A Fable for Growthmen," *American Economic Review*, pp. 638–643.

PHELPS, Edmund S. (1966).*Golden Rules of Economic Growth*, New York: Norton.

PRZEWORSKI, Adam and Fernando Limongi (1994). "Political Regimes and Economic Growth," *Journal of Economic Perspectives*, 7, 3 (Summer), 51–69.

Q

QUAH, Danny (1993). "Galton's Fallacy and Tests of the Convergence Hypothesis," *Scandinavian Journal of Economics*, 95, 4, 427–443.

QUAH, Danny (1996). "Twin Peaks: Growth and Convergence in Models of Distribution Dynamics," *The Economic Journal*, 106 (July), 1045–1055.

R

RAMSEY, Frank (1928). "A Mathematical Theory of Saving," *Economic Journal*, 38 (December), 543–559.

RAPPING, Leonard (1965). "Learning and World War II Production Functions," *Review of Economics and Statistics*, 47 (February), 81–86.

ROBERTSON, Sir Dennis. Letter to J. M. Keynes. In J. M. Keynes, *The General Theory and After: Part 2 —Defense and Development*, Vol. XIV of *The Collected Writings of John Maynard Keynes* edited by E. Johnson and D. E. Moggridge. London: Macmillan (1973).

ROBINSON, Joan (1937/8). "The Classification of Inventions," *Review of Economic Studies*, 5 (February), 139–142.

ROMER, Paul M. (1986). "Increasing Returns and Long-Run Growth," *Journal of Political Economy*, 94, 5 (October), 1002–1037.

ROMER, Paul M. (1987). "Crazy Explanations for the Productivity Slowdown," *NBER Macroeconomics Annual*, Cambridge: MIT Press.

ROMER, Paul M. (1989). "Capital Accumulation in the Theory of Long-Run Growth," in Robert J Barro (ed), *Modern Business Cycle Theory*, Cambridge, Mas.: Harvard University Press.

ROMER, Paul M. (1990). "Endogenous Technical Change," *Journal of Political Economy*, 98, 5 (October), Part 2, S71–S102.

ROMER, Paul M. (1994). "The Origins of Endogenous Growth," *Journal of Economic Perspectives*, 8, 1 (Winter), 3–22.

S

SACHS, Jeffrey and Andrew Warner (1995). "Economic Reform and the Process of Global Integration," *Brookings Papers on Economic Activity*.

SCHMOOKLER, J (1966). *Invention and Economic Growth*, Cambridge, Mass.: Harvard University Press.

SCHUMPETER, Joseph A. (1942). *Capitalism, Socialism, and Democracy*, New York: Harper.

SEARLE, Allan D. (1946). "Productivity Changes in Selected Wartime Shipbuilding Programs," *Monthly Labor Review*.

SEN, Amartya K. (1970). *Collective Choice and Social Welfare*, Edinburgh: Oliver and Boyd.

SHLEIFER, Andrei and Robert W. Vishny (1993). "Corruption," *Quarterly Journal of Economics*, 108 (August), pp. 599–618.

SMITH, Adam (1776). *An Inquiry into the Nature and Causes of the Wealth of Nations*, New York: Modern Library, Cannan Edition.

SOLOW, Robert M. (1956). "A Contribution to the Theory of Economic Growth," *Quarterly Journal of Economics*," 70, 1 (February), 65–94.

SOLOW, Robert M. (1957). "Technical Change and the Aggregate Production Function," *Review of Economics and Statistics*, 39 (August), 312–320.

SOLOW, Robert M. (1970). *Growth Theory: An Exposition*, Oxford: Oxford University Press.

SOLOW, Robert M. (1994). "Perspectives on Growth Theory," *Journal of Economic Perspectives*, 8, 1 (Winter), 45–54.

SOLOW, Robert M. (1997). *Learning from "Learning-by-Doing". Lessons for Economic Growth*, Stanford, CA: Stanford University Press.

SUMMERS, Robert and Alan Heston (1988). "A New Set of International Comparisons of Real Products and Price Levels Estimates for 130 Countries, 1950–85," *Review of Income and Wealth*, 34, 1–26.

SUMMERS, Robert and Alan Heston (1991). "The Penn World Table (Mark 5): An Expanded Set of International Comparisons, 1950–1988," *Quarterly Journal of Economics*, 106, 2 (May), 327–368.

SUMMERS, Robert and Alan Heston (1995). "Penn World Tables, Version 5.5," available from the National Bureau of Economic Research, Cambridge, MA.

SWAN, Trevor W. (1956). "Economic Growth and Capital Accumulation," *The Economic Record*, 32 (November), 334–361.

T

TURNER, Paul (1993). *Modern Macroeconomic Analysis*, Maidenhead (England), McGraw.

U

UZAWA, Hirofumi (1961). "Neutral Inventions and the Stability of Growth Equilibrium," *Review of Economic Studies*, 28 (February), 117–124.

V

VALDES, Benigno (1988). "Cambio Técnico, Rentabilidad y Crisis," *El Trimestre Económico*, 55 (3), 219, pp. 559–578.

W

WICKSELL, Knut (1901, 1934 for the English translation). "A Mathematical Analysis of Dr Åkerman's Problem," in *Lectures in Political Economy*, 2 vols., ed. by Lionel Robins in 1934, London: George Routledge and Sons.

WICKSTEED, Philip H. (1894). *The Coordination of the Laws of Distribution*, London: Macmillan

WRIGHT, Theodore P. (1936). "Factors Affecting the Cost of Airplanes," *Journal of the Aeronautical Sciences*, 3, pp. 122–128.

Y

YOUNG, Alwyn (1994). "The Tyranny of Numbers: Confronting the Statistical Realities of the East Asian Experience," *NBER Working Paper 4680*.

Index

A

Aghion, Philippe, 157
Agriculture:
    the green revolution in, 67
AK model, 106
    (*see also* "linear-in-K" model)
Anisi, David, xvi
Arrow, Kenneth, 78, 100, 119, 123,
    167
Arrow-Romer model, 104ff
    (*see also* "Linear-in-K" model)
Asher, H., 102
Automobile industry (cost reduc-
    tion in [...] due to "learn-
    ing-by-doing"), 102fn

B

β-convergence test, 45–47
    (*see also* Barro-regression)
    (*see also* Convergence)
Backus, David K., 121fn
Baily, Martin N., 92
Balanced growth path:
    in the "linear-in-K" model,
    107
    in Romer's (1990) model,
    145–147
    in the Solow–Swan model, 30
    (*see also* equilibrium)
    (*see also* steady state)
Baldwin, Richard, 112

Barro-regression, 45, 47, 48, 50,
    60, 64, 65, 67, 68, 69, 70
Barro, Robert, xiv, 45, 51, 52, 67,
    121, 125, 162
Blanchard, Olivier, 108
Burda, Michael, 4, 7
Bush, George, 1

C

Caballé, Jordi, xvi
Canada, 11, 117
Capital:
    broad concept (measure) of,
    53–56, 88, 90, 122, 125,
    126
    depreciation of, 25, 26, 27,
    28, 56, 77, 108
    human (*see* human capital)
Capital accumulation:
    fundamental equation of, 26,
    56
    (*see also* fundamental
    growth equation)
    and knowledge creation
    through learning-by-
    doing, 99–104, 119–120
    subsidies to, 113–114, 156
    (*see also* investment)
Capital-augmenting technology:
    16, 17
    (*see also* technical progress)
Capital investment (and external-